START YOUR OWN
HOME-BASED BUSINESS

START YOUR OWN HOME-BASED BUSINESS

NICK DAWS

Corpus Publishing
United Kingdom

© Corpus Publishing 2004

This edition published in 2004 by
Corpus Publishing
PO Box 8, Lydney, Gloucestershire, GL15 6YD
Tel: 01594 560600 Fax: 01594 560550
Email: info@firststonepub.co.uk

British Library Cataloguing in Publication Data
A CIP record for this book is available from the British Library

ISBN 1 899053 17 4

Text and Cover Design IPA

Printed and bound by Bell & Bain Ltd, Glasgow.

Distributed in the UK by Gardners Books, Eastbourne

CONTENTS

Appendices

Index

INTRODUCTION

'May you live in interesting times' is, so I am told, an old Chinese curse. The implication is that most of us would far rather live in ordinary, even slightly dull, times. Interesting times suggests times of insecurity, of disruption, of change. And most of us, while we may agree that 'a change is as good as a rest', are uneasy when the world appears to be changing almost daily before our eyes.

Well, like it or not, few would deny that these are interesting times. Seldom has the pace of change in the world been more rapid. And nowhere has this been felt more than in the world of work. In the UK at least, the last ten years have seen the virtual collapse of manufacturing industry. The whole concept of 'a job for life' has vanished, with many people facing redundancy not just once, but two, three or more times during their careers. Even in sectors which were previously bywords for stability, such as banking and insurance, large-scale redundancies have become the norm. Many jobs advertised today are not permanent – whatever permanent might mean now – but on short-term contracts. Very few people today have the luxury of knowing that they will still have a job this time next year.

All change, however, brings opportunities as well as threats – and I firmly believe that as a result of some of these social and economic changes the prospects for people wanting to start a business of their own have never been better. Many of the organisations which laid off staff now buy in services from freelances or small businesses. Advice and assistance is widely – and in many cases freely – available for people who want to start up on their own. And advances in information and communications technology (computers, mobile phones, the Internet and so on) mean that self-employed people and small businesses can compete more effectively than ever before with large corporations. These developments have also, of course, created a wealth of (home-based) business opportunities for people with relevant skills, such as website designers, computer programmers, and so on.

Starting your own business is, however, far more than just a substitute for traditional employment – it is a positive career choice in its own right. With many jobs today offering little in the way of satisfaction or prospects, more people than ever are looking for alternative ways of finding fulfilment in their work. Not only that, many are seeking more flexible working arrangements which allow them to enjoy more time with their families or pursuing leisure interests. Running your own home-based business can offer great personal satisfaction and the potential of good financial rewards, and it can be as flexible as you wish. A home-based business is also, of course, ideal for many people with disabilities. As a result of all these factors, starting a home-based business has become for many their favoured route to achieving the life they desire for themselves and their loved ones. Every year, thousands more people are 'breaking free' to enjoy the flexibility of self-employment and the satisfactions and rewards of being their own boss. This book will show you how you can join them...

'Start Your Own Home-Based Business' is divided into two parts. Part A takes you through everything you need to consider before starting a home-based business – from requirements for success, through drawing up a business plan and cash flow forecast, to matters such as marketing, financial planning and credit control. Practical, detailed advice is given, with contacts for further information as appropriate.

Part B of the book contains concise profiles of over fifty different home-based business opportunities you could start. Some of these require specific skills, training or experience (e.g. book-keeping, website design), while others are open to almost anybody (e.g. window cleaning, house-sitting). Each profile includes concise answers to the following six questions:

(1) What the work entails
(2) What you need to get started
(3) Who your customers will be
(4) How much you can make
(5) How to sell your services
(6) Where you can get more help.

With regard to the latter, for each profile I have aimed to provide at least one useful resource for further information. Often this is an organisation serving and representing people in the occupation concerned. In such cases you will find an address, a phone number and a web page (if one exists). I have not listed fax numbers or e-mail addresses, as these can easily be obtained by a quick phone call or from the website. This section also includes for some of the profiles information on the excellent distance learning (the new name for correspondence teaching) courses which are now available. In many cases you can study for your new home-based career during your own time, while perhaps still working for an employer.

So why did I write this book? For over ten years I have run a successful home-based writing and consultancy business myself, specialising in careers and self-development. During this time I have met many other home-based workers in a wide range of occupations. Without exception, they all agreed that starting in business was one of the best decisions they ever made, and not one (except on a very bad day) ever expressed any wish to be back in conventional employment. I believe that for many people starting their own home-based business can be the answer to unemployment, job insecurity, work-based stress and the lack of flexibility in traditional employment. If this book serves to ease the path of just one person into the exciting world of running their own business, I shall be more than satisfied.

I should like to close this introduction with a word of thanks and an appeal. Thanks first to the many home-based workers, and the organisations serving them, who assisted me in researching and writing this book. I must also offer my particular thanks to Janet Macdonald, who helped research and write a number of the job profiles, and Liz Fleetham of Wolverhampton Business School, who read and commented on the draft manuscript. And the appeal? I should like to ask you, valued reader, to write in to me via my publishers if you have found this book helpful or you have any suggestions for the next edition. And if, as a result of reading this book, you set up a home-based business of your own, I should be delighted to hear about it.

I wish you every success.

Nick Daws
Burntwood, Staffs
October 2000

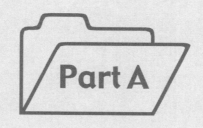

Part A

BUSINESS BASICS

1. WHY START YOUR OWN BUSINESS?

In the UK, and many other countries as well, starting your own business has never been more popular. According to a report from the GEM Project (Global Entrepreneurship Monitor), in the spring of 1999 over 1.4 million people in the UK were attempting to start a business of their own. Less encouragingly, around 500,000 UK businesses close down every year (source: Barclays Bank). So why, despite the obvious risks, are so many people drawn to starting businesses of their own? Their reasons are as varied as the individuals themselves, but the most common include the following.

(1) To make more money

It's a well-known saying, but nonetheless true: nobody ever got rich working for someone else. If you run your own business, the profits will go into your pockets rather than those of someone else (who probably has more than enough already). If your business does well, you can make a lot of money – certainly more than you could ever earn doing a similar job for someone else.

(2) To be independent

In our fast-changing world, few if any jobs now offer long-term security, let alone opportunities for career progression. For many people, one major attraction of starting their own business is to obtain the security now seldom available in paid employment. By starting a successful business they hope to obtain greater independence and financial security for themselves and their loved ones, and perhaps in the long term generate a valuable legacy to pass on to their children.

(3) To gain personal satisfaction and fulfilment

This is a very important reason, especially for people whose current circumstances give them little of either. Being your own boss gives you a measure of freedom and power. You have the chance to exercise and develop your existing skills and learn new ones, and every day to face the excitement of fresh challenges.

(4) To obtain higher status in the eyes of others

Though some may be jealous of their achievements, successful business people are generally held in high esteem by others in the community. By providing goods or services, perhaps employing other people, and paying taxes and duties, they make a real contribution to their community and the quality of life of everyone in it.

(5) To follow through an idea or invention

This is not the most common reason, but many businesses exist because the owner had an idea or spotted a gap in the market, and saw an opportunity to make money from it.

Many people think from time to time about starting a business, but frequently it goes no further than that. Often it takes the spur of a sudden change in circumstances for vague plans to crystallise into something more definite. So perhaps one more reason should be added to this list:

(6) To escape from a sudden, unwelcome change in circumstances

The most common example is unemployment caused by redundancy, but there may also be changes that make your position at work uncomfortable or even untenable. For example, a reorganisation may mean that the nature of your job changes fundamentally, or a new manager may be appointed who decides your face no longer fits in his or her department. Or the change may be nothing to do with your job: perhaps for family reasons it becomes essential for you to spend more time at home (e.g. to care for an elderly relative). Any of these circumstances may provide the incentive for people to seriously consider setting up on their own.

All these reasons and more are potential advantages of starting your own business. There are, however, some possible drawbacks as well, and this is something to be aware of when deciding whether starting a business would be right for you.

(1) Possible variations of income

Instead of having a 'secure' regular weekly or monthly income, a business owner depends for his income on the success of the business, and this is likely to vary from month to month. Of course, an employee's sense of security may well be illusory; if the company employing him is unsuccessful, he will soon find himself out of a job. However, a large business is often able to absorb a temporary downturn in its fortunes by cutting costs and drawing on reserves, so employees are less quickly and directly affected by their employer's difficulties. A business owner, on the other hand, suffers an immediate loss of income if his business passes through a difficult period.

(2) Sacrifices

Starting a new enterprise may involve sacrifices both for you and your family. Many businessmen and women have sacrificed their career prospects in a large organisation in order to go out on their own. If you decide to be your own boss and it doesn't work out, you may find it difficult to re-enter paid employment for someone else. During the business's first few years it may be difficult to find time for a holiday or leisure activities. There may also be financial sacrifices, as in the early years most of the profits from the business may have to be re-invested or used to pay off loans. In the short term, you and your family's general standard of living may well be reduced.

(3) Hard work and stress

In spite of the apparent freedom of being your own boss, the early years of a new business generally require you to work longer hours than you did before. You will have to bear all the stress and worry of the business, and will probably carry this with you even when you are not actually working. There can also be a sense of loneliness and isolation. Many people who decide to set up in business begin (at least) on their own. One common complaint among such people is that they miss the day-to-day banter of the office or shop floor. They also miss having colleagues to turn to when it comes to making difficult decisions or solving problems.

Although at first sight the above may appear rather daunting, it is important not to over-emphasise the possible drawbacks. The truth is that for many people, especially those of a go-getting and entrepreneurial temperament, the attractions and advantages of starting a business greatly outweigh them. One message that should come through clearly, however, is that running your own business is far more than just a means of making a living: it is, quite literally, a way of life. It therefore requires commitment and self-belief, both on your part and that of your family. This is discussed in more detail in the next section.

2. REQUIREMENTS FOR SUCCESS

Deciding to start your own business is unlike applying for a job in one very important respect. While selection for a job usually depends on filling in an application form and attending for interview, no-one else chooses you for self-employment – you must decide for yourself whether you are suitable. Just as it is important to look at your reasons for starting a business, therefore, it is important to examine the qualities and skills you possess personally. These are not simply the specific product- or service-related skills needed for the business you intend to start (essential though these of course are). Rather, they are the general skills and qualities everyone starting in business must have.

So what are the personal qualities you need to succeed in business? Here are the answers some businessmen and women gave themselves.

By far the biggest quality is determination. If things don't go right at first, you have to keep on. Everyone's allowed to make a few mistakes. The main thing is not to be put off when you hit snags.

Eric Lunn, Director, Hinges & Things

You have to commit yourself to it. If you see an opportunity, however small, you must pursue it relentlessly. If you go into business half-heartedly or with your fingers crossed behind your back, then you're likely to fail.

Mr F.M. Daws, Proprietor, Framada Materials Handling

You have to be dedicated, maybe even a bit obsessed! Bags of energy and enthusiasm to get you through the difficult times, which there will be. And, in my line anyway, if helps if you like people and get on with them.

Frances Look, freelance photographer

You need determination, to work long hours – especially at the start, and never give up. Don't let disappointments deter you or affect your morale. But the rewards make all the effort worth it.

**Anthony Todd, Managing Director,
East Cheshire Printers**

A need to provide a high level of service and to understand customer requirements and explore ways of serving their needs in a most cost effective manner.

Mary Lees, Director, Sawyers Packaging

As these quotes reveal, everyone has different views on which qualities are the most important for success in business, but there are certain requirements which come up time and time again.

(1) Determination

Many people talk about starting a business, but only a small proportion do anything about it. Starting a business is a major decision which will change your life and that of your family. It is essential that you are committed to your new career before making such a move; and that once you have started the business you are determined to see it through to success.

(2) Willingness to work

We all think we are willing to work hard, but if you start a business you will soon find out what this means in practice! In the early days at least you are likely to have to work longer hours than the average employee. Although as your business becomes established some of the pressure may ease, you must still expect to work longer and harder than most people in paid employment.

(3) Persistence and perseverance

Successful business people let nothing get in the way of achieving their goals. If they encounter problems, they try to find ways to overcome them. If their first attempt does not succeed, they try a different approach; and, if this doesn't work, another. They are not put off by pitfalls, or discouraged – other than temporarily – by failure. They persevere in their efforts until, eventually, they do succeed.

(4) Stamina

In view of the hours you are likely to have to put in, stamina and at least reasonably good health are important. People running businesses have to avoid taking time off for sickness if at all possible. As a self-employed sole trader in particular, if you are not working you are not generating any income. And if you let down a customer, next time he is likely to go elsewhere.

(5) Self-discipline

If you are in a paid job the chances are you will have a manager or supervisor, part of whose duty is to ensure that you fulfil your obligations to your employer. Your reasons for wishing to start a business may include escaping from such individuals! However, while as a business owner you will have no-one standing watch over you, you will still have obligations to customers, suppliers, employees, officials, and so on. If your business is to go on running successfully, it is important that you have sufficient self-discipline to fulfil all your responsibilities and see a job through to the end.

(6) Willingness to take risks

All business people have to take calculated risks. Whereas in a job you have the relative security of a regular wage or salary, as a self-employed person there is no guarantee what your income will be from one month to the next. You will constantly find yourself having to make decisions about where and how to advertise, which areas to specialise in, when to invest in new equipment, and so on. Although this constant decision-making can be stressful, it can also be satisfying and enjoyable. Solving problems and making decisions can give you a sense of power and confidence.

(7) Ability to cope with stress

Starting and running a business inevitably imposes a range of stresses, both on the businessman himself and on his family. In the beginning at least, long hours, hard work and disruption to family life can cause tension. To be successful in business you need to be able to cope with, and even thrive on, this kind of pressure.

(8) Enthusiasm

Enthusiasm is an essential ingredient of every businessman. If you are half-hearted about your new venture you may have difficulty summoning sufficient determination to overcome problems when they arise. If you are enthusiastic, on the other hand, you will relish the challenges your business presents. What's more, your enthusiasm will rub off onto customers, employees (if you have them) and other people you have to deal with. Most of us would far rather work with or buy from someone who is enthusiastic and enjoys his work, rather than someone who is permanently depressed about it.

(9) Ambition

Most business people have a driving ambition to achieve the best they can for themselves and their loved ones: as well as money, this may include financial security and a better way of life. With such ambitions they can cope with any setbacks along the way, because in their mind they have a goal or vision which drives them on. Ambition and determination together can overcome many obstacles. In business, as in most others aspects of life, if you know what you want and are determined to achieve it, the chances are excellent that you will succeed.

(10) Honesty and willingness to give good service

Every business depends for its continuing survival on a circle of satisfied customers. If people are pleased with the service they have received from you, they are likely to recommend you to others as well as keep coming back themselves. By contrast, if you give poor service then, even if they do not complain at the time, they will not return; and rather than recommend you to others, they will warn them off. If you have a good reputation this will ensure that more people keep coming to you. For this reason, successful business people go to great lengths to obtain and keep a good name for themselves.

EXERCISE

To help assess whether you have the necessary personal qualities for starting and running your own business, complete the checklist below. Circle or underline the description which best describes you.

1. I enjoy a challenge.
    a) always b) usually c) sometimes d) never.
2. I am willing to work long hours.
    a) always b) usually c) sometimes d) never.
3. I actively seek out new experiences.
    a) always b) usually c) sometimes d) never.
4. I am good at taking responsibility.
    a) always b) usually c) sometimes d) never.
5. I am willing to take criticism.
    a) always b) usually c) sometimes d) never.
6. I am good at organising my own time.
    a) always b) usually c) sometimes d) never.
7. I am self-confident.
    a) always b) usually c) sometimes d) never.

8. My general health is good.
   a) always b) usually c) sometimes d) never.
9. I am known as honest and reliable.
   a) certainly b) probably c) possibly d) unlikely.
10. I expect a lot of myself and the people I work with.
    a) always b) usually c) sometimes d) never.
11. I believe success depends on . .
    a) myself b)myself and others c) a range of factors d) luck.
12. I view failure as . .
    a) an opportunity to learn b)an annoyance
    c) a disappointment d) a disaster.
13. In a group situation people look to me to provide leadership.
    a) always b) usually c) sometimes d) never.
14. I can recognise when I need help.
    a) always b) usually c) sometimes d) never.
15. I look for feedback on my performance so that I can do better
    next time.
    a) always b) usually c) sometimes d) never.
16. I am a good judge of character.
    a) always b) usually c) sometimes d) never.
17. I can delegate to others when appropriate.
    a) always b) usually c) sometimes d) never.
18. I can cope with uncertainty about my job and my income.
    a) very easily b) fairly easily c) with some difficulty
    d) with great difficulty.
19. I carry on until a job is complete.
    a) always b) usually c) sometimes d) never.
20. I can cope with stress.
    a) always b) usually c) sometimes d) never.

Now score your responses, giving four points for every a) answer, three points for every b) answer, two points for every c) answer and one point for every d) answer.

If your total is 70 or more, you appear to have the required personal qualities to make a success of starting and running your own business.

If you scored 60–70, you have most of the qualities, but may need to work on certain aspects of your temperament and personality.

If you scored 45–60, you should be able to make a success of starting and running a business, but some areas will definitely need attention.

If you scored 45 or less, you may need to think hard about whether you have the right personal qualities for self-employment.

This exercise should give you some idea as to how well suited you are personally to self-employment. However, people are not always as honest as they could be in assessing their strengths and weaknesses, and sometimes they have an unrealistic view of themselves. It is therefore not a bad idea to copy the above questionnaire and ask your partner, close friend or a relative who knows you well to complete it on your behalf. Compare the answers they provide for you with the answers you gave yourself. Where there are differences, or you disagree with the answer they have given, ask them (in a non-confrontational manner) why they responded that way. Explain that you are not criticising them or the way they completed the task, but simply want to understand your own strengths and weaknesses better.

On the other hand, if the total score given by your partner, friend or relative comes out significantly higher than the score you gave yourself, you may be under-estimating yourself. This may be an encouraging sign that you should have more confidence in your abilities and aptitude for starting and running a business. But do check with the person concerned that they gave honest answers and were not simply trying to please or flatter you!

Friends and Family

Just as it is important to have the right personal qualities yourself, you will also need a supportive family and friends. If you decide to start your business from home, this will inevitably cause changes and disruption in the family routine. Even if you use separate business premises, your friends and family will still have to come to terms with your working long hours and having less time and energy for leisure activities. If you are married or living together, it is especially important that your partner understands the implications of your setting up in business, and supports what you are trying to do.

There is also a positive side, of course. Your family may be a valuable source of help in all sorts of areas, from answering the phone and writing letters, to book-keeping and assisting customers. Having others closely involved with the business can assist when problems arise, as they will bring different ideas and perspectives to the situation. Although it is not absolutely essential to have a supportive family, there is no doubt that you are much more likely to succeed if you have discussed your plans with them and have their wholehearted support.

CHECKLIST

Complete this simple checklist, underlining the answer which applies.

1. Have you discussed your plans for starting a business with your family? — yes / no
2. Do they, on the whole, support your plans? — yes / no
3. Are they willing to assist in the business? — yes / no
4. Do any of them have useful skills which complement your own? (e.g. book-keeping, selling, typing, foreign languages, computers, etc.) — yes / no
5. Will they be able to cope with a variable income? — yes / no
6. Have they accepted that there may be a drop in their standards of living? — yes / no
7. Does anyone else in the family have a job or other source of income which could tide you over while the business is becoming established? — yes / no
8. Could your family cope without you for housework, childcare, gardening, repairs, and so on? — yes / no

The more of the above you can answer 'yes' to, the better your chances of success are likely to be.

Your Skills

To run your business successfully, as well as the right personal qualities and a supportive family and friends, you will need a range of skills. These are described in general terms below. If you lack any of these it does not necessarily mean that you should not set up in business. However, if you feel any of these areas is going to present serious problems, you may need to consider taking on a partner or employee to handle that aspect of the business, or using a specialist adviser or consultant. You might also consider taking other courses to acquire the skills you need.

(1) Technical

These are the skills that you need to actually make the products or deliver the service you are offering. For some types of business you will need to have relevant experience (probably gained as an employee) and perhaps some professional qualifications. For instance, no-one today would set up as a car mechanic without at least some relevant training and experience. On the other hand, for other types of business, including many discussed in Part B of this book, specific qualifications and experience may not be essential. Whatever your business, however, if you expect people to pay you for your work, you will need to have the necessary technical skills to deliver a good quality product or service.

(2) Financial

To run a business successfully you will need a range of financial skills. These include skills in such matters as book-keeping, negotiating credit terms with suppliers, invoicing, credit control, estimating, drawing up budgets and controlling cash flow (the flow of money into and out of the business).

(3) Marketing

Marketing is the process by which you identify potential customers and persuade them to buy your products or services. It includes selling skills, and also such matters as pricing, advertising, sales promotions, public relations, and market research.

(4) Management

If you are going to employ others, you will need a variety of management skills in such areas as recruitment, motivating staff and team building. You will need a knowledge of employment law and health and safety requirements. You will also need to be able to fulfil legal requirements in matters such as deducting tax from employees' pay.

(5) Organisation

Whether or not you intend to employ others, you will need organisational skills to ensure that every aspect of your business runs smoothly. This includes setting up systems for dealing with orders and enquiries, keeping customer records, and so on. It also includes time management, i.e. ensuring that your time is used as efficiently as possible.

(6) Planning

Every businessman also needs planning skills. Good financial planning is crucial to the success of a business. Planning skills are also needed to take best advantage of new opportunities which may present themselves, and to avoid any problems due to changing market conditions. Good planning can avert many problems before they happen.

Many of these skills can be acquired through taking courses, reading books (including this one!), talking to professional advisers, and so on. They will also develop naturally with practice and experience once your business is up and running. However, if you are to succeed in running a business of your own, the above are the most important skills you will need to master.

3. THE BENEFITS OF WORKING FROM HOME

There are many practical advantages to running your business from home. Some of the main ones are listed below.

Save money – If you work from home you will avoid having to pay rent and other running costs (including business rates) on business premises. You will also save on travel expenses (see below).

Save on travel – You also avoid wasting many potentially productive hours in your car or on public transport. Many people (e.g. with jobs in London and other major cities) spend two or more hours a day just commuting; added up over a year, the total amount of time 'lost' in this way can be quite staggering. With many roads approaching gridlock during the morning and evening rush hours, the savings in terms of both time and your blood pressure can be substantial. You will save money on petrol and season tickets; and a further benefit is that you will avoid having to venture out every day during the winter months on dangerous, icy roads and pavements. Of course, you will still have to do some travelling, for reasons such as going to the bank or post office, visiting clients and selling your work.

Feel more comfortable – For a start, you can wear whatever clothes you like. You don't even have to dress or shave if you don't wish (though you will, of course, need to make an effort with your appearance when meeting clients and selling your services). You can take as many tea and coffee breaks as you like, whenever it happens to suit you. You can also arrange your office furniture, lighting and so on exactly as you wish.

Benefit from flexibility – Many aspects of family life can be easier to arrange if you work from home. For example, if you want to pop out at 3.15 to collect your youngest child from school, there is nothing (and no-one) to stop you. You can choose your own hours, working early in the morning or late at night if these options suit you best. You can be around during the day when the plumber or the meter reader calls; you can put out the washing and bring it back in if it starts to rain; and you will not miss important deliveries because you are toiling away at a separate workplace.

Enjoy tax advantages – If you work from home you can claim a proportion of your household expenses (heating, lighting, phone, mortgage/rent, etc.) against tax. Any alterations or repairs to the property which are directly relevant to your business activity can also be set against your business income.

Gain greater home security – The fact that you are likely to be around in the day can help deter burglars (most burglaries in residential areas take place during the daytime). You will also be on the premises – and therefore able to take prompt action – in the event of fires, burst pipes and other such emergencies. Some insurance companies are starting to recognise this fact and offer lower premiums for homeworkers – though this must be set against the fact that work-related computers and other equipment may have to be insured separately for an additional premium (see Insurance).

Enlist support from your family – Working from home means you may be able to get help from your family in your business activities. This might include such matters as answering the phone, making appointments, typing invoices and letters, meeting and greeting visitors, and providing other forms of practical assistance (e.g. repairing the car or troubleshooting your brand new multimedia computer which obstinately refuses to function!).

Enjoy the lack of pressure – With a home-based business you can work as many or as few hours as you wish. If you want to work a fifteen-hour day, you can do so (though hopefully not every day!). Equally, however, you can work part-time if you prefer, perhaps to fit in with your family responsibilities. You can also set your own pace, with no-one standing over you telling you to work harder or faster. For older people, or those with disabilities which slow them down, this can be a particular attraction. As long as your business is bringing in enough money to meet your needs and those of your dependants, you can work as hard or as lightly as you wish – you have complete control over your 'terms and conditions'. It should, however, be said that, although you won't have a boss looking over your shoulder, you will still have customers, who will expect a good quality product or service from you within a certain deadline.

4. ...AND A FEW DRAWBACKS

Although working from home has many attractions, it does possess a few potential drawbacks as well. Some of the main points to consider are set out below.

May disrupt family life – Running a business from home means you and your family's domestic lives will inevitably be affected. Obviously you will need a space in the house to work which might otherwise be used by other family members. In addition, many self-employed individuals have to work long and irregular hours, and your family may need to get used to you being in and out at all times. You may have to work during the evenings, public holidays and weekends, when most 'normal' people are at leisure. Furthermore, in many businesses clients may wish to contact you by phone outside standard office hours (this applies especially if you provide a service to private individuals, e.g. window cleaning or gardening). Family members will therefore need to become accustomed to receiving calls from clients and be briefed on how to handle them. If you have other heavy phone users in the house (e.g. teenagers!) you may need to consider having a separate line installed for business calls.

May be too many distractions – Family and domestic matters can also interfere with your business. Friends and relatives who would never dream of interrupting you at a 'proper' job may think nothing of phoning up or arriving unannounced, not realising (or perhaps caring) that you are 'at work'. Regular interruptions of this nature can seriously reduce your productivity, and hence your income. Even if you avoid this problem, working from home offers a huge range of potential distractions, from pets and family matters, through shopping and household chores, to gardening and watching television. You will need to be self-disciplined, or you can fritter away many working hours on non-productive (in business terms, at least) activities such as these.

May be lonely – Running a business from home can be lonely at times. This applies especially if you live on your own, where in some businesses (e.g. writing or computer programming) you may not speak to another person face-to-face (apart from perhaps the post office clerk) for days on end. Even if you do have a family – or at least a spouse/partner – you may find the isolation during the day difficult to bear. This applies especially if you have previously worked in a busy office or factory, or you have a naturally sociable temperament.

Clients may be deterred – Customers who come to see you in person may be put off to find that you work from home. However unreasonably, they may deduce from this that you are not serious about your business and that you might fail to deliver a professional standard of product or service. Even if you conduct your business entirely by mail, some people find what is obviously the use of a private address off-putting. You can get around this problem to some extent by using a PO Box (see Help From The Post Office) or a separate accommodation address.

Can be hard to get away from work – If you work from home, you may find that work and domestic life become indivisible and it is very hard to 'switch off' and relax when the day's work is done. People who have previously worked in a separate establishment often find the journey between home and workplace provided a valuable psychological dividing line. When your home is also your workplace this line is gone, and the distinction between work and leisure can therefore easily become blurred.

May need greater home security – If you have high-value, easily portable equipment such as computers, fax machines and so on, this may make your home a tempting target for burglars. If, as with many businesses, you have to publicise your address on letterheads, advertisements and so on, this will unfortunately increase the risk of your property being targeted. You may need therefore to increase the level of security in your home, perhaps fitting a burglar alarm, security lighting/cameras, window locks, and so on.

Planning and other restrictions may apply – There are often planning restrictions on running businesses from homes in residential areas. This is most likely to be a problem if your proposed business is likely to cause noise or other irritation to your neighbours: printing, for example, or car repairs. If you live in rented accommodation, the landlord may object to your running a business from his property; and if you are buying your house with the aid of a loan or mortgage, the lenders may be unhappy. There may also be terms in the lease or deeds of your property prohibiting its use for business purposes. This and similar matters are further discussed under Planning Permission.

None of these problems is insurmountable, but it is undoubtedly true that working from home is more likely to be suitable for some businesses – and individuals – than others. The best types of business for running from home are small and office-based, rather than those which require workshops and machinery or selling direct to the public. These are the types of business opportunity which feature predominantly in Part B of this book.

5. CHOOSING YOUR BUSINESS IDEA

And so we come to the nitty-gritty – what business will you start? For some people the answer to this may be obvious. If you are a skilled car mechanic, bookkeeper, photographer or gardener, for example, starting a business within your field of expertise is likely to offer you by far the best chances of satisfaction and success. If, however, you don't have a special skill or interest to base a business around, you will need to give this decision some careful thought.

There is a huge range of home-based businesses you could run. Many are listed in Part B of this book. They can be roughly divided into five main categories:

1. Professional – Computer programmer, graphic designer, accountant, architect, personal tutor, interior designer, etc.

2. Creative – Writer, photographer, artist, desktop publisher, sculptor, etc.

3. Service – Childminder, introduction agency proprietor, private investigator, proofreader, indexer, babysitter, upholsterer, carpet cleaner, etc.

4. Craft – Woodworker, toy-maker, picture-framer, french polisher, jewellery-maker, and a range of other craft-based occupations.

5. Physical – Window cleaner, gardener, personal fitness trainer, builder, odd-job (wo)man, car cleaner/valet, curtain-maker, etc.

Of course, any attempt to categorise in this way is somewhat arbitrary. Creative workers such as photographers and artists also have to use physical skills and provide a 'service' to their clients. Likewise, many people in businesses listed above under 'Service' (e.g. childminding and proofreading) quite reasonably regard themselves as professionals as well. Nevertheless, this basic division may help set you thinking about the range of businesses you could start and what type might suit you best.

The actual choice of business is entirely up to you. For many people, starting their own business based on skills acquired through working for an employer is both a logical and an attractive proposition. On the other hand, if you do not enjoy your work and wish to do something different to make a living, clearly you will need to look elsewhere for this.

A hobby or interest has provided the basis for many a successful business. Gardening, photography, craftwork and working as a tourist guide are all examples of businesses which could arise from this source. Of course, you may need to improve your skills and knowledge before you can ply your trade for money – but in most fields there are courses you can take which will (given a modicum of aptitude and ability on your part) bring you up to a professional standard. Courses relevant to specific occupations are described in the corresponding articles in Part B under 'Where Can I Get More Help?'

Even if you don't have a hobby or interest you could develop into a business, there are still plenty of options open to you. Many of the businesses listed in Part B require basic skills which can be acquired relatively easily: household cleaning, babysitting, window cleaning, pet boarding, commission selling, renting a room, and so on. Or you may be able to learn a skill from scratch by taking a course. Interior design, financial advice work and many alternative therapies are examples of businesses you could start after completing a period of study and passing the relevant examinations. Both open learning and standard college courses in these and similar occupations are widely available. Though it must be said that if you choose this path you may have to wait a bit longer before you are able to get your business up and running – a period of years in some cases.

Buying a Franchise

One other option is to buy a franchise. Franchises are basically ready-made business formats. You pay a fee – which is often quite substantial – and in exchange are helped to set up in business using the franchisor's name and business method. Generally speaking, a franchise gives the right to exclusive use of the organisation's established name within a specified area.

The use of the organisation's name is an essential ingredient of any franchise, but in addition most franchises offer all or some of the following:

(1) Help in choosing premises
(2) Advice and assistance in setting up
(3) Training, if required
(4) Publicity material and general marketing support
(5) Operating methods for the business.

The price you pay is usually made up of an initial fee paid to the franchisor, plus a royalty – a specified percentage of your turnover or profits. There is usually also some loss of independence. The prices you can charge may be set by the franchisor, for example, and you may have to buy all your supplies from the franchisor or his nominated supplier.

Not all franchises are suitable for people wanting to set up home-based businesses – even if you wanted to, you would be highly unlikely to get planning permission to turn your home into a Macdonalds' franchise. Many franchised businesses, however, (e.g. carpet cleaning, driving instruction and fast food catering) can perfectly well be operated in this way. You can obtain information on a wide range of franchise opportunities from the British Franchise Association, Thames View, Newtown Road, Henley-on-Thames, Oxon, RG9 1HG. Tel: 01491 578050. Web: www.british-franchise.org.uk.

Buying a franchise, especially of a well-known and established company, can be expensive. Unless you have a large amount of capital you are likely to have to borrow to meet the cost. On the other hand, potential lenders may be more sympathetic if funds are going on a proven business concept. In any event, before entering into any franchise arrangement it is important to obtain professional advice from a solicitor or an accountant.

Other Considerations

Of course, personal preferences are not the only considerations that come into play when deciding what business idea to pursue. Other things you will need to consider include:

Your health – If your physical health is poor, it is likely to be a mistake starting a business which involves regular strenuous effort, e.g. window cleaning. You must be honest with yourself here. Yes, a healthy outdoor business might help build up your stamina – but if, due to ill-health (perhaps brought on by over-exertion), you keep letting your customers down, you will soon have no business left. If health is a factor, you may be better considering an indoor, office-based business, even if this is not your ideal preference.

Your aptitudes and abilities – Again, be honest with yourself here. You might like the idea of being a freelance photographer or writer, but have you really got what it takes to succeed in these competitive professions? For example, it would probably be a mistake to try to launch a career as a freelance writer if all your work has ever received is rejection slips. If appropriate (and possible), get your work appraised by an independent expert, ideally someone who is already successful in your chosen field. This person should be able to give you objective feedback on your abilities and highlight any areas in which you need to improve. Do not rely on encouraging comments from friends and family: they will inevitably view your work through rose-tinted glasses, and in any event are unlikely to be aware of the standards required by professionals in your field. Of course, if you are really determined to make a go of your chosen occupation, you should not necessarily be deterred if you get an unfavourable response initially. This may, however, indicate that it could be wise to spend some extra time polishing and developing your skills before you start to rely on them for an income.

Your other commitments – For many people a major attraction of starting a home-based business is that they can combine earning a living with their other domestic commitments. But this in turn, of course, imposes restrictions on the type of business which you can run. If you need to be at home to look after young children or an elderly relative, for example, you cannot start a business which requires you to work in other people's houses much of the time, e.g. gardening or household cleaning. Similarly, you may only be able to work at certain times, or need to be free at short notice. These requirements will also have a major impact on the type of business you may be able to run.

The market – Whatever the type of business you decide to start, unless there is a large enough group of people willing to pay you for it ('a market') your venture is doomed to failure. Realism, once again, is all-important here. You may have spent your whole life perfecting your skills in producing life-sized wood carvings of British waterfowl, but how many people will want to buy them and for what price? How will you bring your product or service to the attention of potential buyers – and will it be worth your while to do so for what they are prepared to pay? You must think long and carefully about your proposed business and how you will make money from it. This matter is further discussed in the next section, Market Research.

How much capital you have – Some businesses (e.g. manufacturing) require relatively large amounts of capital to get started, to pay for such things as special equipment, raw materials, stock, transportation, operating licences, advertising, and so on. Others (e.g. window cleaning) require very little in the way of capital expenditure. Bear in mind, however, that even in a 'low cost' business you will still need to have sufficient funds to cover your needs and those of your family while your business is becoming established. Financial considerations are further discussed under Raising Finance.

How much you need to earn – Some (a few) home-based businesses can bring in £50 or more an hour, while in others you will be fortunate to earn this amount in a day. If your business is intended to provide a second income – to augment a pension, for example – then earnings may not matter especially to you. In this case you may simply wish to start a business doing what you enjoy, even if it will never bring in a fortune. By contrast, if your business will have to support a family (not to mention a mortgage, car, foreign holidays, school fees and so on) you will need to zero in on those opportunities which offer the best potential for such an income.

Whatever you decide to do, it is important that it meets all your requirements. If you start a business which is unsuitable, for whatever reason, you will not enjoy doing it. And if you cannot do it properly the business is most likely to fail, thus undermining your self-confidence, and perhaps preventing you from doing something else which you could do well.

Narrowing Down the Choice

Having read this far, and examined the range of ideas in Part B, you may well have a number of ideas for businesses you could run. How then can you narrow this down to select the opportunity which would be best for you?

When making this decision, as mentioned above, you will need to take into account a range of considerations, both business and personal. Business considerations include the amount of capital needed to start the business and its earning potential, while personal considerations include your aptitudes and abilities, domestic responsibilities, health and so on. To work out which idea might be the best for you, write down now your favourite business ideas (up to six) on a piece of paper. Then make another, separate list of everything you require from your venture. To give you an idea, your list might include items such as the following:

- Regular hours
- Flexible hours
- Can be operated part-time
- No night work
- No need to employ others
- Low start-up cost

- Involves meeting people
- Does not involve personal selling
- Little paperwork
- No heavy lifting
- Involves working outdoors
- Involves travelling
- Low risk of failure
- High level of profits
- Will exploit existing skills
- Can be combined with family responsibilities
- Will provide potential for expansion.

Now look at your list and decide which are the most important requirements for you personally, and which the least. Give each requirement a weighting (a numerical score) to signify its importance, on a scale from one to ten. For example, if the most important item on your list is 'low start-up cost' you might give this a weighting of nine or ten. An item which you consider of lesser importance might rate five or six, while an item of relatively little importance might merit a weighting of just one or two.

The next step is to rate each of your own business ideas against the weighted requirements. Taking each business idea in turn, award it points on a scale from 0 to 10 for each of your requirements. Give high points if the idea meets the requirement well, and low points if it does not.

When you have finished scoring each business idea, multiply the points you have awarded it on each requirement by the weighted importance factor. For example, if you have given the idea a score of eight on low start-up cost and the importance weighting you gave for start-up cost was seven, then the total score is $7 \times 8 = 56$ on that requirement. The overall score for each business idea is then obtained by adding together all the total scores for that idea. The example below should make this clear.

EXAMPLE

To illustrate this method, take the example of George. A single man in his late twenties, George has recently been made redundant by a printing company. They have been his employers since he left school. As part of the settlement he receives a lump sum payment, and decides to put this towards starting a home-based business of his own.

George wants a business which will provide a steady living doing something he enjoys. His interests include gardening and DIY, and he would like to apply these skills in his new business if possible. Although he has a lump sum to invest, he is keen to make his money stretch as far as possible. He realises that, although he does not have a family to support, he will still need to live off his redundancy payment until the business is operating successfully, and he doesn't want to run up too many debts initially.

While he has no objection to making a fortune, George's greater priority is finding a business with good long-term potential and low risk of failure. He enjoys meeting people, and wants work which will give him the opportunity to do this. He wants to work outdoors at least some of the time. He also likes the idea of working flexible hours, though he attaches less importance to this. George's list of weighted requirements therefore looks something like this:

Requirement	*Importance weighting*
Low risk of failure	10
Low start-up cost	8
Applies hobbies/interests	8
Chance to meet people	6
Outdoor work	5
Flexible hours	3

After careful consideration George has come up with a shortlist of three potentially suitable business ideas. These are:

1. Gardening
2. Window cleaning
3. 'Odd Job' service.

Using the scoring method explained above, George's ideas come out as follows.

		Gardening		Window cleaning		'Odd Job' Service	
Requirement	Importance	Points	Score	Points	Score	Points	Score
Low risk failure	10	8	80	8	80	7	70
Start-up cost	8	7	56	9	63	8	64
Hobbies/interests	8	9	72	3	24	9	72
Meet people	6	7	42	7	42	8	48
Outdoor	5	9	45	9	45	5	25
Flexible hours	3	6	18	5	15	7	21
Totals			313		269		300
Maximum possible score			400		400		400
% of total possible score			82.50		67.25		75.00

In this example, the business which is best suited to George's requirements appears to be the gardening service: it scores higher than the other two, and meets over 80% of his requirements.

As a guide, your highest scoring business should meet well over 50% of your requirements. If it does not, you may be advised to look at some other ideas, or re-consider your requirements.

This exercise should help you clarify which business would suit you best. It does have a few shortcomings, however. For one thing it is based entirely on your own views of what the business would entail, and these may or may not be accurate. In addition, the exercise can only help you decide which business might best meet your personal requirements. It will not tell you whether that business is likely to be a success.

Nevertheless, while the result of this exercise should not be taken as gospel, it does provide a reasonably objective way of comparing one idea with another.

If You Still Can't Decide...

It may be now that you have come down to a choice between two or three different ideas. Each has its attractions but also its drawbacks, and you really can't decide between them. What more can you do to help reach a decision?

One suggestion – which is a good idea even if you have already decided on a business – is to find out more about what each of your possible businesses would involve in practice. See if you can get part-time or temporary work in a similar field. If this proves impossible, speak to others already doing this type of job or go and watch them at work. Once you have more information, you are very likely to find yourself re-grading your business ideas against your list of requirements.

Depending on your proposed business, perhaps you could even try starting up in a small way yourself, working in your spare time initially without giving up your main job. This can provide an excellent opportunity to see how you enjoy doing the work, and may also give you a better idea of how much demand there is likely to be for your services.

Overall, the more information you can obtain about your proposed business before you decide to proceed, the better is the chance that it will meet your expectations and requirements.

6. MARKET RESEARCH

For your business to succeed, one essential requirement is that there are enough people who will want to buy your product or service. If there are not, all the planning and preparation you put in will be in vain. In addition, if you hope to borrow money to finance your business, any potential lender will want to see that you have given careful thought to who your customers will be. Market research is the means by which you establish this.

Who Will Be Your Customers?

Think for a moment about your proposed business – what kind of person is most likely to be a customer? It is very unlikely that your answer to this question will be 'anyone'. If you plan to run a car valeting or repair service, for example, your first answer might be 'car owners'. If you thought about it a little more you might add such things as 'car owners who live no more than five kilometres away' and 'car owners who don't have the time, the inclination or the skills to do the work themselves'. Already you have begun to exclude large numbers of people who are not car owners, not DIY enthusiasts and do not live locally, and in so doing started to focus your attention on those people who will be your potential customers.

If your answer to the question above really is 'anyone', then you need to think very carefully about how viable your proposed business is likely to be. If you plan to offer something needed and bought by everybody – soap, for example, or writing paper – the likelihood is you will be entering a marketplace already dominated by big firms. Because these companies produce and sell in huge quantities, their production costs are low. They can also afford to operate on very low profit margins (that is, to sell their products at only slightly more than it costs to make them). Furthermore, such companies usually spend large amounts on advertising. New businesses attempting to break into this market will have to do the same and more if they are to establish themselves and compete effectively with the existing companies.

Few small businesses have the resources to compete in such a marketplace. Rather, what you will need to do is find a gap, or niche, in the market where you can sell your product or service to a particular group of customers at a price which allows you to make a reasonable profit. The purpose of your market research will be to find such a niche in the market.

Segmenting The Market

As stated above, for a small, home-based business, trying to sell to everybody is unlikely to bring success. You need to find a smaller group of people who could be interested in the product or service you plan to offer. Having identified such a group, you will then have to decide what products or services to offer these people, how to bring your offer to their attention, and how to persuade them to buy.

Segmenting the market is the term used to describe the process of dividing the whole population into a number of separate market 'segments'. These segments are groups of people with something in common. Once you have identified a particular segment (or segments) as your potential customers, you can start to design your marketing plan – that is, your plan for turning these people from potential into actual customers.

There are many ways of segmenting markets, and it is up to you to decide which methods might be most relevant for your business. Some of the most common methods are listed below.

(1) By geographical location

This will be relevant for many small businesses serving a local community. You might decide to segment the market into potential customers living within (say) a 3 km radius, a 10 km radius and a 20 km radius. For many products and services people prefer to buy locally if they can, as this saves them time, effort and (usually) money.

(2) By age

You could segment the market into children, teenagers, young adults, parents, middle-aged people and older people. Each of these groups might have different requirements. If you plan to offer a mobile hairdressing service, for instance, you may need different approaches according to whether you wish to appeal to young, fashion-conscious people or to older people with more traditional requirements.

(3) By type of customer

There are many ways of segmenting the market by type of customer. Often, these will be specific to the business concerned. In the case of a private investigator, for example, you could segment your potential market into solicitors, local authorities, companies and private individuals. Another way of segmenting by type of customer – when selling craft items, say – would be into retailers, wholesalers and end-users. Each of these potential markets would need to be treated differently. Retailers and wholesalers would expect credit terms, for instance, while private customers are generally prepared to pay immediately.

Other ways of segmenting the market include by gender, occupation, religion, income level, leisure interests, car ownership, marital status, family size and so on. Understanding the nature of the people in your target market segment is vitally important when you are trying to sell to them. For example, an office caterer providing food and drinks for a predominantly middle-class workforce might need to offer quite a different range of products from a mobile snack bar in the middle of a factory estate.

Any of these forms of segmentation can be further segmented. For example, you could sub-divide private vehicle owners into car owners, van owners, motorbike owners, and so on; and these groups themselves could be further sub-divided into Ford owners, Nissan owners, etc. The purpose of this is to find one or more market segments which will (you hope) provide the customer base for your new business. You will then be able to plan every aspect of your business with these people in mind.

To be attractive to your business, a market segment should ideally have the following qualities:

1. There are enough people in it to make serving the group profitable.
2. The segment is growing, or at least stable, rather than shrinking.
3. There are unsatisfied needs among this group of people which the business could profitably meet.
4. There is not so much competition among existing firms that another operator would be unable to attract a sufficient share of the market.

Your market research will help you discover the size, level of competition, and profit potential of particular segments. Having completed the research, and clarified the make-up of your chosen groups, you then face a choice:

(1) You can ignore the differences between segments and try to develop a product or service which concentrates on meeting the needs of a wide range of potential customers, **OR**

(2) You can recognise the differing needs of people in different market segments, and try to offer a range of products or services tailored to meet as many as possible of these, **OR**

(3) You can recognise the differing needs of people in different market segments, but choose to offer a narrow range of products or services concentrated on no more than a small number of chosen groups.

None of these strategies is necessarily better than any other, and each may be appropriate at a different stage in your business's development. When starting out, however, (3) is often the best strategy for gaining a foothold in the market, so long as there are sufficient potential customers in that particular market segment.

Why Do People Buy?

As well as identifying who will be your potential customers, another important question to be addressed by your market research is 'Why will they buy?' The reason for this is not hard to see. Unless you know what your potential customers are looking for, how can you be sure you will be offering what they want?

If your business will involve making and selling a product, for example, your customers may fall into two main categories, retailers and private individuals. In the case of the former, the most important factors in determining whether they will buy from you are (a) whether they think your products are likely to sell, and (b) how much profit they will make from each sale. Private individuals, by contrast, may have a wide range of reasons for buying a particular product, including:

- Cost
- Perceived value for money
- Appearance (including colour, shape, design, etc.)
- Reliability
- Quality
- Performance
- Delivery time
- Safety
- Reputation/recommendation of others

- Image (for example, the product is associated in the customer's mind with being young, successful, glamorous).

With service businesses, likewise, people may have a wide range of reasons for buying. In the case of a gardening service, for example, a customer might buy for any (or all) of the following reasons:

- Wish to save time and effort
- Age/poor health/disability
- Wish to get professional results
- Recommendation of neighbours
- Seen the gardener's work elsewhere
- Inexpensive
- Good value for money
- Convenient
- Trust/liking for the individual concerned
- Range of services on offer.

The reasons people have for buying one product or service rather than another are not always the obvious, logical ones. They may, for instance, prefer to do business with someone local, or an older person, or someone they like the look of, rather than a competitor who fails to meet these criteria. It is essential, therefore, to find out what people in your target market really want from the product or service you plan to provide. Knowing this, you will then be better placed to decide exactly what to offer, and how to market your business to make it most attractive to your potential customers.

Doing the Research

Market research is essential to identify who will be your customers and find out something about their requirements. But how do you go about doing this in practice? In Part B, suggestions specific to each business are provided under the heading 'Who Will My Customers Be?' This section will address the question in more general terms. A wide variety of market research methods are available, but they can be roughly divided into 'desk research' and 'field research'.

Desk Research

Desk research, as the name suggests, is research you can do without leaving your desk – or, at most, by means of a trip to the local library. You can obtain a surprising amount of useful information by this method alone. Some of the most useful sources include:

Directories – There are directories listing the major companies in most trades and industries (the best-known UK publications include Kompass, Key British Enterprises and Kelly's Manufacturers' and Merchants' Directory). These publications can give you invaluable information about the size of a particular market, the main players, and potential customers and suppliers. Clearly, such directories will be less useful if you plan to run a local service business (e.g. window cleaning); but in cases where you will be selling your services to other businesses (e.g. writers, computer programmers and graphic designers) they can provide invaluable information about the sector concerned.

Government information/statistics – The government, via its publishing arm the Stationery Office, publishes research findings and statistics covering such matters as population changes, industrial production, imports and exports, and so on. These are obviously less useful for finding out about local trading conditions, but can provide valuable information on overall trends.

Trade magazines, newsletters and journals – There are national and international publications serving almost every trade and occupation, from Toy Trader to PR Week, Homebrew Supplier to Construction Weekly. These can provide invaluable information on trends and current issues in the business area concerned. As well as reading the articles, look at the advertisements. They can tell you a great deal about potential suppliers, customers and competitors.

Competitors' literature – This is perhaps the most useful source of all. By studying the advertising material produced by your competitors you can learn a lot about whom they see as their target market and how they sell to them. Not only that, you can learn from any mistakes they make and adapt some of their better ideas yourself!

Finally, do not neglect the mass of valuable research information on the internet. A growing number of small businesses in every sphere now have websites, and this can provide a wonderful quick and easy method for checking out the competition. If you plan to start a childminding business, for example, enter 'childminding' in a search engine such as Search UK (www.searchuk.com). This will lead you to a number of websites advertising childminding services, as well as a range of organisations serving and representing childminders both locally and nationally.

Field Research

While desk research can provide useful background information about the area of business you plan to enter, much of this is bound to be fairly general. To get specific information about potential customers and their requirements, you will almost certainly need to do some practical 'field' research as well.

A lot of this can be informal. If you plan to start a local service business, for example, ask around your friends, neighbours, colleagues and relatives. Find out who (if anyone) they employ at present for the service in question, and the reasons they have for using them. Ask them if they have any complaints about their present supplier, and if there are additional services they would like which this person does not at present provide. Ask what it would take to persuade them to switch to a new supplier. Other informal research methods include talking to people already in similar businesses (maybe in other parts of the country or offering different services, so they will not see you as a potential competitor). Or observing other businesses and using your own personal judgement – what would **YOU** require if you were a potential customer?

Researching potential competitors, as mentioned earlier, is also essential. If possible, obtain copies of the sales literature produced by these businesses. You could also try contacting them, posing as a potential customer, to find out their prices, procedures, sales methods, and so on. This may seem a little underhand if you have no intention of buying, but the information you can obtain in this way is invaluable – and you may be certain that, once you are in business, others will do just the same to you. Once you have obtained this information, try completing the simple exercise below.

EXERCISE

Researching Your Competitors

Start by identifying the three other businesses who will be your main competitors (if you can only identify one or two, just use these). Write the name of each business on the top of a sheet of paper, and put below it, in a few sentences, where the business is located and the products and/or services it sells. Also include here any information you have been able to obtain about the prices they charge or their hourly rates.

Now, for each of these businesses, write down (a) the business's particular strengths, and (b) any weaknesses you have been able to discern. For example, with a shop, the strengths might include friendly service and a prime high street position, while weaknesses might include high prices or a limited range of goods.

Finally, for each of these businesses, list as many advantages as you can think of which your business will have over them. To give you an idea, these might include a wider range of products or services, free delivery, a 24-hour emergency service, free initial consultation, money-back guarantee, expert advice, and so on.

This exercise should help you to clarify who will be your main competitors and how you will encourage people to buy from you rather than from them. It is worth continuing this exercise even when your business is up and running. For one thing, the other businesses, if they start to lose customers to you, are quite likely to try to win them back by offering extra benefits themselves. It is a good idea to keep a file or folder on each of your main competitors and, as well as your observations about them, put in copies of their advertising leaflets, price lists, order forms and so on.

If you are going to sell a product via retailers (or wholesalers), you can also approach them for help and advice. They will have a good knowledge of what their customers want, and should be able to tell you what does and doesn't sell. This approach will not work if you plan to sell directly to end users, of course.

Finally, if you really want to do your research properly (and impress any potential lender or backer) you could consider doing a small-scale survey. This involves contacting a good cross-section of people who might be your customers (not just friends and colleagues) to find out what they want and what influences them when deciding what to buy. One good way of doing this is by producing a simple questionnaire. Questionnaires are important tools in market research, and worth looking at in more detail.

Questionnaires

The only way to get accurate information about people's needs, views and habits is to ask them. Questionnaires (written lists of questions) provide a planned and structured way of doing this. Using a questionnaire ensures that you ask everybody the same questions, and makes it much easier to compare and analyse the replies. There are a few basic rules to good questionnaire design:

(1) Keep it short and simple – Most people will not object to answering a few simple questions, but a multi-page document which will take up hours of their time is quite a different matter. Think carefully about what you need to find out, and ask only the most important things. There should be no more than five to ten questions in total. Wherever possible use yes/no questions and multiple choice (where the person answering has to choose from a list of possible answers), as these are easier to complete and to analyse.

(2) Don't ask 'loaded' questions – A loaded question is one which invites a particular answer. If, for instance, you ask 'Would you use my service if it was cheaper than the existing ones', most people will answer 'Yes' without much thought. It is better to ask neutral, factual questions such as 'Where do you have your car serviced at present?' or 'What would you consider a reasonable price for having all your carpets professionally steam cleaned?' The information you obtain from questions such as these will be much more useful to you.

(3) Don't ask too many 'open' questions – All questions can be either open or closed. A closed question allows only a limited number of replies – two in the case of yes/no questions, perhaps half a dozen with multiple choice. This makes closed questions quick and easy to answer. By contrast, open questions (such as 'Do you think a mobile car repair service is a good idea?') admit a huge range of possible answers.

Occasionally open questions may produce interesting and unexpected replies which can affect your whole thinking about the business. But they can also lead to lengthy discussion and debate, and replies to them can be very difficult to compare and analyse. For that reason, it is normally best to have no more than one or two open questions on your questionnaire.

(4) Ask the right people – there is no point in talking to people who are not going to be potential customers. Finding the right people may require house-to-house interviews or stopping people in the street. It will also depend on the type of business you plan to start. For example, if you hope to start a desktop publishing service, you will need to talk to people in local small businesses who are likely to be your main clients.

(5) Ask as many people as you can – The more people you interview, the more useful and accurate your results are likely to be. Rather than try to cram everybody's answers on to one

piece of paper, it is best to make photocopies of your questionnaire and complete one for every person you ask. This makes adding up the figures at the end much easier.

Your Marketing Plan

Once you have completed your market research, you should be in a good position to prepare your marketing plan. This will set out how you propose to attract customers for your business (and, as already noted, without customers no business can survive). Specifically, your marketing plan should answer the following four questions:

(1) How will you advertise your product or service?
(2) What other forms of promotion will you use?
(3) How will you sell your product/service (e.g. retail, wholesale, agents)?
(4) What features and benefits will you emphasise when trying to attract customers?

Let's look at each of these in a little more detail.

(1) How will you advertise your product or service?

If you are providing a local service, the main places you are likely to want to advertise include local newspapers, directories, magazines, and so on. On the other hand, if you aim to sell nationally – perhaps by mail order – you will need to use national newspapers and magazines, and perhaps other media such as posters, TV and radio. In the latter case your advertising costs are likely to be high, and you might consider using an advertising agent to write and place your advertisements for you. Advertising agents are discussed in more detail under Where to Get More Help.

(2) What other forms of promotion will you use?

Advertising is by no means the only possible method of bringing your business to the attention of possible customers and persuading them to buy from you. Other possibilities include:

- Sales promotions (e.g. free gifts or special opening offers)
- Taking a stall at an exhibition
- Preparing a card or leaflet and distributing them to potential clients
- Public relations (persuading the local media that what you are doing is newsworthy and merits free coverage)

- Publicity stunts (another way of obtaining publicity and media coverage)
- Sponsorship (e.g. persuading the local football team to wear the name of your business on their shirts, in exchange for your practical and financial support).

Advertising and promotion will be discussed in more detail under Marketing and Selling.

(3) How will you sell your product or service?

You have a range of choices here, depending on the type of business you intend to start. If you are making a product, for instance, you might decide to sell it through shops or wholesalers, or you might try to sell directly to customers yourself. You might alternatively, or in addition, take on an agent and pay him a commission (a proportion of the selling price) for every product he sells.

Each method has advantages and disadvantages. If you sell through retailers or agents, for instance, they will take part of the profit on every sale. On the other hand, if you attempt to sell directly to customers yourself, you are likely to have to spend a lot more time and money on advertising and promotion. The method you choose to sell your products or services will have important implications in areas such as pricing, cashflow and budgeting.

(4) What features and benefits will you emphasise when trying to attract customers?

Your market research should have given you some idea of the features people in your target segment are looking for in the products or services you intend to provide. In your marketing plan, you should therefore be able to specify what will be the main 'selling points' you emphasise in your advertising.

Assessing Market Trends

Identifying potential market segments and the needs of the people in them are essential if your business is to succeed. Markets, however, are constantly changing. If your business is to prosper in the long-term, it is important to avoid relying on a market with poor future prospects. You should be especially wary of starting a business based on providing goods or services which may be merely a fad, with demand liable to collapse when the next fashion takes over.

Obviously it is impossible to predict how exactly the world will change in the future, but when planning your business it is important to try to take into account not only what the marketplace is like today, but how it may be in five, ten or twenty years time. Market research can be invaluable for spotting and predicting future trends, which can affect even apparently stable occupations such as gardening. For example:

- The growing number of elderly people in the population could lead to an increase in demand for lawn mowing and basic garden care services.
- More people taking foreign holidays in exotic locations might lead to a greater demand for exotic plants and people skilled in cultivating them.
- The trend for both couples in a relationship to go out to work may mean they have less time for activities such as gardening and be more inclined to employ a part-time gardener.

As the above list shows, there is a positive aspect to the need to predict trends. Social changes – more widespread car ownership, for example, or people living longer – can bring new opportunities for far-sighted businessmen and women who anticipate such changes and prepare for them.

7. PLANNING PERMISSION

The good news is that most home-based businesses do not require planning permission. The rules say that permission is not required provided your work use 'does not change the overall character of the property's use as a single dwelling'.

So a graphic artist or writer (to take a couple of fairly random examples from Part B) working in a spare bedroom would not in most cases require planning permission. The same applies even in the case of small-scale manufacturing and service businesses – for example, making toys or craft items, or carrying out clothing alterations and repairs. Planning permission is not normally required so long as your activities do not affect the overall domestic character of the building. If, however, the non-residential use ceases to be subsidiary, perhaps because your business has expanded, planning permission will be required for a change of use. A planning authority might consider the following evidence that a material change of use has occurred:

- A significant alteration to the appearance of the dwelling
- A significant increase in volume of visitors or traffic

- A significant increase in noise, fumes or smell
- The installation of special machinery or equipment not normally found in a dwelling
- The laying out of rooms in such a way that they could not easily revert to residential use at the end of the working day.

In practice, the attitude of the planning department is likely to be influenced by any negative comments they receive from your neighbours. It follows that an important consideration is how much disruption your business activities are likely to cause. If you know your business is likely to be noisy or create fumes or some other nuisance, you may need to think about ways in which you could reduce the nuisance to your neighbours. A freelance musician might have to consider adding sound-proofing to her practice room, for example.

If you need to physically extend your property to accommodate your business, you almost certainly will need planning permission. A full discussion of the planning laws is outside the scope of this book, but broadly in England and Wales you will need permission for new building work if:

- For a terraced house (including end of terrace) or any house in an official conservation area, the volume of the original house would be increased by more than 10% or 50 cubic metres (whichever is the greater).
- For a detached or semi-detached house, the volume of the original house would be increased by more than 15% or 70 cubic metres (whichever is the greater).
- In any case, the volume of the original house would be increased by more than 115 cubic metres.

There are also certain other stipulations. For example, you must apply for planning permission if (irrespective of the points above) the addition would be nearer to any highway than the nearest point of the original house, unless there would still be at least 20 metres between the house as extended and the highway.

Applying for planning permission involves contacting the planning department of your local authority (their number will be in the phone book), and obtaining and completing the necessary application forms. You will also have to pay a fee. In addition, you are likely to require building regulations approval from the local authority's building control department – though your chosen contractor will normally handle this on your behalf. One final point is that you should check the conditions in your mortgage or lease, as this may place conditions on uses to which the property may be put. If you are in any doubt about what you may or may not do, it is advisable to consult a solicitor.

8. FORMS OF BUSINESS ORGANISATION

Even if you only want to run a small home-based business on your own, you should know something about how businesses generally are organised. There are three most common forms of business organisation:

(1) Sole trader
(2) Partnership
(3) Company with limited liability.

Each of these types of organisation has its advantages and its disadvantages. It is impossible to say which is best, because none is best in all circumstances.

Sole Trader

This is the oldest, simplest and most common form of business organisation. It is also the most straightforward to set up. Basically, the owner or proprietor of the business *is* the business. Whether you trade under your own name or use a business name such as Garden Designs, you are solely responsible for everything the business does. Being a sole trader does not mean you cannot employ anyone – it simply means that you are the only owner of the business (often called the proprietor). This form of organisation is common in small service businesses of all kinds.

Operating as a sole trader is simple and cheap. It also has the great advantage that all the profits belong to you personally, so if your business does well you can make a lot of money. There are other benefits as well. A sole trader makes all the decisions himself, so this type of business can be very flexible, adapting quickly to changing circumstances. If, for instance, your customers start asking for new products or services, you can make the changes needed to provide them quickly and easily. There is no-one to argue with you if you wish to alter the way the business is run. Without doubt, operating as a sole trader can provide great personal satisfaction.

Being a sole trader does have its drawbacks, however. Just as all the profits of the business belong to you, so you personally are responsible for all its debts. If the business cannot pay its creditors, you, the business owner, can be made bankrupt – that is, you may be forced to sell your personal possessions, your house, your car, and so on to pay off the business's debts.

As a sole trader, you are liable not only for what you do, but for what your employees (if you have any) do as well. For instance, if they fail to install or repair an electrical appliance correctly and it causes an injury, you personally may be sued. It is therefore essential that you insure against such mishaps. The business is also heavily dependent on your good health, and you should insure against the possibility of this failing.

Most sole traders operate businesses which do not require substantial amounts of capital (money invested in the business). They largely provide their own money at the beginning. However, when the time comes to expand, the owner may have to borrow in order to increase the assets of the business, and this is where other people may enter the picture.

It is at this stage that one of the other forms of business organisation may be considered, because they make more money available. However, they do involve a reduction in personal control and direction of the enterprise.

Partnership

In this form of business there are two or more owners. They divide the profits between them, and also share liability for any debts which arise. Partnerships are common in all fields where personal service is involved. Many professional practices such as accountancy, law and medicine are organised in this way.

A great advantage with a partnership is that there is usually more money available to be invested in the business. The worries and responsibilities are shared among more people and, of course, there are more people to contribute to the business's success. Everything does not depend on one person. If one partner is ill, or just wishes to take a holiday, the whole business will not come grinding to a halt.

A big disadvantage of a partnership is that if it fails you can be called upon to pay all the debts of the partnership. This includes the debts of your partners if they cannot pay their share – even if the debts were incurred without your knowledge.

In addition, there tend to be stricter legal requirements governing partnerships, and this means more rules concerning how you organise and run the business. Responsibility for decision-making will be shared between you and your partners, thus also reducing your freedom of action, and perhaps leading to disagreements.

Furthermore, partners will often put different amounts of money into the business. In some cases, one partner may have supplied most of the money, while the other has brought the expertise. This may cause disagreement over how profits should be shared. It would not be reasonable for profits to be shared simply in proportion to money invested; the partner who put up less money would naturally expect some reward for his expertise, though deciding what this should be might be difficult. It is essential that such issues should be settled at the start in a formal partnership agreement. If you are thinking of starting a business as a partnership, you should certainly seek legal advice.

Company

A company – properly called a joint stock company – is where a group of individuals put their money together to make a 'joint stock' of capital. The people who put up the money are called shareholders. They all own a share of the company, and expect to receive a share of its profits.

The shareholders are also called 'members' because they are part of the company, but the company is a legal entity quite separate from the members who own it. In law, a company is regarded as an individual in its own right. It can make a profit or a loss; it can be held responsible for the actions of its employees; it can be sued; and, if the worst comes to the worst, it can go bankrupt (though in the case of companies this is called 'going into liquidation').

The amount of the company each shareholder owns is directly proportional to the money he puts in. The shares of large companies are bought and sold on the stock exchange. Such companies are called public companies, and anybody can buy their shares through a stockbroker or bank. The shares of many smaller companies, however, are owned entirely by the people who work in them.

Limited Liability

Nowadays nearly every joint stock company in the world is formed on the principle of limited liability. In the UK such companies must put the letters 'Ltd' (the abbreviation for Limited) or PLC (short for Public Limited Company) after their name. In other parts of the world they put letters like 'S.A.', 'N.V', 'GmbH' and 'Inc'. These are all very similar in meaning.

Limited liability means that if a company fails and has to close down, the individual shareholders will not be held responsible for the company's debts. Each shareholder only loses the money he spent on buying his shares. Unlike a sole trader or a partner, his personal possessions cannot be sold to pay the company's debts; his liability is limited to the amount he invested (hence the term 'limited liability').

Because of the principle of limited liability, establishing your new business as a company may appear an attractive option. Potential lenders and creditors are very well aware of the principle and its implications as well, however. If you apply for a loan or credit terms, they will naturally want to ensure that their money is returned in the event of your company failing. Particularly if you are setting up a new business, therefore, they may require you to personally guarantee any debts, e.g. by allowing them to place a legal charge on your property. In this case, if your company does subsequently fail, the creditor can still pursue you personally for any debts outstanding.

Company Directors

Although a company is regarded in law as a separate person, it cannot carry out any business by itself. People must be appointed to manage and run the business, and these people are called the company directors. The minimum number of directors in a private company is one (though in this case someone else must fulfil the role of company secretary). A public limited company must have at least two directors.

In a small company, such as a family business, the shareholders are often themselves the company directors; they both own the company and run it. With larger companies it is usual for shareholders to appoint directors with the necessary skills to manage the company on their behalf. The shareholders meet just once a year, at an annual general meeting, to express their approval or disapproval of the way the directors are managing the business; to appoint new directors if required; and to accept or reject the directors' recommendations on how the profits are to be distributed.

Again, in a small company all or most of the directors will be closely involved in the running of the business. In a larger company many of the directors may only work part-time for the company, simply attending board meetings at which general policy decisions are taken. They leave the day-to-day running of the company to one director, known as the managing director, or a small number of executive directors. Unless they are also shareholders, directors are not entitled to a share of the profits. However, they are entitled to a fee for the work they do for the company, plus their expenses. The managing director and executive directors, who work full-time for the company, also receive a salary, just like any other employee.

The directors may employ staff to work for them and managers to supervise those staff, but the directors have the overall responsibility and are answerable to the shareholders for the success or failure of the enterprise. The shareholders have the right to demand not only that the directors act in good faith, but also that they exercise skill and care in managing the business.

Which Type of Organisation?

Each type of business organisation has its advantages and disadvantages, and you must choose the type which is most suitable for your needs.

The sole trader approach is likely to be the first choice for many small home-based businesses. Its advantages are:

(1) It is easy to set up
(2) The owner has complete personal control
(3) All profits belong to the owner personally.

The disadvantages of being a sole trader are:

(1) The liability of the owner is unlimited - he may be made personally bankrupt if the business fails
(2) The growth of the company is limited by the amount of money the owner either has or can borrow as a personal loan
(3) If the owner is ill, the business may not be able to carry on; although sometimes a good employee may be able to manage the business for a short while.

Setting up in partnership can overcome some of the above drawbacks. A partnership is more complicated to set up than a sole trader business, but less so than a limited company. The advantages of a partnership are:

(1) It offers greater scope for financial investment and growth
(2) It allows the skills of several people to be combined, rather than relying on one person
(3) If one partner is ill, the others can continue the business; the business may also continue on the death of one partner.

The disadvantages are:

(1) As with a sole trader, the liability of the partners is unlimited; however, in this case, the partner accepts liability not only for his own decisions but for those of his partner or partners. It is therefore essential that a partnership is only entered into with people whose integrity and ability can be relied upon
(2) Although there is likely to be more money available for a partnership than for a sole trader, there will generally be much less than for a limited company
(3) Each partner has less direct control than a sole trader.

A limited liability company is the safest type of enterprise, but it is also the most complex. Its advantages are:

(1) No individual is liable to the company for any amount in excess of the value of his shares; thus, everyone knows how much he is committing himself to from the start
(2) If the company fails, individuals will not normally face personal bankruptcy and the loss of their property and possessions
(3) The amount of money available for investment is much greater than with other forms of business
(4) More expertise is generally available.

The disadvantages are:

(1) The business is more complicated to set up and will generally require the professional services of a lawyer and an accountant
(2) There is a cost involved in registering as a legal company
(3) The person who sets up the business does not own it - no individual does. He may well be the majority shareholder (that is, the person who owns most of the shares) and have a considerable amount of control, but he cannot have the complete personal control of the sole trader. What he does will be subject to the power of other shareholders, and to the requirements of very strict laws.

In summary, each type of business organisation has both advantages and disadvantages. Many people starting out opt for sole trader status, and perhaps subsequently expand into partnerships and companies as their businesses grow and develop. When starting out, the important thing is to decide what type of organisation will be most appropriate for your business. If you decide to start off as a sole trader no special action as needed, though you should of course notify the Inland Revenue and Department of Social Security (see Tax, National Insurance and VAT). If you are considering setting up in partnership or as a limited company, greater formalities are required. In this case it is highly advisable to obtain professional advice from a solicitor and/or an accountant (see Where to Get More Help).

9. YOUR BUSINESS NAME AND IMAGE

One essential decision you need to make before you start trading concerns your business's name. An obvious possibility for one-person businesses is simply to use your own name. Using this alone, however, tells people very little about what you do. Many businesses take advantage of this opportunity to explain their activities and project a sales message. A simple approach would be to use your name, and add a word or two about the business – for example, Pete Martin Investigations or Rehman Curtains & Upholstery.

You can also use your business name to express your product or service's main selling point. For example, if you are running a children's entertainment service with conjuring tricks, you might decide to call yourself 'Magic Parties'. If you are a plumber offering a 24-hour emergency service, you might choose the name 'Instant Plumbing'.

Avoid choosing a very long name, as people will have difficulty remembering it. Another reason is that you will have to answer the phone in your business's name. Saying 'Littleton Vehicle Cleaning and Valeting Service' twenty or thirty times a day could soon have your tongue in knots! A simple, easy-to-pronounce name, no longer than three or four words, is usually best.

There are some words which you may not use in your business name without official clearance. In Britain, such words include 'royal' and 'authority'. If you are in any doubt about the legality of the name you wish to use, a solicitor should be able to advise you.

Finally, you should try hard to avoid giving your business the same name as another which is already trading. If the other business thinks you are using their name to cash in on goodwill they have built up with their own customers, you could end up in court accused of 'passing off'. This could happen even if you copy the other business's name unintentionally. The local phone book should reveal whether another business in the area is already using your proposed name. You could also make enquiries at your local chamber of commerce.

Your Business's Image

Your business's name is one aspect of its image: the way your business appears to other people and the impression they get of it. Often this goes beyond purely factual matters to feelings and emotions: for example, a business's image may be young and dynamic, or safe and traditional; witty and creative, or honest and straightforward. Apart from the business's name, another important contributor to your image is your letterhead and logo (if you have one).

Most businesses have to send letters to people such as customers and potential customers, suppliers, banks, government officials and so on. Your letterhead is, literally, the heading you use for this. A suitable letterhead can help to give your business the kind of image you want. Just as when choosing your business name, therefore, you should give careful thought to the design of your letterhead.

Letterheads are usually printed on white paper. Tinted papers, such as cream and pale blue, are also popular but may be a little more expensive. Weight of paper is usually measured in grammes per square metre (gsm). Eighty gsm is about the minimum for a letterhead, and if you want your image to be an up-market one you may prefer to use a weight of 100 gsm or more.

One other decision you will need to make concerns the colour of the printing. Black is cheapest and photocopies well. Full-colour letterheads can look impressive, but cost more to print. If you want colour on your letterheads, consider using just one or two colours, perhaps on tinted paper to give the effect of an extra colour. Finally, if you have a computer/word processor, you can of course design a letterhead on this and print it out either in colour or black-and-white (depending on your printer). Modern word processing and desktop publishing programs can give excellent results, but you may need to spend a little time experimenting in order to get a finished effect you like.

Your letterhead will need to include most or all of the following:

- The name of your business
- Your address
- Your telephone number
- Your mobile number
- Your fax number
- Your e-mail address.

If you are using a business name other than your own, it is customary (and a legal necessity in some countries) to include your own name as well – e.g. at the foot of the page, 'Proprietor: J. Johnson'. This helps people who may be contacting you for the first time by giving them a name they can ask for. Limited companies are required to provide a range of information on their letterhead, including company registration number and country of registration.

One other thing you may decide to include on your letterhead is information about the business and/or an advertising slogan. For example, you could include details about the products or services you supply, and a short sales message: 'Photos to remember', 'Keeping your garden green' or whatever!

Your letterhead may also include a logo. This is a symbol or emblem which you hope people will come to associate with your business. Large companies spend sizeable amounts designing and publicising their logos, and there is no doubt that they can make a valuable contribution to a business's image. For small, home-based businesses logos are probably less useful. But if you have a good idea for one, by all means use it if you can. The present author, for example, has on his letterhead a stylised typewriter image originally obtained from a copyright-free clip-art disk. Another example of an attention-grabbing letterhead, this time incorporating a cartoon, is shown in Figure 1.

If you can't, or don't want to design your own letterhead, most printers will do this for you, or you may wish to commission a graphic artist (see Where to Get More Help). It should be possible to adapt your letterhead for use on business cards, compliments slips, invoices and so on. In addition, if your business has transport, such as a van, a version of the letterhead and/or logo should appear on this also. The overall aim is to create a clear, distinct identity for your business in people's minds, so that whenever they see the name, letterhead or logo, they will be know

Figure 1 – If you want to be noticed, get a letterhead that stands out! Freelance writer John Matthey commissioned a cartoonist to produce his, based on a verse he provided. He says, "It was the best £90 I've ever invested as it never fails to provoke a comment and puts me way ahead of the rest."

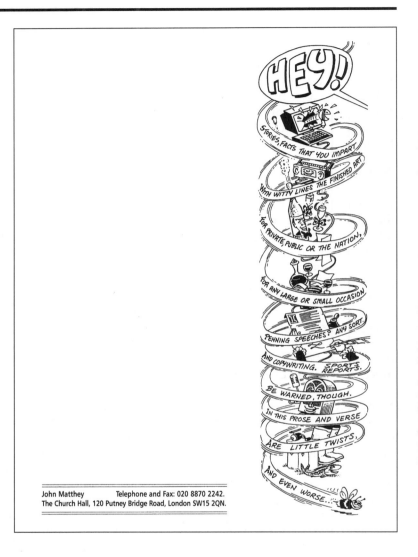

John Matthey   Telephone and Fax: 020 8870 2242.
The Church Hall, 120 Putney Bridge Road, London SW15 2QN.

instantly to whom it refers. This is part of what large companies call their corporate image. Even if yours is just a one-person home-based business, there is no reason why you cannot do likewise!

10. BUSINESS PLAN AND FINANCIAL FORECASTS

So far we have been examining various matters which must be taken into account before starting a home-based business. These aspects are brought together in an important document called your business plan. This is the document which sets out, in words and figures, all the plans you have made for starting and running your business.

Preparing a business plan is far from being a mere academic exercise. Your business plan will fulfil three important functions:

(1) It will help you clarify and organise your thoughts
(2) It will help you raise finance
(3) It will help you monitor your business once it has started.

Let's look at each of these in a little more detail.

(1) Organising Your Thoughts

When you are planning a business there are so many different things to consider that it is very easy to become confused. Putting the whole thing in writing can help you clarify your thoughts and assess the whole project more objectively. In addition, to complete the plan you will have to answer a lot of questions. This forces you to go out and do the necessary research to find answers, which in itself is an excellent discipline.

(2) Raising Finance

If you need to apply for a loan, your business plan will demonstrate to the bank manager or lender that you have carefully considered every aspect of the proposed business, and that you know exactly how much money you need to borrow and what you will require it for. This will help reassure him that his funds will be wisely used. Even if you do not plan to apply for a loan, a business plan could help save you from losing your own money.

(3) Monitoring Your Progress

The business plan sets down the path along which the business should be moving. When you first start your business there will be a vast number of things to do, and it is easy to delude yourself that you are doing well simply because you are busy. Your business plan – in particular the cash flow forecast – will guide you through this period. With the plan at your side, you can take stock at regular intervals (every month perhaps) of how your business is doing. If you are failing to meet your targets, you can then decide on what remedial action to take...and the sooner the better!

Style and Presentation

Business plans can be set out in many different ways, though the information contained is much the same. Some general guidelines are given overleaf.

(1) Your plan must be neatly and professionally presented. It should be typed (never handwritten) and enclosed in a cover or binder which includes the name of the business and the name and address of the person (or persons) behind it. If an accountant has been closely involved in preparing the plan, his or her name and address should be given also.

(2) The plan should be written in the third person - that is, 'the proprietor' or 'Mr/Ms Rogers'. You should avoid referring to yourself in a business plan as 'I' or 'me'. This is simply about appearing business-like.

(3) The plan should be as concise (i.e. brief) as possible, whilst including all the necessary information that a financial backer or other interested party would want to see.

(4) The text should avoid too many salesman's phrases such as 'this wonderful product' or 'this incredible opportunity'. The tone needs to be confident but objective. Rather than make wild claims and sweeping generalisations, in a business plan, as far as possible, you should stick to facts you can prove.

(5) The plan should clearly demonstrate the viability of the proposed business. Remember that potential backers will be looking for evidence of two things in particular: market research, and financial planning and control.

The Contents

Your business plan will need to include most or all of the following sections.

- Introduction
- Product or service details
- Personnel
- Market research and marketing plan
- Premises, equipment and transport
- Suppliers and sub-contractors
- Legal aspects
- Financial information
- Risk assessment
- Financial requirements
- Appendices.

Let's look at each of these in a little more detail.

(1) Introduction

This is where you explain the nature of the business and its proposed structure (e.g. sole trader, partnership, limited company). It should be no longer than one or two paragraphs. If the plan has been written for a specific purpose - e.g. to support an application for a loan - this should also be mentioned here.

(2) Product or Service Details

In this section you describe in some detail the product or service you will be providing. If it is a product, you should show clearly how it will be made, explaining all the stages involved. If instead you are providing a service, you need to explain precisely what this is and what type of customers you expect to require it.

(3) Personnel

In this section you include information about the person or people who are behind the business and will be managing it. If you intend to be a sole trader, this will of course be yourself. In partnerships and limited companies, it will also include your partners or fellow directors.

You should describe briefly your past work experience, especially where this is obviously relevant to the new business. Include any educational or occupational qualifications, and any previous experience of running a business. You should also mention here any business-related training you are undertaking. If you are receiving active advice and support from a business development agency (for example), state this here also. Your overall aim is to demonstrate to a potential lender or backer that you, as the person behind the business, are well prepared for self-employment, and have the experience and training to make it a success.

Finally, in this section you should mention whether you intend to employ any staff. You should indicate how many you will need, what skills they will require, how much you expect to have to pay them, whether they will be full- or part-time, and what training they will need.

(4) Market Research and Marketing Plan

This is a very important section which will normally take up at least a page of text, and in many cases more. Its purpose is to convince the reader that there will be enough demand for your product or service to make the business viable within the market in which you intend to operate.

This section should therefore summarise your market research, and in particular answer the following questions:

(1) Who will be your customers, and what will be their requirements?
(2) How large will your potential market be?
(3) Who will be your competitors – their names, addresses and details?
(4) What are the main strengths of these competitors?
(5) What will be your advantages over them – or, to put this another way, why will people buy from you rather than them?

All your answers should be backed up with facts and figures from your market research. When you are describing the market size, for instance, you should explain clearly how you have arrived at this figure. Statements such as 'There is considerable demand for...' or 'Many people require...' are worthless without some market research data to back them up.

Also in this section you should describe your marketing plan. This concerns how you will advertise, promote and sell your product or service. As stated in the section Market Research, it should answer the following questions:

• How and where will you advertise your product or service?
• What other forms of promotion will you use (e.g. direct mail, exhibitions, telephone selling)?
• How will your product or service be sold (e.g. wholesale, retail or through agents)?
• What features and benefits will you emphasise when trying to attract customers?

Marketing is further discussed in the section Marketing and Selling.

(5) Premises, Equipment and Transport

This section will state the premises to be used. For most readers of this book this will be their home, so you should state this, with perhaps a few words on why this is ideal for your purposes (low cost, convenience, etc.). If you will be working from an office in your home, or perhaps a converted garage or shed, this should be mentioned as well. Remember, the aim is to convince backers that working from home is a sensible option for your business and you have all the facilities and space required.

Similarly with equipment and transport, you should explain what you need, how it will be obtained – e.g. by leasing, hire purchase or outright payment – and whether it will be new or second-hand. If you will require a lot of equipment, it may be worth including more details in the Appendix.

(6) Suppliers and Sub-contractors

Many businesses rely on other businesses to supply them with raw materials, components or services. Any problems in obtaining these can result in disaster for the business, especially if it is a new one. In this section you should therefore explain who your main suppliers and subcontractors will be and why you have chosen them, stating alternatives where possible. You should also comment on any discussions you have already had with suppliers, agreements reached, credit facilities negotiated, and so on.

(7) Legal Aspects

In this section you should include details of any legal matters or requirements which may impinge on your business. For example, if your particular business requires a permit or a licence, you should state here how this will be obtained, what it will cost, what delays are likely between applying and receiving it, and what are the criteria you and the business will have to meet to qualify.

Also in this section you might mention patents (where you are making an original product and wish to prevent others copying it), planning permission (where such permission is required to operate your proposed business) and so on. It is most important that your business fulfils all the legal requirements before you start trading, and backers will want to see that you have taken this into account.

(8) Financial Information

This is probably the most important part of the whole business plan, because it must demonstrate to potential lenders that you have a clear plan and targets for your business's finances, both now and over the coming months. Specifically, it will show that you know how much money you need, what you need it for, how much you expect to receive and to pay out during the business's first twelve months, and how much margin for error you have given yourself.

This section should also explain your policy on pricing. With products you should state the mark-up you intend to use, while for service businesses you should state your hourly rate (for more details, see the section Pricing Your Services). It is customary to mention the normal mark-ups or hourly rates of your particular industry, and give the reasons if yours differ from this. This is very important, as new businesses often under-price, often with dire results.

The section should also include a forecast profit and loss account and a cash flow forecast (see pages 66–72). The former shows the profits you expect to make, while the latter shows the predicted flow of cash into and out of your business (especially crucial in the first few months). With all financial projections you should avoid being over-optimistic and allow reasonable amounts for contingencies (especially overheads, which always seem to be larger than anticipated). You should also state any assumptions you are making, e.g. concerning credit you are given by suppliers and have to extend to customers.

(9) Risk Assessment

In this section you will discuss the risks which are attached to your project, and how you propose to control them. Every business carries some element of risk, and any potential backer will want to see evidence that you have taken this into consideration. Potential risk could come from a number of sources:

- A competitor setting up near you;
- A major customer going into liquidation or taking his business elsewhere;
- Your main supplier or sub-contractor ceasing to trade;
- Customers taking longer than anticipated to pay their bills;
- A long-term decline in demand for your product or service;
- Lower than expected levels of sales;
- Changes in the law making your product/service harder to sell;
- Increases in taxation;
- Variations in interest rates;
- Variations in foreign exchange rates (where the business is involved in trading with other countries);
- Accident or illness;
- Flood or fire.

In this section you should explain the main risks your business is likely to face, and how you intend to monitor and control them. You should also comment on any contingency plans you have to meet setbacks, such as who will take over if you are ill.

(10) Financial Requirements

This is a crucial section, especially when the plan is being used as part of a funding application. Here you state clearly the total capital the business requires, how much you (and your partners/fellow directors) are putting in, what loan will be required, how much share capital (where the business will be a limited company), and what overdraft facilities, if any, you may need. Where you are applying for a loan, you should also state here what security you can offer (e.g. your house, or a friend/relative who will act as guarantor).

(11) Appendix

A variety of things may be enclosed in the Appendix at the back of the plan. They may include:

- CVs (Curriculum Vitae) of the people behind the business.
- Alternative cashflow forecast showing the effect of reduced sales.
- Other financial information, e.g. break-even analysis, operating budget, projected profit and loss account and projected balance sheet.
- Detailed product information and technical data (where appropriate).
- Detailed information about equipment and machinery.
- Detailed market research information.
- Correspondence or agreements with potential suppliers and customers.
- Sales literature, leaflets, photos and so on.

Financial Forecasts

The two main financial requirements for any business are to make a profit and to generate sufficient cash to make payments to suppliers, employees and others as they become due. The objective of the financial forecasts section of your business plan is to show that your business will achieve both of these requirements. Your forecasts should cover at least a twelve-month period, perhaps more if a substantial investment is required.

Forecast Profit and Loss Account

Your forecast profit and loss account attempts to predict how much profit your business will make during its first twelve months (usually) of trading. It shows the anticipated income from sales, the direct costs and overheads which must be met out of this, and the business's anticipated net (taxable) profit. The example below shows the projected profit and loss account for a one-person home-based business.

EXAMPLE PROFIT AND LOSS ACCOUNT

SALES		25,000
OVERHEADS		
Rent	800	
Heat, light and power	100	
Advertising	600	
Telephone	330	
Insurance	220	
Transport	2,800	
Stationery and postage	480	
Professional fees	400	
Bank charges	200	
Interest on loans	560	
Other	300	
Depreciation	350	
TOTAL		7,140
NET PROFIT		17,860
Drawings		12,000
Tax		3,420
Retained in business		2,440

The figure for sales income will be taken from your marketing plan. Other figures should be estimated month-by-month in order to arrive at an annual figure. A few other points to note are as follows:

1. For a home-based business, the figures for items such as Heat, Light and Power will be a proportion of the household bills. Your accountant will advise you on what you can claim.

2. Depreciation represents an allowance for the decline in value of fixed assets such as computers and motor vehicles. Inland Revenue regulations do not normally allow you to claim the

entire cost of such purchases against tax in the year in which you bought them. Rather, the cost must be spread over three years or more. Your accountant will be able to advise you about this.

3. The net profit figure (also known as the operating profit) is the amount of profit your business makes after all direct costs and overheads have been deducted. This is the figure that is used when calculating your tax liability.

4. Drawings are money taken from the business for the proprietor's own use – your wages, if you like. Money paid to yourself is not an allowable expense against tax, so this takes a separate line at the bottom of the profit and loss account.

5. As in this example, the projected profit and loss account should also show that an allowance has been made for tax and for some money to be retained in the business for future investment. Note that in the case of a sole trader or partnership, money set aside for future investment is still treated for taxation purposes as taxable income for the year concerned. If you expect to end the year with considerable cash reserves, therefore, you should discuss with your accountant the desirability of forming a limited company.

Cash Flow Forecast

The cash flow forecast is an essential component of any business plan. It is concerned with predicting the flow of cash in and out of the business. Cash is the life-blood of any business, and failing to pay attention to this essential element is one of the commonest reasons for business failures. By assessing the predicted flow of cash into and out of the business, you can:

- Identify possible cash shortages before they occur and take action to avoid them;
- Identify times when you may have surplus cash, and ensure it is used efficiently;
- Ensure that cash is always available when required, e.g. for paying staff wages;
- Encourage more efficient methods of using resources and saving costs;
- Make soundly-based decisions about your business.

A cash flow forecast lists month by month your business's predicted income and expenditure, and shows your net financial position (i.e. how much you will have in the bank) at any time. The cash flow forecast is especially important in the early days of your business, as it will enable you to see how much money you are likely to need in the early months before you start to receive a steady flow of income from your clients. An example cash flow forecast for a part-time home-based business is shown in Figure 2. The exercise below will help you draw up a cash flow forecast of your own.

EXERCISE

This exercise is designed to help you prepare a cash flow forecast for your proposed business. Obviously at this stage many of the figures will be estimates, but try to be as accurate and realistic as you can. Use only whole figures, rounding up or down as appropriate. The table below is shown for six months to fit on the page, but you should copy it and extend it to cover the first twelve months of trading. If any of the categories does not apply to your business leave them out (e.g. packaging costs may be incurred by people making products but not by those offering a service). Some rows have been left blank for you to put in categories of expenditure specific to your particular business.

CASH FLOW FORECAST

Month	1	2	3	4	5	6

RECEIPTS
1. Sales – cash
2.   – debtors
3. Loans received
4. Capital introduced
5. Other receipts
6. **TOTAL RECEIPTS**

PAYMENTS
7. Cash purchases
8. Payments to creditors
9. Proprietor's drawings
10. Staff wages
11. Capital items
12. Transport
13. Packaging
14. Rent/rates
15. Loan repayments
16. Overdraft interest

17. Professional fees
18. Advertising
19. Postage and stationery
20. Telephone
21. Heating/electricity
22. Insurance
23.
24.
25.
26.
27. Sundries
28. **TOTAL PAYMENTS**
29. **NET CASH FLOW**
30. **OPENING BALANCE**
31. **CLOSING BALANCE**

To help you complete the form, here are some notes together with the item number they refer to.

Line 4 – This shows any money which you or your partners or fellow directors are putting into the business as permanent capital.

Lines 7/8 – These are for payments you make to suppliers for stock or materials. Cash payments are made immediately and included on line 7. Payments to suppliers who allow you credit facilities are shown on line 8. Remember that, in a cash flow plan, all payments are shown in the month when they are actually made, not when the debt is incurred.

Line 9 – This is money drawn from the business for the personal use of the proprietor or (in the case of partnerships) proprietors.

Line 11 – This refers to the purchase of capital items such as equipment or machinery. Note that in the budget forecast the cost of such items may be spread over a period of years using depreciation, but in a cash flow forecast they must be shown when they are paid for.

Line 17 – Includes such things as accountant's fees, legal fees, and so on.

Lines 23–26 – Include any other items appropriate to your business.

Line 29 – To calculate **NET CASH FLOW**, deduct **TOTAL PAYMENTS** (line 28) from **TOTAL RECEIPTS** (line 6). This will show you the extent to which the total amount of cash in the

Month	Pre-start	1	2	3	4	5	6	Total
Capital from proprietor	500							500
Income								
Business cards		75	162	188	200	200	175	1000
Personal stationery		200	250	300	300	300	400	1750
Other printing				50	50	100	200	400
Total income	500	275	412	538	550	600	775	3650
Payments								
Start-up costs	100							100
Stock of paper/cards/ envelopes/chemicals			70	95	110	120	140	535
Heat & light				62			62	124
Telephone				63			63	126
HP repayments			50	50	50	50	50	250
Wages for proprietor		400	400	400	400	400	400	2400
Insurance premium		10	10	10	10	10	10	60
Total payments	100	410	530	680	570	580	725	3595
Net cash flow	400	(135)	(118)	(142)	(20)	20	50	55
Opening balance	0	400	265	147	5	(15)	5	
Closing balance	400	265	147	5	(15)	5	55	55

Figure 2 – A simple cash flow forecast prepared for a part-time home-based printing business.

business has increased or decreased during the month concerned. In the first few months it is quite likely that payments out will be greater than receipts, so the calculation will give you a minus figure. Using the normal accounting convention, such figures should be shown in brackets, e.g. (1250).

Line 30 – This shows the amount of cash you have at the start of the month. It is the same as the closing balance of the previous month (line 31).

Line 31 – The closing balance is the amount of money you have at the end of the month. It is the opening balance plus or minus the net cash flow (line 29).

When completing your own cash flow forecast, follow this simple procedure:

(1) Use a pencil, rather than a pen, so that you can make changes and corrections easily.

(2) Work **ACROSS** the sheet, starting at the top with sales – that is, estimate your cash sales for each of the first twelve months you are operating, then income from debtors.

(3) Miss out line 3 at this stage, but fill in lines 4, 5 and 6, still working across the page.

(4) Next, fill in lines 7 to 28, missing out for the moment lines 15 and 16.

(5) Subtract line 28 from line 6 to get the **NET CASH FLOW** (line 29). Complete this for the whole year.

(6) Now calculate the opening balance (line 30) and the closing balance (line 31) for every month. In the first month the opening balance will be zero and the closing balance will be the same as the net cash flow. In subsequent months, the opening balance will be the same as the closing balance of the previous month, while the closing balance will be the opening balance plus or minus that month's net cash flow.

(7) When the tasks above have been completed, you will almost certainly have a number of negative figures in line 31. If this is the case, you will need to borrow money to keep your business afloat. Looking at the chart, try to estimate how much is negative for a long-ish period (six months or more), and how

much is negative for a shorter period. The long negative part can then be met by a loan, while the shorter part can be bridged with an overdraft (see the next section Raising Finance). If there are **NO** negative figures in line 29 you will not need a loan or overdraft, and lines 3, 16 and 17 will all remain zero.

(8) Put your loan requirement into line 3, and check that the sum of that amount and the overdraft does not exceed your line 4, since lenders normally prefer not to put more money into a project than the proprietor. If the figure you need to borrow considerably exceeds the amount you have available to put into the business, you may need to consider forming a partnership or a limited company to raise extra funds.

(9) Finally, assuming the requirement in (7) has been met, put the loan repayments and/or overdraft fees in lines 16 and 17, and re-calculate the totals accordingly.

Having worked out exactly what your business's financial requirements are likely to be, we can now move on to the important topic of raising finance.

11. RAISING FINANCE

Whatever the type of home-based business you plan to start, you will need to find some money to finance it. Part of this will be needed to cover the cost of equipment and materials, and part to cover your own living costs until the business is bringing in a regular income. You will need to establish whether you can raise all this money yourself, or whether you will need to obtain a loan (or grant) for some of it. To do this, you will need to calculate how much capital you yourself can raise. When working this out, remember to include the value of all of the following:

• Cash
• Savings
• Stocks and shares
• Your car
• Insurance policies which can be cashed in
• Any other material possessions which could be sold (e.g. jewellery).

From this you will need to deduct any:

* Other outstanding loans
* Bills due for payment.

This will give you a figure for your total net worth. Of course, this is just a theoretical maximum, and it may neither be necessary nor desirable to put all this money into the business in practice. For example, if you have an old car, it may be more valuable to you and your business as a means of transport than whatever price you could sell it for. If you redeem a life insurance policy early, you may end up receiving a very poor return for the money you have paid in. The same applies if you sell stocks and shares at the wrong time (i.e. when the price is low). Nevertheless, if you really do need to raise the maximum possible, the calculation will give you some idea of how much this would be.

Capital Requirement

Having worked out the maximum you could raise, you must now compare this with the total amount of money you will need to start your business – your capital requirement. Once you have done this, you will be able to make plans for how you will bridge the gap.

Your capital requirement will be made up of two things. These are:

1. Permanent capital – This is money needed for the purchase of equipment, vehicles and so on which will become permanent possessions of the business, otherwise known as fixed assets. For many businesses the largest fixed asset they require is premises. Clearly this will not be an issue with a home-based business!

2. Working capital – This is money needed to meet the day-to-day running costs of the business. Running costs include such things as printing, postage, stationery, telephone bills, raw materials, and so on.

Running costs also include the money you need just to cover your own living expenses. Often this is more than you might think. To work out how much you need just to survive, complete the exercise over the page.

EXERCISE

PERSONAL SURVIVAL BUDGET

Cost Per Month

Mortgage/rent
Loan interest
Local rates/taxes
Water
Gas/electricity/oil
Telephone
Life insurance
Other insurance
Pension
Food
Clothing
Travel/car
Holidays
Subscriptions/newspapers
Children
Other items
Unexpected contingencies

TOTAL:

LESS any other family income:

SURVIVAL INCOME:

This is the minimum you need every month just for you and your family to survive.

In working out your initial capital requirement, you need to take into account both permanent capital and working capital. Once your business is running successfully, your working capital needs should be covered by the income the business is generating and perhaps by short-term borrowing such as a bank overdraft. In the first few months, however, the business is unlikely to be receiving much income, and you may need to find most of your working capital from other sources.

Raising Money From Other Sources

Having calculated (1) how much capital you can raise, and (2) how much you need to start the business, you should now have a good idea of how much money you need to find from other sources. Knowing this figure is important, because it will have a considerable bearing on how you proceed next.

If you need to raise a relatively large proportion of the total, and this money is required for investment in fixed assets such as a computer, vehicle or special equipment, your need is for permanent, long-term capital. While you may be able to raise some of this by means of a loan through a bank or other financial institution, you might also need to find a backer or partner willing to provide capital which will be permanently invested in the business. This may mean that you form a partnership or limited liability company with other participants, rather than operating on your own as a sole trader.

On the other hand, if your needs are proportionately small and the finance is required mainly for working capital (as will be the case with most home-based businesses), you may be able to negotiate the necessary bank overdraft facilities to cover these, while finding most of the permanent capital yourself. In this case, you may choose to operate as a sole trader to keep complete personal control of the business.

Borrowing Money

It is no disgrace if you find you need to borrow some money when starting out. Few businesses are able to operate solely on the owner's funds. Those who try frequently fail because they are undercapitalised (that is, they do not have sufficient capital to meet their working requirements). Most businesses have to borrow to some extent. What is generally needed is:

(a) A mixture of long-term and short-term finance, and
(b) A balance between what is provided by the owner of the business and what by outside lenders.

Borrowing needs to be matched with the purpose it is required for. That is to say, if you need money for a short period only, you should apply for short-term finance such as a bank overdraft. This is an agreement with your bank that, over a short period, you can draw out more money than you have in the account, so long as you later pay the money back to the bank with interest. On the other hand, when funds are required for long-term purposes – say the purchase of a vehicle or computer equipment – a long-term loan is likely to be more appropriate.

Different types of finance are suited to different purposes. For example, it would be a mistake to buy expensive machinery with a ten-year lifespan using short-term finance such as a bank overdraft. For one thing, over ten years you would pay much more in interest charges than with a long-term loan; and for another, by doing this you would be tying up a valuable source of short-term finance for things such as working capital. This is summed up in a well-known piece of advice for businessmen: don't borrow short to pay long.

So far as the balance between your own and outside finance is concerned, as a rough guide most financial institutions will expect you to put up at least half the total cost of any business venture. The exact amount they will be prepared to lend you is governed by a range of factors, including the type of business you propose to start, your past business and financial record, how much security you can offer against the loan, and so on.

Types of Finance

There are three broad categories of finance, short-, medium- and long-term. Let's look at each of these in turn.

(1) Short-term Finance (up to one year)

This is normally used for such things as:

- Financing seasonal/cyclical fluctuations in trade
- Financing general working capital requirements
- Purchasing minor fixed assets with a short working life
- Providing temporary, bridging finance while long-term finance is arranged.

There are many potential sources of short-term finance. The most common are listed below.

Overdrafts – a bank overdraft, already mentioned, is the most popular form of short-term finance. Overdrafts have the advantage of being simple to set up, and are also very flexible. Generally speaking, the bank specifies a maximum you are allowed to borrow up to, and you can use as much or as little of this as you require. On the other hand, interest rates for overdrafts are generally higher than for medium or long-term loans, and they are repayable on demand. This makes them unsuitable for long-term borrowing.

Trade credit – most suppliers are willing to extend credit terms to business customers. That is to say, they will allow customers a certain period of time – thirty days perhaps – from delivery before requiring payment. In effect, therefore, this is a short-term loan. If you go beyond the agreed period, however, interest may be charged and, ultimately, trade terms may be withdrawn.

Hire purchase – this is a way of purchasing items by instalments. By paying an initial deposit and regular sums over a period of time, a business acquires ownership of the goods. The business has use of the goods from the initial deposit, but they do not officially become the property of the business until the final instalment has been paid.

Leasing – this is a method of financing the use of an asset rather than its actual purchase. It is used by businesses to finance things such as motor vehicles, computers, photocopiers and machinery. The leasing company retains ownership of the items, and charges the business a rental for their use. Leasing finance may be short- or medium-term, according to the duration of the lease.

Factoring – this is a popular source of short-term finance for established businesses. Companies known as 'factors' take over the business's trade debtors in exchange for an agreed reward (usually a percentage of the amount outstanding). This means that the business has the use of money owed to it immediately, and does not have to spend its time pursuing overdue accounts. As mentioned, factors are only concerned with taking over a business's trade debtors, so this form of finance will not be of interest if you are just starting out.

(2) Medium-term Finance (1–5 years)

This is normally used for financing fixed assets with medium-term life such as cars and computer systems, and meeting increased working capital requirements. It may also be used to replace a persistent overdraft.

The main source of medium-term finance is bank loans, which are usually repaid by monthly instalments. Loans may be made at a fixed interest rate, where the amount of each repayment is fixed at the beginning of the loan and cannot alter; or at a variable rate, where the interest rate can go up or down according to economic conditions, with monthly repayments varying accordingly. Fixed rate loans make budgeting easier; but if interest rates generally fall, there is a risk of getting locked into a situation where you are paying for your loan at a rate which is no longer competitive. Bank loans are typically given over a period matching the expected life of the asset they are to purchase.

(3) Long-term Finance (over five years)

Long-term finance is used for financing major fixed assets with a long life and for providing semi-permanent working capital. The main sources of long-term finance are bank loans, mortgage loans and equity finance (share issues). Most home-based businesses are unlikely to require long-term finance when starting up, though it may become relevant if you subsequently decide to expand, perhaps into specialist business premises.

Applying for Finance

If you need extra finance beyond what you can raise yourself, you will generally need to apply to a lending institution such as a bank or finance house. Such institutions are in business to lend money, but will not of course give you a loan just because you ask for it. A lender will want to ensure that his (or his depositors') money will be wisely used, and returned with interest in due course. As discussed in the last section, he will want to see a business plan showing that you have thought out every aspect of your proposed business, and a cash flow projection showing your anticipated financial situation and requirements.

In addition, the lender will want to assess you personally, trying to assess how well or badly you will run your business. He will look at such things as:

- Your character, background and previous experience
- Your previous financial history, how thrifty you have been, and how you have handled any existing accounts you may have
- What funding you require: what type of finance you are looking for, how much, and for how long
- How much you are prepared to put into the project (he is likely to be looking for a substantial contribution, probably matching that from the bank)
- How and when the borrowing will be repaid
- What security you can put up in the event that you default on repaying the loan.

Obviously not all potential borrowers will be able to meet the banks' ideal, and many loans are made to people who fall short of this – particularly to those with a sound business proposition, but lacking a track record in business. In borderline cases, the lender has to rely on his personal judgement.

When applying for finance, it is therefore important to present a smart, businesslike image. Even if you are nervous inside, you need to appear well-prepared and confident (though not over-confident) about your business and its prospects. As mentioned, you will also need to present a business plan showing you have taken into account every aspect of your proposed business.

What Happens if You Can't Get a Bank Loan?

If you have a good case for funding and present it (and yourself) well, there is every chance that you will succeed in your funding application. If you are turned down, however, you may need to re-think some of your plans. You have two possible courses of action.

One is to reduce your capital requirements, for instance by starting part-time or reducing the range of services you offer initially. Once a lender can see that you are trading successfully, he is likely to be much more willing to provide a loan. Alternatively, you may be so successful working this way that the profits generated mean you no longer need extra money at all!

The other solution is to find an alternative source of finance. A range of organisations exist to provide help and support for people starting businesses of their own, and some can also assist with loans or even grants. Depending to your age and background, the area where you live and the type of business you plan to start, any of the following organisations may be well worth approaching.

1. The Prince's Youth Business Trust (PYBT) – The PYBT helps unemployed young people between the ages of 18 and 30 start businesses of their own. They offer both grants and cheap loans (typically in the region of £2,000–£2,500). Each applicant is also allocated a business adviser to help with all aspects of setting up and running their business. For more information, call the PYBT on 0800 842842.

2. Business Link Networks – Business Link is a joint initiative between Training and Enterprise Councils (TECs), Chambers of Commerce, local enterprise agencies and business owners. There are around 240 centres in England providing support, advice, services and information. While they do not offer grants or loans themselves, they will certainly be able to let you know of possible sources of finance locally. For more information on your nearest Business Link centre, phone 0345 567765.

3. Training and Enterprise Councils (TECs) – TECs are local

consortiums which support and represent business and industry in their area. They run training courses and offer financial advice for anyone thinking of starting a business, and also provide grants and loans. Check in the phone book for the number of your local TEC, or enquire at your nearest Business Link centre. Note that from April 2001 TECs will be replaced by local Learning and Skills Councils (LSCs). These are expected to offer a similar range of services to businesses, but will have a greater emphasis on education and life-long learning.

4. Chambers of Commerce – Chambers of commerce provide their members with training, business support and finance. They also have extensive libraries containing information on marketing and looking for trading partners. For more information on your local chamber of commerce and what it can offer, phone their national information line on 0345 567765.

5. Regional Development Agencies (RDAs) – There are nine Regional Development Agencies in England whose role includes promoting economic development and regeneration in the regions concerned. Especially if you live in a deprived urban or rural area, they may be able to assist you with loans, grants and other forms of business support. Contact your local Business Link centre or TEC/LSC to find the Regional Development Agency covering your area, or check the website at www.localregions.detr.gov.uk/rda/info/index.htm.

6. Business Angels – If you have an original idea which you think could make a lot of money, it may be worthwhile approaching a business angel. In return for investing in your business they will expect a share of future profits and a say in how the business is run, so it is important to choose someone with whom you believe you will be able to build a good working relationship. Contact the National Business Angels Network on 020 7329 4141.

7. Your Local Council – All local councils offer advice and practical support for people in their area starting new businesses. Typically these will include a range of publications, advice on legal matters such as licensing and rates, and practical support such as low-cost start-up units. They may also be able to provide grants and loans in suitable cases. Look at the page for your local council in your phone book. The phone number you require for more information may be listed under Business Services or Economic Development.

8. Shell 'Livewire' Programme – This well-established scheme helps young people aged 16–30 set up businesses of their own.

They provide a range of information and advice, and business start-up awards of up to £10,000 via an annual competition. For more details call 0345 573 252, or see their website at www.shell-livewire.org.

If you are still unable to come up with the cash you need, another option (mentioned earlier) may be to bring in a partner or partners. This could be either to help you with the day-to-day running of the business or simply to provide finance in exchange for a share in the profits (a 'sleeping partner'). Or, of course, you may have a friend or relative who would be prepared to lend you the money so long as it is repaid (with interest) once the business is running successfully.

If, however, none of these approaches proves fruitful, perhaps you would be best advised to try a different business altogether. Part Two of this book includes plenty of ideas for low-cost home-based businesses. By starting a less expensive business initially, even if this is not what you ideally want to do, you may be able to raise sufficient capital to finance the business you really do want to start!

12. HELP FROM THE POST OFFICE

Almost anyone running a business from home will need to use the services of the Post Office, and specifically their letter collection and delivery arm Royal Mail. Indeed, many businesses would be unable to operate without their help. As well as daily postal deliveries and collections, they offer a wide range of special services tailored to the needs of businesses. Below are listed some of the main services which may be useful to you in running your home-based business.

Private Box: A private box provides you with a short and easy to remember alternative business address (e.g. PO Box 321). It can be useful if your postal address is on the lengthy side, or if you don't want customers and suppliers to know that you are operating from home.

Mail posted to a private box is held at the local delivery office until you pick it up, or you can pay an extra fee to have it delivered to your usual address. A private box costs £52 a year or £42 for a half-year. If you want your mail delivered to your home rather than going to collect it, you pay the same amount again – so the total cost is £104 a year or £84 a half-year.

Keepsafe: If you are going to be away from home for a period of up to two months, you can have your mail held by the post office and delivered on a day of your choice. The Keepsafe scheme costs £5 for up to two weeks, £8 for three weeks, £10 for four weeks and £15 for two months. You can obtain an application form from your local post office. A week's notice is required.

Special Delivery: This is the service to use with urgent and/or valuable items. Royal Mail guarantees that your package will be delivered by the next working day in mainland Britain and Northern Ireland, and within three days at most in the more remote islands (e.g. Orkneys). Prices start at £3.35 for a single item weighing up to 100g. Compensation is payable if items are damaged or lost (an item being defined as lost if it has not been delivered 10 days after the deadline). The normal maximum compensation is £250, but for more valuable items you can opt for a higher level by making an additional payment at the time you send the package. Special delivery items are handled by a different network from other postal items. You can track their progress and confirm their safe arrival on the Royal Mail's website at www.royalmail.co.uk.

Business Collection: If you do a lot of business via the post, you may find it helpful to arrange for a postman to come and collect your outgoing mail from your premises. If you spend over £15,000 a year on postage, the Royal Mail will provide this service free. Even if you do not spend this amount, however, they will collect your post for a fee. This is £420 a year for a daily collection from Monday to Friday, or just £210 if you agree to have your post collected before 3 p.m. A single, one-off collection of 1,000 items or more, or items with more than £200 postage value, is free. A single collection of fewer than 1,000 items, or items with less than £200 postage value, costs £5.

Business Reply and Freepost: These services allow customers to contact you at your expense. With the Business Reply service, specially printed cards or envelopes (either first or second class) are supplied for customers' use. Business Reply is a good choice when using mailshots or magazine inserts to advertise.

With Freepost (second class only), customers reply by putting your Freepost address on their own envelopes. This can be ideal if you want to encourage a good response to local radio or press advertising, but you can also use your Freepost address on printed reply cards or envelopes in mail shots. There is an annual licence fee of £57 covering both these services. You then pay an additional 0.5p per item handled.

Mailsort: This title covers a range of services which provide discounts ranging from 13% to 32% for bulk mailings. To qualify, you must post a minimum number of items (over 4000 letters or 1000 packets at a time), 90% of your mail must be fully and accurately postcoded, and all of it must be sorted and prepared according to Royal Mail's instructions. You can make additional savings if you apply barcodes to your mail. The Royal Mail will advise you on this.

Household Delivery Service: The Royal Mail provides a door-to-door delivery service for leaflets, special offers and other promotional material. This can provide a handy, economical way to target potential customers in your area. You can select the addresses to be delivered to according to a wide range of criteria. These include postcode area, district or sector; TV region; geo-demographic (i.e. certain types of property only); residential/business, and so on. Costs vary according to the number and weight of items you are sending. Prices range from £28 to £53 per 1000 items.

Admail: Admail enables your customers to respond to any address you like. You can use this service if you wish to use a more prestigious address in your advertising, or perhaps somewhere more local in an area you are targeting. Royal Mail will forward all responses to your home address, or to another destination if you prefer. Your Admail address can be short and therefore memorable, which is useful if you want to use it in advertising. All letters are redirected by first class post. Costs range from £100 for 30 days up to £600 for a year. Discounts may apply if you have more than one contract.

Franking: If you send out regular mailshots, a franking machine may be a good investment. It will save you time and trouble buying and sticking on stamps, and the results look more professional. Alternatively, if you have a one-off mailing of at least 500 letters or packets you can take them to a Main Post Office and pay the standard postage in a lump sum. The Royal Mail will then frank the letters for you and deliver them in the normal way.

The Direct Mail Information Service: The Direct Mail Information Service (DMIS) undertakes regular in-depth research into the direct mail industry in the UK. You can get free outline reports from DMIS on topics such as direct mail trends, customer loyalty, response rates to mailshots, and so on. More information is available from The Direct Mail Information Service, 5 Carlisle Street, London, W1V 6JX (tel. 020 7494 0483). They also have a website at www.dmis.co.uk.

For more information about any of the above services, a good starting point is one of the Royal Mail sales or customer service centres found in most large towns and cities (look in the phone book under 'Royal Mail'). Take a look also at the Royal Mail website at www.royalmail.co.uk.

13. PHONES AND FAXES

Just as most home-based businesses depend on the Post Office for their smooth running, so too do they rely on having an efficient telephone service. Most home-based businesses depend on the phone for a range of reasons:

- For many businesses this is the most convenient way for customers and potential customers to get in touch.
- You can easily contact suppliers, advertising media, your professional advisers, and so on.
- If you have business partners or associates, or employ staff, it will be easier for them to contact you (and vice versa).
- If you want to use the facilities of the Internet to aid your business, you will need a phone line to connect with it.
- Likewise, if you want (or need) a fax machine, you will need a phone line to connect it to.

It follows that nearly all businesses need a phone. To save costs you may decide to start off by using your home phone for the business as well. If you do this, however, you will need to brief other family members on how they should answer calls. If your teenage children aren't prepared to sacrifice all their street cred by saying 'Johnson's Window Cleaning Service' whenever they pick up the receiver, simply getting them to state the phone number is a good compromise. In contrast, a laid-back voice saying 'Yeah?' gives a poor first impression, and may result in a lost sale.

Some people are confident and at ease on the phone, while others are at best uncomfortable with it. The best advice if the latter applies to you is to try to relax and be natural, and remember that this form of communication, like all such skills, improves with experience. Always keep a notebook by the phone, so that you (and anyone else who answers) can keep a record of any messages. This is much better than writing on scraps of paper, which can easily become mislaid.

BT Network Services

As well as the basic phone service, a wide range of additional services is available from BT (British Telecom). You will have to pay an extra charge for many of these, but this is generally quite modest. Those services of the greatest potential interest to home-based workers include the following.

Call Minder: Call Minder is a network-based answering service. It provides an alternative to having your own answering machine (see below) which may be attractive to some home-based workers. Call Minder will automatically answer your calls when there is no reply or if you are already speaking to someone else (something an ordinary answering machine cannot do). You can retrieve your messages by dialling a special code from your home phone (free) or any tone-based phone in Britain or overseas (for which there is an extra charge).

Call Diversion: Call Diversion enables you to automatically divert incoming calls to almost any number in the UK, including mobile phones. In addition to the quarterly fee, you are charged for the portion of the call from your home number to the number diverted to. Call Diversion can be useful if you are spending a period of time away from home, say working at a customer's premises. Diversion can be switched on and off at will by entering the appropriate code numbers from your home phone.

Call Sign: Call Sign gives you an extra phone number on your line, identified by a different ringing tone. Without having an extra line installed, you can therefore have a separate number to give to clients and in your advertising. When the phone rings, you (and your family) will know by the tone whether it is a business or personal call. You could also use the Call Sign service to identify incoming faxes.

Caller Display: Caller Display lets you see who is calling before you pick up the phone, and records details of any callers while you've been out. As well as paying the extra fee for this service, you will need to obtain a special receiver which includes the necessary LCD display panel. These are available from BT and other specialist suppliers.

Ring Back: With this service, if the number you are calling is engaged, you simply dial '5' before you put the phone down. Your phone will then ring once the other person's phone is free (a special ringing tone is used to indicate this). Pick up your phone, and their phone will start to ring.

Free Services

Friends and Family: This free service enables you to specify up to ten numbers you call frequently (including one international number), and you will then get a discount (10% at the time of writing) when phoning those numbers. You can change all or any of your Friends and Family numbers at any time.

Best Friend: You can also nominate one of your ten Friends and Family numbers as your 'best friend', and get an additional discount (20% at the time of writing) on calls to this number. Sad as it may sound, a growing number of home-based business owners give their internet access provider as their 'best friend', in order to ensure they get net access at the lowest possible rate.

Call Return: This service allows you to find the number of the last person who called you, whether you answered the phone or not. You dial 1471 and a recorded voice will tell you the number of the last person to call, and the time they rang. If you do not want your number to be made available in this way, you can dial 141 before any number you ring. Call Return is a free service and you do not have to register to use it.

If your business really takes off, you may find it desirable to have a second phone line installed. BT runs regular special offers to encourage people to get a second line, and it is well worth contacting BT Customer Services on 150 to see what deals may be available. Internet users can check on prices and services by visiting BT's website at www.bt.com.

Finally, it is worth noting that the information provided here has referred specifically to BT, but a growing range of alternative telephone providers now also offer their services to home users. People in many areas have the option of using a cable company for their phone, and this can provide a cost-effective solution, particularly if you want the company's home entertainment package as well. Other phone companies use BT lines but with different tariffs which again may be more attractive than BT's. Against this, it should be noted that not all of the network services listed above may be available to people using a telephone provider other than BT.

Answering Machines

A telephone answering machine (TAM) is a particular asset for one-person businesses, as it means that if you are away from the phone the machine will take messages for you and perhaps prevent a lost customer. A wide range of machines is available from suppliers such as BT, electrical stores (e.g. Dixons and Tandy) and specialist phone shops. Prices start at around £30 and go up to £200 or more. The more expensive machines have a wide range of extra features, including automatic dial-back, call forwarding, remote playback of messages, and recording the date and time of incoming calls. For many home-based businesses, however, a basic machine costing under £50 will be perfectly adequate.

Answering machines do have some slight disadvantages. For one thing, some people dislike them and will refuse to leave a message. Another is that a person hearing an answering machine on the other end of the line will get a clear impression that you are a small – probably one-person – enterprise. A more personal alternative to the machine would be to engage an answering service to take calls on your behalf. Such services ensure that the phone is always answered by a human being, and they will take messages and pass them on to you. To identify such services in your area, look under 'Telephone Answering Services' in Yellow Pages.

Mobile Phones

If your business takes you away from home a lot, you might benefit from a mobile phone. Mobiles use radio rather than fixed lines to transmit messages, so they will operate almost anywhere. There are four digital mobile phone companies in Britain – Cellnet, Vodafone, Orange and One-2-One – and each offers a range of different tariffs. These vary widely, some being more cost-effective for low users, others for those who make more frequent use. If you are considering obtaining a mobile phone, research all the options carefully, and choose the network and tariff most appropriate to your needs. As well as the cost of the mobile itself (often very low in the UK), there is likely to be a charge for connecting you to the network, a monthly rental, and a bill for every call you make.

Mobile phones can be expensive to use, and it is important to check that the benefits will justify the costs involved. Before making any purchase, therefore, obtain at least the current issue of a consumer periodical such as What Mobile? to check their recommendations. Some retailers such as Peoples Phone and Carphone Warehouse claim to offer unbiased advice on which mobile phone company and tariff would suit you best, based on your circumstances and anticipated pattern of usage. The quality of advice can vary, however, and it is best to speak to two or three potential suppliers before signing any contract.

Fax Machines

Fax machines – more properly called facsimile machines – provide a means for transmitting written documents over telephone lines at the same price as an ordinary phone call. They can also be used as basic photocopiers, and many businesses now find them indispensable.

If you wish to obtain a fax machine, you will of course need a telephone line to connect it to. If you want the fax to be switched on all the time, you will need a separate line and phone number for it. Some modern fax machines, however, can automatically determine whether an incoming call is a fax or voice call, and will route the call accordingly; thus you will need one line only. Fax machines can either be rented or bought.

Another alternative, if you have a computer with a modem (a device for connecting your computer with others via a phone line), is to use this for sending and receiving faxes. Most modern computers come pre-installed with software which will enable you to send, say, a word processed document to a fax machine. Many will also enable you to receive faxes, though this facility can be more awkward to set up and use. An alternative is to use a net-based service such as FaxMe (www.faxme.co.uk). This free service provides you with a phone number for incoming faxes, which are then converted to emails and forwarded to your email address. This is further discussed in the next section, Computers and the Internet.

14. COMPUTERS AND THE INTERNET

Many home-based businesses will benefit from having a computer, and for some types of business (e.g. desktop publishing, website design) they are indispensable. Home computers can help with a huge range of tasks, from preparing invoices to keeping accounts. They can also give you the means to access the vast resources of the Internet (of which more later). Here are some of the main areas in which having a computer can be useful for home-based businesses.

Word Processing

A word processing program in effect makes a computer work like an electric typewriter, but with many additional features. Most importantly, when you are writing a letter or other document, the words are not immediately printed on paper as would be the case with a typewriter, but instead appear on a monitor screen. You can then edit your document – correcting mistakes, removing and adding text, and moving text around – until the letter is exactly how you want it. Only then do you need to print it out. With the help of a word processor, even inexperienced typists can produce highly professional-looking letters and documents.

Another big advantage of word processing is that documents can be stored electronically for re-use in future. This is a particular benefit when there are certain documents you send out regularly with only slight variations, e.g. invoices, statements and quotations. You can store such documents in the computer, then simply make any necessary amendments to things such as name, address, date, amount and so on before printing them out. Many word processors also include a 'mailmerge' facility, whereby you can combine a standard letter with a list of names and addresses to produce a series of letters, each individually addressed to a person on your list.

Word processors also include a range of other facilities to help make writing quicker and easier and documents more professional-looking. Most include a spellchecker, which will identify any spelling mistakes in your document and substitute the correct version. Other facilities include automatic page numbering, bold text and italics, underlining, changing the size and style of text, and many more. Currently the most popular word processing program is Microsoft Word, followed by Corel, WordPerfect and Lotus AmiPro.

Desktop Publishing

Desktop publishing (DTP) is similar to word processing, but the term tends to be used to describe the production of more elaborate documents such as newsletters, magazines and brochures. As well as text, such documents may include a wide range of visual elements, including diagrams, illustrations, graphs, photos, and so on. They are frequently set out in multiple columns, and use full-colour artwork. Modern word processors have a good range of desktop publishing facilities, though serious professionals use dedicated DTP programs such as PageMaker or Quark Express. The latter are not as good at manipulating text as straightforward word processing programs, so most also include the facility to import text created on a word processor.

Desktop publishing programs – and modern word processors – can enable you to produce high quality artwork for publicity materials and the like without the need to employ a professional artist or designer. However, the programs do take some time (and possibly training) to master, and to use them well you really need some knowledge of design principles. In addition, if you are going to use features such as photos, you will need a piece of equipment called a scanner to convert them to a form which the computer can use.

Spreadsheets

Spreadsheet programs enable you to store and manipulate numerical information. They are therefore ideal for purposes such as accounts and cash flow forecasts. Once your spreadsheet has been set up, you can simply enter the appropriate figures into it and it will automatically perform routine tasks such as adding up columns of figures for you.

Spreadsheet programs can also be used to calculate and print out invoices and quotations. For example, if you need to charge a client for twelve hours of work at £17.50 per hour plus expenses, a spreadsheet program can be set up to perform this calculation automatically for you and print out the appropriate invoice. Finally, most spreadsheet programs have the facility to convert the information contained within them into charts, graphs and diagrams. Putting information such as sales and advertising expenditure into this format can be very helpful when looking for underlying trends.

Popular spreadsheet programs include Lotus 1-2-3 and Microsoft Excel.

Databases

A database program is rather like a filing cabinet or card index, but because it is computerised it offers many advantages over manual systems. In a database program you can store the names, addresses and other details of customers and potential customers, suppliers, business contacts and so on. The computer allows you not only to keep and easily update these details, but to print them out on labels, envelopes, invoices, mailshots and so on. Database programs make it easy to find any record you want, for example by typing a single keyword such as the person's surname.

Database programs will also enable you to sort records, and select only those which meet certain criteria. For instance, you could, at the touch of a few keys, get a list of all your customers over the age of 25 (assuming age is in the information you keep), or all of those in a particular town or village. Databases are a particularly valuable tool in sales and marketing. For example, you could keep a database on all your customers, recording such details as when they last ordered, what they ordered, and how much. You could then get a list of all those customers who have **NOT** ordered from you in the last six months, and write them a letter reminding them about your services.

The one main drawback to database programs is that all the information has to be keyed in the first place, and then kept up to date. Where there are large numbers of records, and large amounts of information stored on each, this can become a tedious and time-consuming exercise. In the end it is up to you to decide what information will be most useful to your business, and avoid putting irrelevant information onto the database just for the sake of it. Some popular database programs include Microsoft Access and Lotus Approach.

Integrated Packages

As well as individual programs for specific purposes, computer programs are increasingly sold in integrated packages or 'suites' (new computers are often sold with an integrated package such as Microsoft Works pre-installed). A typical integrated package might include a word processor, a database, a spreadsheet, and one or two other programs such as an electronic address book and a desktop publishing program.

The programs in integrated packages are designed to be used closely together, which can have many advantages; for example, you can use names and addresses from your database to create mailmerged letters with your word processor. The individual programs in an integrated package may not be quite as powerful or versatile as stand-alone programs, but for many home-based businesses they are likely to be a good choice and excellent value for money.

Which Computer Should You Buy?

There is a vast range of computers, with new models appearing every day as manufacturers try to outdo one another with regard to price and performance. Especially if you are new to computing, it is important not just to buy the first machine you see, but to take some time to assess what you want and what is available. A huge range of magazines about computers is published today, and it is worth getting hold of some of those aimed at non-expert readers to try to get a feel for the market. A personal recommendation is

Computer Active, an inexpensive, yet informative, weekly publication aimed primarily at home-based users.

If you have decided to buy a home computer, you will have a number of choices to make. The first is fairly straightforward – Macintosh or IBM-compatible. Almost all personal computers fall into one or other of these categories. The great majority sold through the shops are IBM-compatible, and most home-based business owners may prefer to obtain such a machine, if only because of the wide range of programs available to run on them. The main rival system is Macintosh. Macintosh computers (e.g. the attractively designed iMac) are particularly strong on desktop publishing, and if you intend to do much of this, this may be an option you will wish to consider.

How do you know whether a computer is IBM-compatible or not? Look for information about the operating system. If a computer uses some version of DOS/Windows, it is IBM-compatible. The same applies if the silicon chip inside the computer is described as a 'Pentium'. Whilst IBM-compatible computers are manufactured by a huge range of companies, Macintosh computers are produced only by Macintosh themselves.

As well as the actual computer, you will also need to purchase a printer. There are three main types, each with their advantages and disadvantages.

Dot Matrix: These are generally the least expensive machines, but as you might expect they also give the poorest quality output. A tiny group of pins strikes an ink-coated ribbon and presses the ink on to the paper. Dot matrix printers are cheap to run, and modern ones offer reasonable quality. They may be worth considering if you are on a very tight budget.

Inkjet: These machines work by spraying tiny blobs of ink on to the page. Modern inkjet printers give good quality results, and are likely to be the only realistic choice if you want to print in colour. Their drawbacks are: (a) the relatively high running costs; (b) the fact that they need special, coated paper to give the best finish; and (c) the ink tends to spread, meaning that text does not always print as crisply as one would like. Note, also, that most inkjet ink is water-based, meaning that these printers are not suitable for printing labels and envelopes (they will smear in the rain!).

Laser: Laser printers give the highest quality output. A laser beam in the machine draws the characters in your document onto a drum. The drum attracts ink powder (toner) to the characters, and they are then transferred to paper. At one time the high price would have ruled out laser printers for most home-based businesses. However, nowadays some excellent low cost black-and-white models are available (I am happy here to give a plug for my Brother HL-730 laser printer, which is still producing top-notch results three years after I bought it). Laser-printed documents look crisp and professional, and the running costs are generally lower than inkjets. They also tend to be the fastest printers, especially for long documents.

Buying Your Computer

Buying a computer for your business can be a daunting prospect. To avoid expensive mistakes, follow the checklist below.

(1) Decide exactly what you want your new computer to do for you. Will it be used mainly for word processing, or do you intend to use spreadsheets, databases, desktop publishing programs, and so on? Even if you only intend to use the computer for one or two applications initially, bear in mind that you may wish to add others later on.

(2) Speak to a number of possible suppliers, and explain exactly what you want your computer system to be able to do.

(3) Avoid getting sidetracked into detailed discussions about technical specifications – ensure that the supplier sticks to discussing what the computer will do for you.

(4) Ask to see the complete system working. Get the supplier to demonstrate the features which you yourself wish to use.

(5) Buy proven products which have been used successfully by others, not new and untested ones.

(6) Wherever possible buy an existing software package rather than having one designed for you from scratch. The latter procedure can be time-consuming and expensive.

(7) Be prepared to spend a little bit extra to get a system which will meet your needs now and in the foreseeable future. If you buy the cheapest system now, you may find yourself having to buy a new, more powerful system within a few months. As well as the inconvenience, this can work out more expensive than buying the more powerful system straight away.

(8)   Particularly if you are new to computing, see whether the supplier will install the computer for you and take you through the initial steps of starting it up and using it. A growing range of suppliers offer this service, though the cost will be incorporated in the price you pay.

(9)   Find out what after-sales support is available. Is there a period during which, if the computer breaks down, the supplier will replace it or repair it free of charge? In this case, will you have to take the computer back to the supplier, or will he come to your premises? Is there a telephone number you can ring for advice and support? Ensure that any guarantees made by the supplier are put in writing.

(10) And finally, never rush in to buying a computer. Before you sign on the dotted line, think carefully about what you need and whether the system you are buying will meet those needs. If possible, get a second opinion from a friend, colleague or relative who has some knowledge of computers.

The Internet

As mentioned earlier, one big advantage of having a home computer is that it will enable you to access the resources of the internet. I assume many readers of this book will have little if any experience of the net, so let's start with the basics. The internet is a world-wide network of inter-connected computers. It began in the USA and is still American dominated, but it is not under the control of any particular government or agency. Anyone with a suitable computer and a modem can dial in (via an internet access provider) and gain access to information stored on many thousands of computers. Not only that, you can advertise your business with your very own 'homepage' on the web, and communicate with other computer users across the world for the price of a local phone call.

The internet actually consists of a number of different networks and services. Probably the best known is the world wide web (web for short); this is the most technically sophisticated area of the internet. Viewers explore web sites using a browser program, and can move quickly and easily from one site to another via so-called hyperlinks (a process popularly known as surfing the web). Other services of interest to home-based business owners include newsgroups and – of course – e-mail.

How Do You Join Up?

At the risk of stating the obvious, the first thing you will need is a computer. Most home computers sold in the last five years can cope with e-mail and newsgroups, but if you intend to use the facilities of the world wide web you will need something fairly modern. With apologies in advance for the jargon, the least you will need is a 486 or Pentium PC with at least 4 (preferably 8) Mb RAM. The good news is that, if you are buying a computer today, almost any new machine on sale will easily meet these requirements.

To get on the internet you will also need a modem. As discussed earlier under Fax Machines, these are devices which enable you to connect your computer with others via an ordinary phone line. Many computers sold today have internal modems built in, but failing this you will need to buy one. If you are buying a modem, here are two pieces of advice:

(1) Get an external modem rather than an internal. External modems are slightly more expensive, but they are much easier to fit. Furthermore, an external modem has a row of lights on it, which can be very useful for seeing whether or not anything is happening while you are connected.

(2) Get one as fast as possible – a minimum of 28,800 bps (bytes per second). Again, this does not matter with e-mail, for which even the very slowest of modems will be adequate; but if you intend to use the facilities of the world wide web, a fast modem is essential.

Finally, you will need to open an account with an internet access provider (IAP). These are companies which will provide you with the means to access the internet and make use of its various services. Your IAP will give you an e-mail address and a number to phone in order to connect with the internet.

There is a wide range of IAPs vying with one another for your custom. Some charge a monthly subscription, but a growing number are free (they make their money through advertising and a small slice of the cost of access phone calls). The UK's leading free access provider is FreeServe, and you can get a CD including all the software you need to join up with them free of charge from any Dixons electrical store. Some other free IAPs, with contact phone numbers for further information, include Virgin Net (0500 558800), LineOne (0800 111210) and Freezone (0870 744 1111).

The free services generally offer telephone support on premium rate helplines costing up to £1 a minute to call. If, however, you feel you will need a lot of hand-holding initially, you might prefer to join a service which charges a monthly subscription but provides telephone support either free or at standard rates. Two of the best known IAPs in this category are CompuServe (0990 000200) and AOL (0800 3765432). Both of these also offer their members a considerable amount of proprietary content in addition to internet access.

This is not the place for a lengthy discussion of the pros and cons of different service providers; newsstand magazines such as *Internet* publish all the detailed, up-to-date information you could possibly need. It is, however, well worth contacting some of the IAPs mentioned above and asking them for further information.

What Can You Do on the Internet?

As mentioned earlier, there are three main Internet services which are likely to be relevant to home-based businesses. In order of technological sophistication, these are e-mail, newsgroups and the World Wide Web. Let's look at each of these in turn.

(1) E-mail

E-mail is, of course, short for 'electronic mail'. It provides a simple method of exchanging messages with other Internet users, be they on the next street or the other side of the world. The main benefits of this are (a) the low cost, and (b) the speed of delivery (compared with conventional mail services). You don't have to be connected all the time in order to receive your incoming mail. All IAPs offer a mailbox facility, whereby messages sent to your e-mail address are stored till you next log on to collect them.

When you sign up with an IAP, the provider will give you an e-mail address (some offer more than one, so that colleagues, or other members of your family, can have their own e-mail addresses as well) and provide software enabling you to send and receive e-mails. Once you have written your e-mail, you can send it to anyone you wish as long as you know their e-mail address. A typical e-mail address would be: jane.smith@aol.com.

Most IAPs supply a program called an off-line mailer which enables you to create and store messages in your own time. Then, when you next dial your IAP, all your messages are transmitted and incoming mail placed in your mailbox to be read when you come off-line. All this can be done in a few seconds of phone contact, making e-mail not only cheaper than the post but also faxes and ordinary phone calls. Furthermore, you can contact 1, 2 or 50 people with a single message.

For small business owners, e-mail offers several potential attractions. Principally, you can correspond quickly and cheaply with clients and potential clients across the UK, and even in other countries. And, once you have an e-mail address, clients will have a quick, cheap and simple way of getting in touch with you; the advantages of this will be obvious. You may be able to submit invoices and other correspondence by e-mail, thus saving on postage and stationery. And in certain types of business (e.g. freelance writing and editing), you may actually be able to submit your work via e-mail, again saving time and money.

(2) Newsgroups

These are, if you like, the next step up after e-mail. A newsgroup is basically an electronic noticeboard devoted to a particular subject. Anyone accessing a newsgroup can read messages other people have sent in and, if they wish, reply or 'post' a message of their own.

There are many thousands of newsgroups devoted to any subject you can imagine (and quite a few you probably can't). They are divided into families each of which shares a common prefix such as rec (for recreation) or misc (miscellaneous). Examples include rec.arts.film and misc.writing.

Newsgroups are full of enthusiasts who like nothing better than to talk about their pet subject. They might not appeal to everyone as a way of passing the time, but they can come sometimes be very useful for business owners as a means of solving problems. For example, a mobile mechanic needing to find a spare part for a vintage sports car might post a request in the newsgroup uk.rec.cars.classic, with a very good chance that someone reading his message would respond with the information he required.

(3) The World Wide Web

The world wide web (often shortened to the web) is the largest and fastest growing part of the internet. It is also the part which receives by far the greatest publicity. Indeed, new users could be forgiven for thinking that the web **IS** the internet!

There are literally millions of documents on the web. Some are businesses advertising their wares, while others are run by universities, government institutions, and so on. Quite a few are run by clubs and societies and, of course, by private individuals. As well as text, web pages can contain photos, sound and video clips, animations, and so on. In addition, web pages have one other very important feature – the so-called hyperlinks. These are short cuts to other documents on the web. By clicking on a hyperlink you can be transported instantly to another web page, even if it is on a computer the other side of the world. This makes the web a very powerful tool for research.

Every document on the web has a unique URL (uniform resource locator). This is an internet address for a particular website. Once you know the URL of a site, you have all the information you need to visit it. For example, the URL of the Friends of the Earth site is http://www.foe.co.uk. To access websites, as previously mentioned, you need a program called a browser. All IAPs include a browser as part of the suite of programs they provide for new subscribers, and it installs along with the other software.

The web is an invaluable source of information on any subject imaginable, but finding the information you want from the mass of documents on the web can be tricky. Indeed, one writer says, 'The internet is like an enormous library in which someone has turned out the lights and tipped the index cards all over the floor.'

Fortunately it's not completely needle-in-a-haystack, however. Help is at hand in the form of search engines. As the name suggests, these are programs which will help you find documents on the web relevant to the subject you are interested in. They all work slightly differently, but typically you enter a key word or phrase, and the search engine then checks its records and comes up with a list of sites in which your word (or words) can be found. You can then go directly to these sites via the hyperlinks provided. A few of the best-known search engines, with their URLs, are listed:

Alta Vista	http://www.altavista.digital.com
Ask Jeeves	http://www.ask.co.uk
Excite	http://www.excite.co.uk
Google	http://www.google.com
Hotbot	http://www.hotbot.com
Infoseek	http://www.infoseek.com
Lycos	http://www.lycos.co.uk
Search UK	http://www.searchuk.com

| Webcrawler | http://www.webcrawler.com |
| Yahoo | http://www.yahoo.co.uk |

Search engines are powerful tools, and the best news is that most – including all those listed above – are free to use. They can be used for a wide range of purposes, including identifying suppliers and potential customers, researching the latest developments in your field, and finding online stores selling books and other products (frequently at lower prices than those you will pay in the high street).

Setting Up Your Own Web Homepage

One other big attraction of the world wide web is that you can use it to advertise your business by creating your own 'homepage'. Various firms will do this for you – for a price – but it is actually not difficult to create a basic homepage of your own. Most IAPs provide space on the web as part of their service package. They will also usually provide the basic software (tools) to create a homepage suitable for publishing on the web. As a general principle, it is important that your business homepage should be attractive, informative and (if possible) entertaining. People who are surfing the web have a huge range of sites they can visit – and if yours does not immediately grab their interest, they will swiftly move on somewhere else.

15. TAX, NATIONAL INSURANCE AND VAT

As Benjamin Franklin famously observed, there are only two things any of us can be sure of in this life: death and taxes. As a self-employed business person, it will be your responsibility to keep records of your business income and expenditure so that you can declare them to the authorities, and in due course pay tax on them.

Book-keeping is discussed a little later on in the book. It is, however, worth emphasising that, while all business income must be declared for tax purposes, you can set against this any expenditure directly related to your business. This will include obvious things like the cost of raw materials, stationery, postage, printing and photocopying, business bank charges, a proportion of your home phone bills, and so on. In addition, you should be able to deduct the costs of any journeys related to your work, including visits to clients, printers, your bank, etc. Should you decide to join a relevant trade or professional organisation, you can claim their membership fee. You can also set against income the cost of any business-related training you undertake. Finally, if you are working from home, you can claim a proportion of your household bills (gas, electricity, water, etc.) against tax. If you are a home-owner, however, this may have implications for your liability to capital gains tax when you sell your house, so it would be advisable to speak to an accountant about this first.

Income Tax

The amount of income tax you have to pay depends on a range of factors. As you will probably know, everyone in the UK has a tax-free personal allowance (see below). Once your earnings in a year exceed this, you start to pay tax at whatever may be the going rate. For the year 2000/2001, tax was due at 10 per cent on the first £1,520 worth of taxable earnings. On taxable earnings from £1,521 to £28,400, tax was due at 22 per cent. Any income above this was taxed at a rate of 40 per cent.

Note that the figures above are based on your income from all sources. If you have another full-time or part-time job, this may well use up your tax-free allowance, and in that case you will pay tax at the appropriate rate on all your freelance earnings.

For the year 2000/2001, the basic single person allowance was £4,385. The married couple's allowance was withdrawn from April 2000, except in the case of couples where at least one partner is over the age of 65. Self-employed people declare their income to the Inland Revenue on self-assessment tax returns. They pay tax (including Class 4 National Insurance – see below) by two instalments in January and July each year; unless the amount owed is very small, in which case it may be collected in one instalment or by an adjustment to your personal allowance for the following year.

If your business is set up as a limited company different rules apply, and you will need to take advice from an accountant. You are most likely to be paid in the form of a salary from the company, on which you will have to pay tax monthly like any employee, and dividends, which for tax purposes are treated differently again. Your accountant will advise you on the most tax-efficient combination of payment methods for your particular circumstances.

As soon as you start earning money from your home-based business, you should notify the Inland Revenue; they will then send you the necessary forms to fill in. The tax office to contact will be the one covering the area where you live (assuming you are working from home). This may well be different from your former

PAYE tax office, which will have been based on your employer's address, not yours.

Up-to-date information about tax rates, allowances and so on is available from the Inland Revenue's website at www.inlandrevenue.gov.uk.

National Insurance

The Contributions Agency (formally part of the Department of Social Security, now a division of the Inland Revenue) must also be informed of your business activities for national insurance purposes. The position is somewhat complex, but the main points are summarised here. An employee taxed under the PAYE (pay as you earn) system normally pays a fixed proportion of his or her earnings (in 2000/2001 10% of weekly earnings in the range £76.01 to £535) in national insurance contributions. This is deducted directly by the employer, who also makes a further contribution himself.

A self-employed person, by contrast, pays his/her national insurance in two parts. Class 2 contributions are fixed payments made every week, normally by direct debit. For 2000/2001, the weekly rate for self-employed people was £2. If you believe your earnings from self-employment are likely to be low, you can apply for exemption from paying Class 2 National Insurance. The low earnings limit for the 2000/2001 tax year was £3,825. If you wish to apply for exemption, you can do so on leaflet CA02 'National Insurance for self-employed people with small earnings'. This is available from local tax and DSS offices or direct from the Contributions Agency (address below). It is, however, worth noting that if you do not pay Class 2 contributions, it may affect your pension rights and your entitlement to some social security benefits.

Class 4 contributions are an additional levy made on earnings within certain set limits. Unlike Class 2 contributions, they do not provide any entitlement to social security benefits, and are really just another form of taxation. They are assessed and collected by the Inland Revenue along with income tax. In the year 2000/2001, Class 4 contributions were payable by self-employed people at a rate of 7% on earnings between £4,385 and £27,820. You pay Class 4 contributions only on income within these two bands, so the most you would have had to pay in the year 2000/2001 was $(27,820 - 4,385) \times 7\% = £1,640.45$. This is the amount you would have paid if you earned £27,820 or more.

For any enquiries about National Insurance, or to provide notification that you are setting up in business, write to: The Contributions Agency, Self Employment Directorate, Longbenton, Newcastle-upon-Tyne, NE98 1YX. You can phone their enquiry line on 06451 54655 (local rate). Information is also available via the website www.inlandrevenue.gov.uk/nic/index.htm.

Value Added Tax (VAT)

If your taxable turnover – as opposed to net profit – exceeds a set figure at the end of any twelve-month period, you are obliged to register for VAT. Once registered, you will then have to charge VAT at the current rate – 17.5% at the time of writing – to your clients, and pass this on to the local VAT office (a division of Customs and Excise) at regular intervals.

Many small businesses attempt to postpone VAT registration because of the extra paperwork it entails. However, registration can have some advantages. Although you have to collect VAT from your clients, you can also reclaim the VAT you pay on business supplies (materials, stationery, training courses, etc.). Because of the relatively high VAT threshold in the UK (already over £50,000 and raised most years), the majority of people running home-based businesses are unlikely to have to register when starting out.

It is, however, possible to register voluntarily even if your turnover is below the threshold if you believe that the ability to reclaim the VAT you pay on your supplies will justify the extra paperwork. To do this, you will need to satisfy Customs and Excise that your activities constitute a proper 'business for VAT purposes'. Bear in mind, also, that if you take this course you will have to add VAT to all your customers' bills (unless your particular line of business is zero-rated, e.g. selling books or children's clothing). If customers cannot reclaim this themselves, it may make your service or products less attractive to them.

If you would like more information about VAT registration at any stage, you should ask for Notice 700/1 'Should I be registered for VAT?' from your local Customs and Excise office. Information is also available on the Customs and Excise website at www.hmce.gov.uk.

Business Rates

If part of your home is used exclusively for work purposes, you could in theory find yourself liable for business rates in addition to your ordinary council tax bill. However, the government has said that where business use is subsidiary to domestic use, rates will probably not be levied. In practice, so long as you have not turned your whole home into a shop or factory, you would be unlucky to find yourself under the scrutiny of the valuation officer (and rather foolish to raise the question yourself). Note that if you decide to claim some of your housing costs as work expenses, you may run a greater risk of being levied for business rates.

16. PRICING YOUR SERVICES

For many people running small businesses, putting a price on their products and services is one of the hardest tasks they have to perform. Setting prices is something of a balancing act. If you set your prices too low you may fail to cover all your costs and end up losing money rather than making it. Clearly no business can survive long in those circumstances! On the other hand, if you set your prices too high, people may be unwilling to buy from you, especially if they can buy the same product or service more cheaply from one of your competitors.

It follows from this that in setting prices both the cost of providing the product or service, and the price that the customer will be willing to pay, must be taken into account. In different types of business, however, this applies in different ways.

Pricing a Product

If your business will involve producing a product (e.g. toys or craft items), the price you charge will have to cover the cost of the raw materials plus your overheads (heating, lighting, advertising, stationery and so on) and also give you a reasonable profit. The simplest way to price each unit is therefore as follows:

$$\text{Selling price} = \text{cost of materials per unit} + \frac{\text{total overheads}}{\text{total production}} + \text{mark-up}$$

The total overheads includes, for this purpose, the cost of labour, whether it is yours or (later on) that of your employees. The selling price therefore covers all your fixed and variable costs, while the mark-up is what will give your business its profit. This may be best explained by an example.

EXAMPLE

Nita plans to set up a home-based business making soft toys. She intends to buy the materials and kapok (stuffing) and assemble the toys herself. Nita estimates that she can make one soft toy per hour, with raw materials costing £2 per toy. Working forty hours a week, she can therefore produce 40 toys every week. She must now work out what she should charge for her labour per hour.

One simple approach to this problem is to is to charge what you would have to pay an employee to do the job. After all, if the business really takes off and Nita has to take on someone to help her, she will need to pay this person the 'going rate' for the job. If this rate is much more than she has been paying herself, she will either have to raise her prices or lower her profits, neither of which is likely to be an attractive option. By studying job advertisements in her local paper, Nita estimates that the usual rate for this type of job is around £160 for a 40 hour week. To work out an hourly rate, she adds another 50% to this, to take into account such things as paid holidays and sick leave, extra taxes, and the higher overheads taking on an employee would entail. So, in Nita's case, the hourly rate comes to (£160 + 50%)/40 = £6.00 an hour.

Nita must now work out her total fixed costs (overheads) per year. By paying herself £6.00 per hour and working 49 forty-hour weeks (leaving three weeks for holidays), Nita's annual 'wages' come out as 6.00 x 49 x 40 = £11,760. Nita estimates that her other overheads will be around £3,000 every year, giving her a total overheads figure of £14,760. Nita's yearly production will be 40 x 49 = 1960 toys, and she decides to aim for a mark-up of 30%. The pricing calculation therefore comes out as follows:

$$\text{Selling price per toy} = £2 + \frac{14,760}{1,960} + 30\% = £12.39$$

Having worked out a selling price, Nita must now check whether people will be prepared to pay such a sum for one of her toys. She hopes to sell most of her production through shops. As a rule-of-thumb, non-food products sell at about double the retailer's cost price, so a likely retail price for one of Nita's soft toys would be around £25.00. Retailers will soon tell Nita whether her toys will sell at that price. If not, Nita will have to reduce her prices. This could be by either cutting the cost of raw materials (though potential savings here are limited), increasing her productivity (i.e. producing toys at a faster rate than one per hour), cutting her rate of pay (though this in unlikely to be an attractive option) or changing the design.

*   *   *

One point arising from this is that Nita is paying herself a wage but also making a profit from her mark-up. Perhaps it may seem as though Nita is paying herself twice, and you might wonder why she does not simply pay herself a wage and have done. However, if all Nita makes from her business is the £6.00 an hour she pays herself, she might as well be doing a paid job for someone else and letting them worry about marketing, book-keeping, pricing and so on! The profit is extra income which recompenses Nita for the risks and extra work entailed in running a business, and that is why you should normally budget to make one. Nita may decide to take all of her profits herself – in which case she will be taxed on it as income – or she may choose to re-invest some or all of it in new equipment such as an electric sewing machine which may improve her productivity.

One other point is that Nita's calculations assumed she would be working the whole time just on making toys. In practice this is unlikely, as any business owner also has to spend time on many tasks which do not make any direct contribution to profit. These may include:

- Book-keeping
- Seeing customers and potential customers
- Getting money from customers when it is overdue
- Buying materials and finding better sources of supply
- Preparing advertisements, leaflets, letters, price lists, etc.
- Planning and organising future work
- Maintaining and repairing equipment
- Dealing with officials
- Travelling
- Dealing with correspondence, etc.

In deciding what to charge, remember that you will need time for all of these things and more, in addition to the time you can devote to productive, profit-making work. If you are a sole trader, you are likely to find at least 25% of your time will be spent on these other matters.

Pricing a Service

Many home-based businesses, instead of making products, involve providing a service. In service-based businesses pricing is normally based on an hourly rate for the job, plus the cost of materials.

If you are running a service business then, rather than a product, what you are really selling is your time. Putting a price on this is therefore crucial. One possible approach is to decide on your target annual income, then work out the number of hours you will be able to charge to customers during the year. By dividing your target income by the number of chargeable hours, you will come up with the amount you need to charge per hour to achieve your target income.

Bear in mind, however, that you will not be able to spend every hour of the day on chargeable work. Some time, inevitably, will have to be spent on tasks such as book-keeping, marketing, administration and so on. Typically, in a service business around 25 to 50 per cent of your time may have to be spent on tasks that are not immediately chargeable to a customer.

As with a manufacturing business, you will need to include in your hourly rate an amount to cover your overheads and an amount to provide a profit. The total hourly rate you charge will be according to the following formula:

$$\text{Hourly rate} = \frac{\text{Target annual income} + \text{total overheads} + \text{target profits}}{\text{Total chargeable hours per year}}$$

This calculation will give you an hourly rate, but you need to check how it compares with other, similar businesses. This is where market research is so important. If your hourly rates are much higher than other businesses, you will have problems attracting customers, and need to look at ways of bringing your rate down. Possible options would include working longer hours, or reducing your target income, overheads or profit margin.

EXAMPLE

Mark plans to start his own building business. He decides that he will work 49 weeks a year, and will aim for an average of 30 hours a week chargeable work. This gives him 1,470 chargeable hours per year. His target income for the first year is £12,000. The hourly rate he will need to earn to achieve this therefore comes out as:

$$\frac{12,000}{1,470} = £8.16 \text{ per hour}$$

The actual rate Mark charges his customers, however, needs to include in addition an element to cover his overheads and an element for profit. Mark estimates that his annual fixed costs (excluding what he pays himself) will come to £4,000 and he will aim for £2,000 profit in his first year. Mark's total hourly rate which he must charge customers to meet all these requirements is therefore:

$$\frac{12,000 + 4,000 + 2,000}{1,470} = £12.24 \text{ per hour}$$

*   *   *

Charging for Materials

As well as your hourly rate, the fees you charge clients will also need to cover the materials you use and any other variable costs. (An example of another variable cost would be the cost of subcontracting part of a job – that is, paying someone else to do it instead of doing it yourself.)

One common way of charging for materials is 'at cost'. However, this need not necessarily mean that you charge the customer the same amount as you paid for them. To do so would be to ignore the hidden costs of such things as the time you take to find and buy materials, the cost of keeping them in stock, the cost of travelling to pick them up, and so on. Some businesses define 'at cost' as the retail price which a private customer would pay, whereas they themselves purchase at trade or wholesale prices. This difference helps recompense their other costs. Depending on your business, this may well be a sensible policy.

The Perils of Under-charging

Before leaving this topic, it is worth making the point that many people when starting out in business make the mistake of under-charging. Their reasons include:

- They forget the need to cover all their overheads and make a reasonable profit
- They believe they lack the experience or skills to command higher rates
- They think they will have to charge less than existing businesses to win customers away from them
- Or they simply take the view that any work (and income) is better than none.

In the short term under-charging may well attract customers. However, it is very likely that the income generated will be insufficient to cover all your costs and still leave you with enough income to live on. Furthermore, once your customers have become accustomed to paying 'bargain basement' fees, you are likely to face stiff resistance from them if you try to raise charges later. And finally, many people (rightly or wrongly) associate low fees with shoddy workmanship. Clients whose first priority is a good-quality job may therefore actually be put off if the prices you quote appear suspiciously low.

For the long-term success of your business it is much better to work out target rates of payment according to the principles set out above and use these as your basis for charging. Of course, sometimes a potential client may respond that the fee quoted is higher than he or she expected. In this case, you may have to decide how much you want (or need) their custom. If you have no other work on and the amount charged will still cover your costs and produce some sort of profit, you may decide to accept a reduced fee. However, you should be aware that the client who wants the lowest price is often the one who will be the most demanding of your time and the most critical of your service.

Pricing is an essential aspect of operating a successful business. Concern yourself with what the competition is charging by all means, but ensure that you cover all your costs, including time and expenses, plus a reasonable profit margin. Once you have established your reputation, you can then raise your prices.

17. MARKETING AND SELLING

This is arguably the most important aspect of running any business, large or small. Marketing involves identifying who your potential customers will be (through market research) and tailoring your product/service to meet their needs. It also involves bringing your business to these people's attention and persuading them to buy.

Marketing covers not only advertising and selling, but a host of other factors which can affect your success or failure in attracting work. These include the prices you charge, the range of products and services you offer, your location, public relations, sales promotions (e.g. special offers), and so on. This section will concentrate on advertising and selling – but it is important to bear in mind that these are just two of a number of marketing ingredients which you will need to be aware of and try to manipulate to your business's advantage.

Advertising

Advertising aims to bring a product or service to the attention of potential customers, and persuade them – or start to persuade them – to buy. When spending money on advertising you hope to recover your costs and more – hopefully much more – from increased sales. Advertising is not a precise science, however, and results can never be guaranteed. In general, if you have enough customers coming to you by word-of-mouth recommendation, there is little point in advertising.

If you do decide to advertise, you should have some kind of plan or strategy to guide you. The aim of your advertising strategy should be to bring potential customers from a state of ignorance about your product or service to a desire to purchase it. Your advertising should:

- Get customers' attention
- Help them understand the product or service
- Get them to believe in the benefits you are offering
- Make them want to buy your product or service
- Get them to take action (e.g. fill in a coupon or make a phone call)
- Improve the business's image and reputation.

No one advertisement on its own can be expected to achieve all this. Rather, you will need to use a mixture of different types of advertising over a period of time. The latter point is particularly important. It is easy to believe, if you have taken out a half-page advertisement in your local paper, that everybody in the area now knows about your business. This is a mistake. People forget about adverts almost as soon as they have read them, unless they happen to need your product or service at that particular moment. It is therefore very important, if you are going to use advertising, to advertise regularly.

Regular advertising has other benefits as well. For one thing, if an individual sees your advertisement every week or month, your name is more likely to come into his mind should he at some point have need of your services. For another, if you advertise regularly, people will, in general, be more inclined to see your business as established and reliable, and unlikely to disappear overnight with their money. This is one reason why you will sometimes see businesses advertising 'established 1989' (or whatever). It all helps give an impression of stability and reliability.

On the other hand, it must be said that in some types of business regular advertising may cause a degree of suspicion among potential customers. Tradesmen such as builders and plumbers, for example, tend to obtain much of their work through personal recommendation from satisfied customers. If such individuals advertise regularly, some people may conclude that if they need to advertise that much they cannot be very good! It is difficult to give hard-and-fast advice about this, as so much depends on local factors (e.g. are there many other businesses in the area offering this service, or just a few?). The best advice is to put yourself in the place of a potential customer. If you saw a business such as yours advertising every week, would you be impressed by this or suspicious about it?

Where Can You Advertise?

When deciding where to advertise you have a wide range of media to choose from. Some, however, are more likely to be of interest than others. Large companies may use television, national newspapers, national commercial radio, and so on, but for a small business the cost of this is likely to be prohibitive. In addition, if your business serves just your local community, there is little point spending money sending your message to other parts of the country.

For many home-based businesses, the most fruitful forms of advertising are likely to include local newspapers, magazines and directories; brochures and leaflets; advertising cards; and mail shots. Let's look at each of these in turn.

(1) Local newspapers, magazines and directories

For many small businesses, these are likely to be among the first choice of places to advertise. Your aim should be to choose a publication which is seen by as many people as possible within your target area. For example, if you are aiming to provide a service to householders living within a 5 km radius of your business, you should choose a publication covering that area and preferably (to ensure that your advertising is as cost-effective as possible) no wider.

Having chosen the publication, or publications, you wish to advertise in, you must then decide on the size of your advertisement and what you want to say in it. Most newspapers and magazines offer both 'classified' and 'display' advertising. Classified advertisements – also known as lineage – normally consist of a few lines of text under a particular heading (e.g. builders, car repairs, electrical). They are usually charged at a price per word. Display advertisements – which can also include cartoons, graphics, and so on – are charged for by the amount of space they take up. Small display advertisements are charged per single column centimetre (scc), which is a space one column wide and one centimetre deep. Publications may also quote the cost per 1/8, 1/4, 1/2 or full page. There may be an extra charge if you want your advertisement in a particular position, e.g. on the front or back cover.

Classified advertisements are cheaper, and for many businesses can be a cost-effective way of attracting customers, especially if repeated regularly. They can also be a good way of 'testing' a new publication to see the level of interest an advert in it generates. Display advertisements are obviously more eye-catching than classified, but before going down this route you need to be confident that the extra response such an advertisement may generate will be sufficient to justify the extra expenditure.

What goes on your advertisement is up to you (or your agency, if you decide to employ one), but the guidelines below may be helpful:

* Have a clear, straightforward message
* Use as few words as you can to get your message across
* In display ads, try to come up with a catchy headline which sums up the main benefit your business offers to its customers
* Throughout the advertisement, go on emphasising the benefits of your product or service to the customer
* Keep yourself in the background – talk about 'you' (the customer) rather than 'we' or 'I'
* Avoid making extravagant claims and promises you cannot keep (people will not believe you, and you may end up in trouble with the law)

- Avoid being funny – other people may not share your sense of humour
- In a display advertisement, use pictures or photographs wherever possible
- At the end of the advertisement, make it clear to readers what to do next ('Ring 070 9000 now for an instant quote', 'Return the coupon below for a free brochure'.).

It is also a good idea to study other people's advertisements, both your competitors' and other businesses'. If the same advert is repeated week after week, this is a good sign that it is having the desired effect of bringing in customers. See if you can work out what is making these advertisements successful, and try to apply what you have learned in your own advertising. Do not simply copy other people's advertisements, but it may be possible to adapt ideas, especially from businesses in other sectors, in your own advertising.

Finally, it is important to monitor the effectiveness of your advertising, so that you can see what works and what doesn't. Do not merely rely on personal impressions ('That advert looked good'), as these are often misleading. Keep a count of the actual number of replies you get to each advertisement, and also the number which translate into actual sales. If you are advertising in a number of places, you will need some means of separating out responses to each advertisement. One way of doing this is to include a 'keying device'. This is normally a code inserted in the address which tells you where people have got your details from. For example, if you have an advertisement in the Littletown News asking people to write to you for information, you could put 'Dept LN' after your business's name. Then, every time you get a letter with 'Dept LN' in the address, you will know that it came from that source. If people phone, you can of course just ask them where they saw your number.

(2) Brochures and leaflets

Leaflets and brochures can carry more information than an advertisement, as more space is available to you. The message they convey is also intended to last a lot longer. As most people will not bother to cut out and keep an advertisement, a newspaper advertisement will last only as long as the newspaper it is contained in. After a few days, at most, it will therefore be thrown away. A well-designed and informative leaflet or brochure, by contrast, may be kept for future reference, perhaps for many months.

Brochures are small booklets. They normally consist of a few pages folded down the middle and stapled, perhaps with a card cover. Their most common uses are to send out to people enquiring about your services, perhaps in response to a newspaper advertisement. They may also be sent to existing customers or to people who have bought from you in the past. Brochures may include prices, or – to prevent them going out of date too soon – you may decide to insert a separate price list at the back. Brochures are a relatively cheap and cost-effective method of advertising, so long as they are distributed to people who have a genuine interest in purchasing from you.

Leaflets are even simpler than brochures. They consist of just one or two pages, or perhaps a single page folded over. Because they are so cheap to produce, leaflets can be more widely used than brochures. They can be given out at exhibitions, used in mailshots, inserted in newspapers and magazines (for which you will, of course, have to pay a fee), dropped through people's letterboxes, or even handed out to passers-by in the street.

Although leaflets and brochures are inexpensive, it is important that their appearance should not detract from the image you are trying to project. So they should not look too cheap and tatty, and the style should be consistent with your letterhead and packaging. As with advertisements, the main message in a leaflet or brochure should concern the benefits of your product or service to the customer. Keep the style relaxed and informal, almost as though you were writing a letter to a friend. Unless you are specifically aiming at technical people, avoid going into great technical detail. If such information is needed, it is normally better to keep the main text jargon-free and put product specifications, test data and so on in a separate section at the back.

When writing a leaflet or brochure, the same general principles apply as for writing advertisements, though you can and should go into more detail about your service. In addition, to achieve maximum effect the design must be good. Modern word processing and desktop publishing programs can produce professional-looking results using the templates they come supplied with, but if you do not have one of these (or are not confident about their use), it may be best to obtain professional help. Many high street printers will advise and assist in preparing artwork for a leaflet or brochure, or for a higher quality (but more expensive) service you could try a commercial artist or graphic designer. Advertising agents will also undertake this work, although their charges can be high. For many home-based businesses employing an agency, in the beginning at least, may not be viable or cost-effective.

(3) Advertising cards

Another option well worth considering is advertising cards. These are similar in size to business cards, around 10 x 6 centimetres being typical. Cards are very cheap to produce, and can be used in similar ways to leaflets. They are particularly useful when advertising businesses such as taxi services, which people may need at short notice. Advertising cards can be left in hotels, restaurants, cafes, bars, telephone booths, shops, nightclubs and so on, either in small piles on a table or stuck to the wall (though it may be best to obtain the proprietor's permission first!).

Cards can also be put through people's letterboxes. Because of their handy size, people may be more inclined to put them in a purse or wallet for future use than they would with a leaflet. One idea which some firms have adopted is to print their own message on one side of the card, and on the other include a list of phone numbers such as the local police, hospital, fire service, etc. The aim is to make the card more useful to the recipient, so there is more likelihood that he or she will keep it safe for future reference.

(4) Mailshots

A mailshot involves sending advertising material through the post to potential customers. This approach is also known as direct mail. The effectiveness of a mailshot depends on two things:

(1) The accuracy of the mailing list
(2) The impact of what you have written.

For a successful mailshot, an accurate mailing list is essential. Writing to people who have gone away, gone out of business, died, or are not interested in your product or service is a waste of time and money. The best way of building up a mailing list is to start with people who have bought from you in the past, or at least enquired about your products or services. You can add to this by obtaining names from directories, trade associations and so on. If, for example, you are selling printing supplies, you may be able to obtain the names and addresses of all the printers in your area from a local directory.

You could also consider exchanging mailing lists with other non-competing businesses, buying or renting them. If you buy a list you can use it as often as you like, but lists are seldom sold outright. More often, you will have to rent a list, which means you are allowed to use it once only and cannot copy the names on it (though if any of the people you mail become your customers, you can then legitimately add them to your own mailing list). Specialist agents called list brokers can supply mailing lists in a wide range of categories, usually for rental. Lists available may include anything from single people to over-sixties, art collectors to vegetarians, business opportunity seekers to millionaires! Details of a range of list brokers can be obtained from the Direct Marketing Association (DMA), Haymarket House, 1 Oxendon Street, London, SW1Y 4EE (Tel. 020 7321 2525). Information is also available from their website at www.dma.org.uk.

Mail shots should not be too long. One popular approach is to include a sales leaflet and a covering letter. In the letter you introduce yourself and explain what you are offering, emphasising – as ever – the benefits of your product or service to the customer. The accompanying leaflet should reinforce the sales message and leave recipients in no doubt as to what they should do next. If this is to write for further details, you could include a stamped and addressed envelope. If you want them to phone, ensure your number is printed prominently at the foot of the page.

Bear in mind that large mail shots can be costly. It is therefore essential that they are well targeted at people who have a genuine interest in buying from you, or the profits may not cover the costs involved. For small, home-based businesses, the best approach may be to begin by writing to existing customers with special offers and so on. If this proves successful, you may try writing to other potential buyers as well; but be very cautious before spending large amounts. If you are using a new, untried mailing list, start with a small test mailing – one or two hundred letters perhaps – and only try a larger number if the response to the test mailing proves encouraging.

The Post Office has a range of services such as Mailsort aimed at businesses who wish to use direct mail – see the section Help From the Post Office for more details. It is also worth contacting the Direct Mail Information Service, who provide a range of free information and services (as well as some you have to pay for). Contact: the Direct Mail Information Service, 5 Carlisle Street, London, W1V 6JX (tel. 020 7494 0483). See also their website at www.dmis.co.uk.

Personal Selling

Advertising will begin the selling process but, for most products and services, completing the sale will require some degree of personal involvement, either face-to-face or over the phone. Selling is a skill which comes more readily to some people than to others, but there are certain principles you can learn which should help make it easier.

(1) Face-to-face

This could occur in a variety of situations: a builder meeting a potential client, a toy-maker talking to a retailer, a private investigator talking to a solicitor, a writer or artist arranging a school visit, and so on. You may be 'cold calling', that is arriving unannounced, or you may be calling to fulfil an appointment made as a result of your advertising. Whatever the circumstances, making a good first impression is essential. Your skills (and self-confidence) are sure to improve with practice, but below are some guidelines which should get you off on the right track:

- Make sure that your appearance is smart and businesslike. Though it should hardly need saying, ensure that your grooming and personal hygiene are beyond reproach.

- Take adequate sales material – samples, business cards, brochures, order forms, and so on – and ensure that you know it thoroughly. Bring an up-to-date price list, and perhaps a pocket calculator in case you have to work out a price there and then.

- Prepare a written outline of your sales approach, so that you know what you are going to say when you meet a potential customer and the specific points you want to make. This is not to say you should have a script – it is important to listen carefully to what the customer tells you and respond accordingly – but you should have a general idea of the structure you wish your meeting to follow.

- Whenever possible, make an appointment beforehand rather than turning up unannounced. Cold calling is inefficient, as frequently the person you need to see will be out, in a meeting or otherwise unavailable. In addition, many people are hostile to 'salespeople' who turn up uninvited, and you will have to overcome this initial hostility before you can even think about making a sale.

- If – as recommended – you have an appointment, make every effort to arrive on time. If you are going to be late, phone ahead to warn whoever you are seeing. Even if you are late, don't run upstairs or along corridors. This will make you untidy and out-of-breath, and create an unfavourable first impression.

- On meeting the potential customer, introduce yourself and offer to shake hands. Use the person's name ('Good morning, Mrs Grosvenor'). You will, of course, have confirmed this beforehand, preferably while making the appointment.

- Encourage the customer to talk about his or her needs, as this will allow you to respond in the most appropriate way. Show the customer the benefits your service or product offers, as it is these which the customer buys. For example: 'Using my services will free you to spend more time concentrating on what you do best' or 'Your customers will want to order more of these because they're such good value for money.'

- If your service or product can meet the customer's needs, explain how it will achieve this. On the other hand, if you cannot meet his needs, then say so now. Your credibility will be enhanced, and the customer will be more likely to get in touch with you when he does need what you have to offer.

- If the customer raises objections, listen carefully, making notes if appropriate. Then go through the objections one at a time, showing how you will overcome them. Try to anticipate all the possible objections beforehand and have replies prepared for them. Obviously, your ability to do this will improve with experience.

- When you sense that the moment is right, close (i.e. complete) the sale. Don't risk irritating your customer by carrying on listing benefits once he has definitely decided to buy. Get him to sign an order form if appropriate, and leave a copy which should include the agreed price.

- Aim to end the meeting on a positive, friendly note. Reassure the customer that he has made a wise choice in deciding to purchase from you. Even if he has not made a purchase on this occasion, you should aim to leave him with the impression of a warm, trustworthy person with whom he would like to do business in the future.

Telephone Selling

The telephone can be an invaluable tool for selling. It can be used in a variety of ways. In some circumstances you may be able to close a sale directly over the phone, thus saving the cost and time of going to see the customer in person. This is especially the case when selling to former or current customers. More often, however, the telephone will be used in the first stage of the selling process. By phoning a potential customer, you aim to find out: (a) whether the business uses (or might use) the service or product you are selling; and (b) the name of the person who would make the decision on purchasing.

You can then ask to speak to this person and attempt to make an appointment to see him, or alternatively you could write a sales letter addressed to him personally. After a few days, you could then phone to check that he received your letter, and try to make an appointment to see him in person. Using the telephone as part of your sales strategy has the great advantage that it allows you to contact a large number of potential customers, and narrow these down to the most promising 'prospects' on whom to concentrate your personal selling efforts. Here are a few tips on using the telephone for selling:

(1) Prepare in advance what you are going to say. Write it down and have it in front of you when you pick up the phone to call a potential customer. Practise with a friend or your spouse, or in front of the bathroom mirror. Your aim should be to sound relaxed and natural, not as though you are reading from a script.

(2) Choose the right time to call. With business customers, towards the end of the day when they are winding down may be the best time. If you are calling private individuals, it is preferable to avoid ringing them at work, as they may feel awkward or embarrassed at discussing their personal affairs in front of colleagues. It is best to ring such people at home in the early to middle part of the evening.

(3) When making your call, relax and try to use a normal, conversational tone. Don't worry if you have a local or regional accent – people at the other end often react positively towards this, feeling that the person calling them is more natural and 'real'.

(4) Keep a smile on your face while you are speaking. This will help you relax, and the good humour in your voice will communicate itself to the other person.

(5) Set yourself targets for numbers of calls to make. If you are 'cold calling', there is a good chance that many of the people you phone will be uninterested in what you have to offer. However, if only one in ten wants to know more, this still means that by making 100 calls you should be able to fix up ten appointments.

(6) If the person on the other end is rude or abusive, avoid the temptation to be rude back. Just put the phone down and call the next name on your list. Professional telephone salespeople are trained to welcome every rejection they receive as one step nearer to the next acceptance. It will help greatly if you can adopt a similar attitude yourself.

After-sales Service

Making sales is essential to the survival of every business, but the marketing process does not – or should not – end there. Your aim should not merely be to make a single sale, but to create a satisfied customer who will come back to you – perhaps many times – and recommend your business to his friends and relatives.

Your marketing strategy should therefore include some means of ensuring that your customer is satisfied with the service or product he has received, and reassuring him that you will be there to help if any problems arise later. If problems do subsequently occur and you are able to resolve them, this is a powerful means of generating customer loyalty and ensuring your business gains a good reputation.

The kind of after-sales service which is appropriate will obviously differ from business to business, but one measure worth pursuing in many businesses is keeping in regular touch with former customers, even if they haven't bought from you for a while. You might, for instance, write to let them know of any new services you are offering. You could even send out a regular newsletter, or a copy of your latest brochure or catalogue. Another idea which works well in some types of business is to follow up a sale with a reminder of when the procedure concerned is due to be repeated. For example, a mobile mechanic might write to a customer to remind him when his car's next service is due.

Finally, when complaints arise, investigate them thoroughly and accept responsibility if the fault has been yours. If such is the case, offer a refund, replacement or whatever is most appropriate. A customer with a complaint who feels that he has been treated fairly and sympathetically is very likely to become one of your most loyal customers in future. A generous policy here frequently pays huge dividends in long-term customer goodwill and support.

All of these strategies will help improve your business's reputation and build confidence in your product or service. No businessman who hopes to succeed over a period of years can afford to neglect the importance of after-sales service.

Marketing Awareness

As a small business owner it is important always to be thinking about ways in which your service or product could be marketed better. One method is to observe what others, especially your nearest competitors, are doing, and be prepared to adapt or 'borrow' their best ideas. Listen also to your customers, especially when they ask for a service or product you do not currently provide, and consider whether it would be feasible to offer this. Even if you do not have time for any other market research, by these simple techniques you will stay aware of your market and be able to develop and expand your business.

18. HOW TO GET 'FREE' PUBLICITY

As well as paid-for advertising, you may be able to obtain a certain amount of free publicity for your business if you understand and apply the principles of PR (public relations). Although professional PR practitioners will argue that their jobs concern much more than just getting free publicity, for the small home-based business this is by far the most important aspect of PR.

Media coverage obtained through PR is normally free, though it can be time-consuming to arrange. The aim of this approach is to get information about your business into magazines or newspapers in the form of articles or news stories. This can be a very effective way of publicising your business, as people are often more inclined to believe what they read in a news item than in a paid-for advert.

The main way to achieve news coverage is by sending out a press release. This is a short news story which you hope will be published by the paper, or prompt one of their reporters to write an article based on it. Press releases must contain something newsworthy, as newspapers will not simply print a piece saying how wonderful your business is. Nevertheless, local papers in particular are often under-staffed and welcome good stories they can use, even if the news they contain is not particularly earth-shattering. A few events which might justify a press release include:

- The opening of your business
- Winning a big order
- Winning a prize or award
- Celebrating an anniversary
- Offering a new service
- Developing a new product
- Sponsoring a local sports team
- Assisting a charity or charitable appeal
- Special offers, events, and so on.

A press release should **NOT** be written in the same way as an advert. The idea is to achieve coverage in the news pages, so you should try to imitate the concise, factual style used by newspaper reporters. Your aim should be to produce a story or article which could be used by the editor without requiring any changes. If your press release is published more or less as you wrote it, you can congratulate yourself on a job well done! The main principles of press release writing are summarised below.

(1) On the top of your headed notepaper write the date and the heading **PRESS RELEASE** in block capitals.

(2) Below this, write a heading for the release. This should explain in a nutshell what the release is about – for example **LITTLETON TOY-MAKER GETS CONTRACT WITH HAMLEYS!** or **LOCAL PHOTOGRAPHER WINS NATIONAL AWARD.**

(3) Below this, write the text of your press release. As mentioned, this should be in article rather than advertisement style. Aim to answer as concisely as possible the five **Ws – WHO, WHAT, WHEN, WHERE** and **WHY** (that is, **WHO** you are, **WHAT** you have done, **WHEN** you did it, **WHERE** you did it, and **WHY** you did it). Try to cover all the main points in the first paragraph or two, as the lower half of the release may be cut if the editor is short of space.

(4) If possible, include a quote from yourself or someone else in your business. This can lighten the tone of the release and make it look more like a 'proper' news story (which nearly always include quotes). It will also help greatly if you can include a photograph to accompany the release (or let the editor know that photographs are available on request).

(5) At the end of the release, if at all possible include a phone number where a reporter can contact you to get more information.

You can send your press release to the editor, or to the reporter who covers small business matters for the paper. Don't expect to succeed every time - your release may be competing with hundreds of others - but when you do manage to get coverage the amount of interest it generates can more than justify the effort you put in. Below is an example of a press release so that you can see what they look like.

PRESS RELEASE

July 3 2004
For Immediate Release

LOCAL PHOTOGRAPHER WINS NATIONAL AWARD

Local photographer Jenny Richardson is celebrating after achieving first place in the Kodak National Photographic Awards, 1999/2000. As well as £1,000 worth of photographic equipment, her prize includes an all-expenses paid trip to Kenya to take pictures of wild animals on safari.

This theme of this year's Kodak competition was 'Plants and Animals', and Jenny's prize-winning photos included a number of her cat, Sylvester, playing in her garden. She will soon be taking pictures of much bigger cats in the famous Masai Mara national park.

Jenny's more usual subjects include children and wedding parties. She says, 'Winning this award was a wonderful surprise for me, but I don't intend to become a full-time wildlife photographer. I enjoy working with couples and families in Littleton too much to give that up.'

Would-be clients wanting to book Jenny for a forthcoming wedding or other event can contact her on 0700 344566. Jenny says she will give a 10 per cent discount to anyone mentioning that they heard about her through this article.

Further information: Jenny Richards
     Tel: 0700 344566 (day/evening)

If you find you enjoy writing press releases and have some success with them, you could try your hand at writing short articles, perhaps for trade or technical magazines. You should not necessarily expect to be paid for such articles, but will benefit from the publicity they generate.

Sales Promotions

Sales promotions are closely related to PR. They are designed to generate extra interest in your product or service, but rather than working via the media they aim to appeal to potential customers directly. A few examples of sales promotions are as follows:

* Giving free samples
* Discounts for some types of buyer (e.g. students, unemployed)
* Free gifts with purchases
* Giving talks or demonstrations about your product or service
* Special opening offers
* Fashion shows
* Competitions
* Vouchers giving money off the next purchase
* Mobile demonstrations
* Exhibitions.

Sales promotions aim to attract new customers and retain old ones. As you will note from the list above, they allow you to give your creativity free rein. Promotions are often combined with advertising (e.g. you could mention in your adverts a two-for-the-price-of-one offer) and with public relations (e.g. in the sample press release, the sales promotion of a 10 per cent discount for every customer mentioning the article was used).

Sales promotions are increasingly popular among businesses, with some finding them more effective for generating sales than traditional advertising. You do, however, need to be careful that you are not giving away money needlessly. The aim of sales promotions should be to attract new customers who then become regular clients. Promotions are therefore best used occasionally rather than continuously, and their effectiveness should be carefully monitored.

19. BOOK-KEEPING AND ACCOUNTS

Before you begin trading, it is essential to have a suitable system in place for keeping financial records. Such records are vital, both for the information they can give you about the success (or otherwise) of your business, and when the time comes to prepare your end-of-year accounts.

The Need for Financial Records

There are many good reasons why businesses need to keep accurate financial records. For one thing, as mentioned above, at the appropriate time you will have to use them to prepare accounts for the tax authorities, so that they (and you) know how much tax you will have to pay. If your accounts do not show clearly what you have earned the tax inspector will make his own estimate, and you may find yourself paying more tax than you should.

Keeping good records is to your own benefit as well. For one thing, they will show you how well or badly you are doing at any given time, so that you will not suddenly find yourself having to sell your business, or even your home, to pay off your debts. Before you spend money, you will want to be sure that you can afford to spend it. If you know about money problems as soon as they arise, you have a much better chance of putting them right before they become too serious.

If you want people to lend money to you, they will certainly expect to see your accounts. For example, a bank will want to ensure that the business is likely to do well enough to pay back any loan, together with interest, within the time specified. Finally, if at some stage you decide to sell your business, any potential purchaser will wish to see the books and accounts.

However small your business, therefore, you must keep accurate financial records. The smaller your business, the simpler these can be, but they must still be accurate, detailed and up-to-date. All bills sent out and received must be carefully filed, and you must be organised and methodical in all your record-keeping.

Book-keeping Systems

Particularly if you are operating as a sole trader or a partnership, you have considerable freedom of choice in deciding what books to keep. In making your decision, there are a number of factors to keep in mind.

(1) Simplicity

There is no point in having a system more complex than you require. Especially if you have little knowledge or experience of book-keeping, a simple system such as an analysed cash-book – to be discussed shortly – may be perfectly adequate. In any case, your book-keeping system should be simple enough that you understand it and can easily explain it to someone else if you are away for any reason.

If your books are unnecessarily complex, the danger is that you will spend excessive amounts of time in maintaining them, time you could more profitably use in running your business; or else your books may not be completed fully or correctly, and the information in them will be worthless.

(2) Legal Requirements

While simplicity is important, your books and accounts must meet the requirements of business law. In particular, if you have chosen to trade as a limited company, there are quite strict conditions on what records you must keep and when and how you submit your accounts. Your professional advisers (accountant and solicitor) should be able to advise you on these points. If your business is a particularly complex one, or you know that working with figures is not your strong point, it may be advisable to engage a freelance book-keeper to take on this area of responsibility.

(3) Usefulness

As already mentioned, one of the most important reasons for keeping financial records is to obtain useful information on which to base decisions. A system that is too complex and difficult to understand may not produce information quickly enough to identify problems or exploit profitable opportunities.

(4) Professional Advice

Before making any decision on what book-keeping methods and systems to use, it is highly advisable to consult an accountant. Your accountant will be one of your most important professional advisers, as it is he who will have to translate the information in your books into accounts for the tax authorities. If you consult him at an early stage you can ensure that your systems are set up in the way in which he prefers, and so cut down the time he has to spend preparing your accounts (and hence the amount you have to pay for his services).

A Simple Book-keeping System – The Analysed Cash-book

This is a simple system which will nevertheless meet the needs of many home-based businesses (during their early years at least). To operate it you will require an analysis book, available from all office stationery suppliers (the system can also be easily adapted for use on a computer with a spreadsheet program – see below). Analysis books are large, hard-backed books, pre-ruled with narrow horizontal lines and up to thirty (or more) vertical columns. You can use one book for income and another for expenditure; or, to economise even further, use the front of your book for expenditure and the rear for income.

The use of the system is best explained using an example. The one used here concerns an individual working as a freelance proofreader and editor; but it would work just as well with the great majority of home-based business opportunities discussed in this book. The example page below shows how income is recorded. As you will see, the first column is used for the date of each item, and the second for a brief description of the item itself. The next column is then used to record the amount of the item, while the columns to the right of this are used for income in particular categories. The choice of categories is entirely up to you. In the example the three categories chosen are proofreading, editing and sundry income (money from any other source).

Record of Income (£)

Date	Item	Total	Proofrdg	Editing	Sundry
1/3	Hodson's	350	350		
4/3	HPI Ltd	560		560	
18/3	Hodson's	350	350		
24/3	XYZ	50			50
27/3	HPI Ltd	100		100	
30/3	Farmer's	250	250		
	TOTAL	1660	950	660	50

As you will notice, each item is entered twice (though this is not the same as double-entry book-keeping!). By totalling up all the columns at the end of each month, you will be able to see the total you have earned that month, and the amount contributed towards that by the different types of income. If you keep a running total from one month to the next, you will be able to keep track of your progress throughout the year, and will have the figures all ready for your end-of-year accounts.

Your record of expenditure would look similar. Again, a simple example is shown below.

Record of Expenditure (£)

Date	Item	Total	Stationery	Postage	Phone
3/3	Stamps	10.00		10.00	
7/3	Phone	60.00			60.00
16/3	Envelope	0.45	0.45		
24/3	Stamps	5.00		5.00	
24/3	Folders	8.25	8.25		
30/3	Stamps	20.00		20.00	
31/3	Labels	5.95	5.95		
	TOTAL	109.65	14.65	35.00	60.00

This method of record-keeping helps you keep track of what you are spending in different categories. For example, in the record above, you can see at a glance that you have spent a total of £35 on postage during March. For practical purposes, there would probably need to be a few more categories of expenditure other than those shown above, including perhaps training, travel, insurance, professional fees and subscriptions, bank charges, and – not least – money you have withdrawn for your own use (usually known as drawings).

To claim an item of expenditure against tax, you should if at all possible get a receipt for it. It would therefore be a good idea to have an extra column on the left-hand-side of the page for receipt numbers. You can number receipts consecutively, starting again from 001 each year. Mark the reference numbers on the receipts as well, so that you have an easy way of identifying which item of expenditure each receipt refers to.

A further refinement is that, instead of the single column for 'Total', you might instead have two columns: one for items paid for out of your business account (by cheque, standing order, etc.), and the other for items paid for in cash. This will make life easier when checking your financial records against your bank statements. And when/if the day arrives when you have to register for VAT (see the section Tax, National Insurance and VAT) you could simply add further columns to record VAT paid to suppliers and VAT charged to customers.

Although this is a very simple system, it contains all the information which would be required to draw up a set of accounts. This system has been used satisfactorily by the present author for nearly ten years.

Using a Computer

If you have a computer with a spreadsheet program, it is easy to adapt the system described above to it. Keeping your books on computer has one great advantage: the computer can be programmed to do all the calculations for you (e.g. adding up columns and calculating running totals). This can lead to considerable savings in time and effort. Most spreadsheet programs will also allow you to display financial information in the form of graphs and tables, which can be helpful in terms in seeing long-term trends.

The analysed cash-book system can be used with any spreadsheet program, but you can also buy dedicated programs (again based on spreadsheets) on which to keep your financial records. The most popular of these include Intuit Quicken and Microsoft Money. These are both excellent programs, and the latest versions include the facility to download information from your bank account via the Internet (assuming, of course, that you have an electronic banking facility set up). This can save you time in entering data, and will provide you with a mass of tools for displaying and manipulating financial information. You will, however, need to do some work to adapt the program concerned to your own individual circumstances.

Submitting Your Accounts

It is, of course, quite possible to prepare and submit your annual accounts to the Inland Revenue without involving an accountant. If your annual turnover (gross income as opposed to profit) is below a certain figure (£15,000 for the tax year ended April 1999), you do not have to submit detailed information, just figures for total turnover and allowable expenses. If you are running your business as a part-time sideline, you may opt to do this rather than paying an accountant to produce a full set of accounts which are unlikely to be required. Even so, if you do this you should still keep detailed and accurate financial records, both for your own benefit and for calculating the figures for your tax return. Remember, also, that the Inland Revenue may decide to investigate your return in more detail (a certain number of taxpayers are randomly chosen for this ordeal each year). In this case you are likely to be required to produce the records from which your income and expenditure figures were compiled.

If you are running a full-time profitable business, you are still of course at liberty to produce your own accounts. However, most self-employed people in this category prefer to pay an accountant a few hundred pounds to handle this task for them. There are many advantages to this, including the following:

- Paying an accountant to do this leaves you more time to concentrate on running your business.
- The accountant will have much more experience of dealing with the tax authorities than you do, and is far less likely to make mistakes.
- If the tax inspector has any queries, the accountant should be able to answer them.
- The accountant may be able to suggest (legal) ways you can reduce the amount of tax you have to pay.
- He or she may also be able to suggest additional benefits and allowances you could be claiming.
- And finally, the tax authorities may be less inclined to query a tax return if they can see that it has been completed by a qualified accountant.

Overall, for most small business owners, trying to do your own end-of-year accounts is likely to prove a false economy. Certainly the great majority, unless they have an accounting or book-keeping background, use a professional accountant to prepare their accounts and handle any negotiations with the Inland Revenue. Most accountants, incidentally, will also complete and submit your annual self-assessment tax return as part of their service.

20. INVOICING AND CREDIT CONTROL

In some businesses (e.g. window cleaning) customers expect to pay you there and then, but in others you will be required to present an invoice. This applies particularly where your customers are other businesses rather than private individuals (e.g. desktop publishing, indexing). Businesses generally require some sort of invoice for tax purposes, and in any event they are often not in a position to hand over money or write out a cheque to you there and then.

An invoice is basically just a request for payment within a specified period (typically 30 days). Newcomers to business are often concerned about this, but there is no need to be. An invoice can be quickly and simply produced on your own letterhead or, at a pinch, a sheet of plain paper. In any event it should include the following items:

- Your business name and address
- Your phone number (in case there are any queries)
- A reference number (chosen by you)
- The name and address of the organisation being invoiced
- The amount to be paid
- The date.

An example invoice is shown below.

JONATHON DOE
Website Designer

101 London Road, Middlewood, Worcs, WR7 9LT.   Tel: 01534 792909

TO: Sunlight Conservatories Limited
Unit 7, Colebrook Industrial Estate
Basingstoke
Hants
RG21 4RY

8 July 2004

INVOICE NO: P/751

To design work and consultancy on company website.

20 hours @ £25 per hour

TOTAL DUE: £500

Terms : Payment in 30 days

Please make cheque payable to J. Doe

Signed...

The reference you put on the invoice is up to you, but clearly these should follow one another in numerical order. A simple method, as used in the example, is to use a letter (or letters), followed by a number. If you like, the letter could identify the type of job performed – so a mobile mechanic might use an 'S' prefix for invoices referring to servicing, 'R' for repairs, and so on. In any event, it is important to put some sort of reference number, as large organisations in particular often require one for their payment systems. And when in due course you receive payment, frequently the only indication of what it refers to will be the invoice reference number (often written on the back of the cheque or an accompanying 'with compliments' slip).

As soon as you have completed a job you should prepare your invoice and send it by first class post (the sooner your customer receives it, the sooner you can expect to be paid!). Keep a copy of all invoices, and check regularly to ensure they have been paid (see Credit Control, below). If you send out large numbers of invoices to some customers, you may find it desirable to send them a monthly statement listing the dates and amounts of all invoices outstanding. However, for most home-based businesses this is unlikely to be a necessity.

If you issue more than a very few invoices, it is best to keep a record in a separate invoice book. This need be no more than a list in numerical order, including the following information:

- Invoice reference number
- Date issued
- To whom
- Amount
- Date payment received.

You could also include a column in which to record details of reminder letters/phone calls (see below). Checking regularly in your invoice book will help you keep track of accounts which have not yet been paid.

Credit Control

Most customers will of course pay your invoices within the period specified, but sometimes the required payment fails to arrive. In this case you will need to consider what further action to take.

The best first step, once an invoice is more than a fortnight late, is to phone the debtor up. At this stage you should avoid the least hint of a threat. Your approach should be friendly, your attitude that you are merely 'jogging his [or her] memory' about an overdue payment.

In many cases this will be quite sufficient. There may have been a genuine slip of the memory or, in larger organisations especially, the paperwork may have gone temporarily astray. In such cases, a simple phone call may be all that is needed to jolt someone into action and produce the required cheque.

If this still fails to produce a result, your next step may be either a personal visit or a letter. Personal visits can be productive with private individuals in particular, as they may well be embarrassed into paying the bill there and then. However, making a personal visit to a debtor is admittedly not the most appealing of prospects; and if the debtor concerned is on the other side of the country, visiting may not in any event be practicable. In such cases you may decide to write instead. When writing to a company or individual concerning an unpaid debt, follow the guidelines below:

Be clear and concise
Many people believe that debt collection letters must be written in legal mumbo-jumbo. That is not the case. State in plain English the amount owed and the goods or services the debt relates to, quoting your original invoice number if relevant.

Be firm but polite
The payment may have been delayed for all sorts of reasons, some perfectly innocent, and you may still want to do business with the debtor again some time in the future.

Do not ask why the debt has not been paid
If you ask this, you are inviting the debtor to come up with an excuse rather than the money he owes.

Do not ask for part-payment or payment by instalments
Doing this immediately puts the idea into the debtor's head. If the debtor subsequently contacts you to suggest such an arrangement, you may have to consider it (even if you reject such an offer, a court is very likely to find it acceptable). However, you should always ask for the whole amount initially.

Personalise all letters
Avoid writing to 'The Accounts Department' or 'The Manager'. Try to address all letters to a named individual. Avoid, also, putting

'first reminder' at the top of the letter. This tells the debtor that there are more such letters to come, and he can safely delay payment a bit longer.

Write only two letters

The first of these will set out the debt and request payment, while the second will give warning of legal action if payment does not follow within a specified deadline (say seven days). If the second letter still fails to produce payment, you must then begin legal proceedings (see below).

Taking a Debtor to Court

If your phone calls, letters and visits still fail to produce a result, you may have to consider legal action. However, as soon as you start proceedings you will accrue further costs in the form of court fees and (if you engage one) solicitor's bills. Before going any further, therefore, you should check the following points:

1. Has the debtor got the money to pay the debt? If not, you are merely throwing good money after bad.

2. Do you have written evidence to support your claim? This will be required by the court, particularly if the debtor disputes the amount outstanding.

3. Do you have the full and correct name and address of the debtor? This will be required for the legal forms.

4. Is the debt less than six years old? If it is over that, it cannot generally be collected.

If you can answer these four questions affirmatively then you can – and should – proceed with legal action. If you back off at this point, the debtor will know that your earlier threats of legal action were empty. Your chances of ever recovering the debt then will be zero.

At this stage you may decide to hand over the case to a solicitor or debt collection agency. You should definitely do this if the sum owed is over £3,000, or if there is some dispute over the nature or amount of the debt. However, there is one very straightforward method by which a small business owner, even with no previous experience, can pursue a case where the debt in question is £3,000 or less. This is through the so-called small claims procedure.

The Small Claims Procedure

The small claims procedure forms part of the county court system in England and Wales (in Scotland and Ireland there are similar procedures going under the name of 'arbitration'). The procedure can be used when you are claiming £3,000 or less. It may also be used for sums of over £3,000, though this is at the judge's discretion. The small claims procedure is a simple, straightforward process designed to be used by people without the aid of solicitors.

To begin a small claims case, you will need to attend at your local county court and collect three copies of a form known as a 'default summons'. You should also be given a set of explanatory leaflets explaining what you have to do next. Essentially, you are required to fill in the forms including details of the amount you are claiming and why you believe you are owed this money. You pay a court fee (which is added to the total outstanding) and the summons is then issued. The debtor has a set period (16 days for a limited company, 21 for an individual) to either pay the debt or explain why he disputes it. In the latter case a date for a hearing is then set at which both sides can present their case in front of a judge whose decision is legally binding.

Most debt cases, of course, do not go this far, but it is important that you are prepared to take the necessary action to pursue a debt when required. One other point is that you should keep an eye on the overall average time taken for invoices to be paid. If this starts to creep up, it can have a damaging effect on your cash flow – and may ultimately cause your business to fail if for this reason you are unable to meet the demands of your creditors.

21. INSURANCE

Even if you are running a single-person business from home, you are likely to require some additional business-related insurance. At the very least, you should check whether you need to amend your home contents and buildings insurance.

At one time home insurance companies often refused to cover items such as personal computers if they were used for work purposes. Some insurers still take this attitude, but a growing number are more enlightened (one example is Royal & Sun Alliance, tel. 0800 300 660). In fact there seems little reason why insurance companies should discriminate against home-workers, as the fact that they are around during the day should actually reduce the likelihood of burglaries and other disasters.

Apart from home insurance, other types of business-related insurance you may require according to your particular circumstances include the following:

Public liability: This provides you with protection if a member of the public suffers injury, loss or damage caused by defects in your products, services or premises, or by the negligence of you or your employees. Any business dealing with the public should have public liability insurance, though it is not legally compulsory.

Employer's liability: This is similar to public liability insurance, but covers you for claims from your employees. In Britain public liability insurance is generally compulsory if you employ staff or you are a director of a limited company (in which case you are considered an employee of the company). It is not legally essential for sole traders and partnerships with no employees. Nevertheless, it may still be prudent to take out an employer's liability policy, in case an accident occurs when a friend or relative is helping you. You should also bear in mind that a self-employed sub-contractor working on your behalf may be considered as your employee for insurance purposes.

Business interruption: This provides cover if for some reason you are unable for a period to go on running your business. The circumstances causing this might include a break-in, computer failure, ill health, call for jury service, or sudden family crisis. Business interruption cover compensates you for the loss of income during this period and the possible loss of clients and contracts.

Personal accident/disability insurance: This will ensure your future financial security in the event of you suffering a disabling illness or accident. This is particularly important for sole traders and those with family responsibilities who have no other source of income should they become unable to work.

Motor vehicle insurance: If you intend to use your private car or van for business purposes, you may well find that an ordinary domestic insurance policy will not cover it. If your business will involve transporting other people's goods, you are likely to need an additional 'goods in transit' policy to cover the goods while they are in your possession.

Credit insurance: Insuring against bad debts can be expensive, but is worth considering if most of your business will be done with just a few large companies. What would happen to your business if one of these customers suddenly went into liquidation owing you large amounts of money?

A broker will be able to advise you on your insurance requirements; plenty are listed in Yellow Pages. The services of such individuals are usually free, but most are paid by commission on the policies they sell, so it is in their interests to persuade you to buy as much cover as possible. You will therefore need to weigh up their advice carefully and buy only as much insurance as you need and can sensibly afford. This is obviously something of a balancing act, and it is desirable to review the position every year as your business develops and changes.

Finally, a quick word should be said about Tolson Messenger, an independent UK broker specialising in insurance for home-based businesses. Tolson Messenger offer a range of home insurance policies which also incorporate the additional cover many home-based businesses require. Their Homextra Policy, for example (underwritten by CGU Insurance), includes together with the usual buildings and contents insurance, public liability, employer's liability, business equipment and business interruption cover. Further information is available from Tolson Messenger on 0800 374246 or on their website www.tolsonmessenger.co.uk.

22. WHERE TO GET MORE HELP

As the preceding sections have indicated, running your own business demands a range of knowledge and skills quite apart from those required to make your product or deliver your service. As a business owner you inevitably have to be something of a 'Jack of all Trades'. This means not only exercising a broad range of skills, but also recognising situations where it is necessary to seek advice and assistance from outside advisers. This section will highlight a number of advisers whose help you are most likely to find useful.

Accountant

A good accountant can be invaluable in setting up and running a successful business. Among the wide range of services available from accountants are the following:

(1) Advice on the most appropriate legal and financial structure for the type of business you are starting
(2) Advice on possible sources of additional funds
(3) Advice on what books to keep and (if required) doing the book-keeping

(4) Preparing financial accounts and tax returns

(5) Liaising and negotiating with the tax authorities

(6) Advice on future financial planning to minimise your tax liability

(7) Advice and assistance with controlling creditors and debtors (credit control)

(8) General financial advice, for example with regard to loans and subsidies, grants, pension planning, and so on.

In addition, for small limited companies, an accountant will undertake work concerning the formation of the company, the issue and transfer of shares, annual returns, auditing the company accounts, arranging Annual General Meetings, and general company secretarial work (often in conjunction with a solicitor). .

Finally, a good experienced professional accountant may be an invaluable source of general management advice, particularly for sole traders who may otherwise feel rather isolated when making decisions on the running of their business.

Of course, it is not essential to engage an accountant when first starting out, particularly if you have a knowledge of book-keeping and accounts yourself. On the other hand, you will almost certainly need help from an accountant at some stage, especially regarding such matters as VAT registration and dealing with the taxman. For some of the (many) other reasons why you should consider engaging an accountant sooner rather than later, see the section Book-keeping and Accounts.

Choosing Your Accountant

The first step in choosing an accountant is deciding what you want from him (or her). Not every accountant will offer every sort of service. For example, large city firms are unlikely to offer a weekly book-keeping service, while a sole practitioner may not have the expertise to help with raising capital or setting up a limited company.

Large accountancy firms serve mainly medium to large-sized businesses, and their fees are often high. For an individual starting a home-based business and wanting someone to prepare their accounts and provide general financial advice, a partnership or sole practitioner will often be the best choice. There is a good argument for choosing a partnership rather than a sole practitioner, as there is always a chance that the person concerned will fall sick, move away or even die, leaving you without anyone to handle your accounts. With a partnership, at least if one partner moves on there will be someone else in the business to take over.

Before choosing an accountant, ask around for recommendations, e.g. from other people you know who run their own businesses. Contact a number of accountants, whether or not they have been recommended to you, and ask about their terms. Ask for details of existing customers who would be willing to provide references, and get in touch with these people. Finally, bear in mind that anyone can call himself an accountant, so check that the person you wish to appoint has the appropriate professional qualifications.

Cost

How much an accountant will cost depends on the type and amount of work involved, and this can be difficult to predict in advance. Nevertheless, most accountants will give you an estimate. For a straightforward service involving preparation of accounts and occasional financial advice, most will charge you a single annual fee. For a small home-based business, you should expect to pay somewhere in the region of £250 to £500.

Many accountants spend much time and effort just sorting out their clients' financial records, and the cost of this inevitably has to be passed on. It therefore pays to set up a book-keeping system your accountant is happy with, and keep it neatly and accurately. An hour of the accountant's time spent discussing what books you are going to keep now may save him having to spend many hours later sorting through your records.

Solicitor

Whilst most businesses require the services of an accountant on a fairly regular basis, assistance from a solicitor will generally be needed only when a specific problem or query arises. Situations in which you might need the advice and help of a solicitor include:

(1) Deciding the most appropriate structure for your business
(2) Drawing up a partnership agreement
(3) Buying a business
(4) Evaluating and purchasing a franchise
(5) Forming a limited company
(6) Legal aspects of employing staff
(7) Health and safety requirements
(8) Collecting unpaid debts
(9) Selling your business.

In addition, a solicitor is likely to be needed when a trading agreement has to be drawn up (e.g. an import/export deal or joint trading arrangement with another company). For the benefit of all parties involved, such agreements are usually formalised in legal contracts. Your solicitor will help to draft such contracts, ensuring that they are acceptable to everyone concerned and comply with all the legal requirements.

Finally, businesses may use the services of solicitors when a dispute arises. If one business decides to sue another in court (e.g. for unpaid debts or infringement of a patent), a solicitor will usually be engaged to handle this.

Choosing Your Solicitor

Similar principles apply when choosing a solicitor as with an accountant. Solicitors specialise in different aspects of the law, and you need to choose one with expertise in industrial and commercial matters rather than a specialist in, say, criminal or family law. Most solicitors operate in partnerships, and often there is one partner who specialises in business matters. You should aim to meet this person and satisfy yourself that he has the experience and knowledge you require. As when choosing an accountant, it is wise to take up references.

Cost

Whereas your accountant may charge you an annual fee, a solicitor is likely to charge you for each job you want doing. Before engaging a solicitor, you should ask him for an estimate of costs. If the solicitor says that this is not possible because he does not know how long the job will take, ask him for his daily rate. Many solicitors will quote a package price for certain jobs such as forming a limited company.

To keep costs under control, it is important to give your solicitor clear instructions, and ask him to keep you informed of the costs incurred in any ongoing action. In disputes between businesses, in particular, legal costs can quickly mount up.

Other Sources of Help

In addition to the advisers described above, there is a range of others you may be able to call upon as circumstances dictate. The main ones likely to be relevant to home-based businesses are listed overleaf.

(1) Bank Manager

You might not immediately think of your bank manager as one of your professional advisers. That is because, unlike most other advisers, you do not pay directly for his services (you pay indirectly, of course, in the form of bank charges). Nevertheless, your business bank manager can be a source of advice on a wide range of business matters. As someone with a close knowledge of what other local businesses are doing, he will be well placed to comment on your plans and make suggestions on how they could be improved. Like an accountant, he should be able to advise you on many of the financial and managerial aspects of your business. Many banks also offer advice on matters such as insurance, investments, pension planning, and so on.

A bank manager is not a substitute for an accountant, however. For one thing, while your accountant will give you objective, impartial advice, the bank manager's advice is bound to be influenced to some extent by the fact that he sees you as a (potential) client and source of revenue for his bank. In addition, you may not always wish to discuss business problems with your bank manager, in case (for example) this influences his decision on whether to give you a loan.

(2) Insurance Broker

As explained in the previous section, every business needs insurance. Its basic purpose is to reduce the risk of calamitous loss if some unforeseen misfortune befalls you or your business. Some insurance is essential and legally compulsory, while other types are desirable so long as you can sensibly afford them.

An insurance broker will advise you on the most appropriate insurance for you and your business. He will negotiate on your behalf with insurance companies to arrange the best deal for you. Insurance is a highly specialised area, and a professional insurance broker can be of great assistance in cutting through the jargon and choosing among the many types of policy and cover on offer.

Insurance brokers do not normally work for any particular insurance company and so, in theory, will give you independent advice. However, they are usually paid by commission, so it is in their interests to sell you as much insurance as possible. When dealing with insurance brokers, therefore, it is important to weigh up the advice you are given against how much you can sensibly afford to spend.

(3) Advertising Agent

The job of an advertising agent is to help businesses advertise their products or services. An agent will first advise you on your advertising policy in general. He will design and write your advertisements – in consultation with yourself – and book space for them in appropriate publications. Agents will also produce and book advertisements for other media such as radio when required.

Advertising agents receive commission from the publications in which they place advertisements, so their charges for this type of work are generally quite reasonable. Most agents will also assist with other types of publicity such as press releases and publicity brochures. Higher fees may be payable for this type of work, as the agent does not recoup any of his costs in the form of commission.

For small local businesses whose advertising amounts to no more than the occasional classified ad in their local paper, an advertising agent is unlikely to be required. If you plan to advertise more widely, however, using the services of an advertising agent is highly recommended. A number will be listed in your local Yellow Pages. Call a few and explain the type of business you are in and the level of advertising support you require. The agency will tell you soon enough whether they are able to assist you; if so, you will be invited in to discuss your requirements in detail with one of their executives.

(4) Designer/Graphic Artist

If your business will involve producing or selling a product or products, you might wish to hire a designer to advise you on matters such as colour, shape, features and so on. A graphic designer, otherwise known as a commercial artist, can help with tasks such as designing your logo and letterhead, creating an 'image' for your business, preparing attractive packaging material, and so on. Graphic artists and designers normally charge an hourly fee.

(5) Website Designer

As mentioned in Computers and the Internet, a growing number of small businesses are creating websites as a means of advertising themselves and communicating with their customers. It is actually not difficult to produce a basic website yourself if you have some degree of computer literacy, but for anything more ambitious (especially if you hope to sell directly from your site) it is wise to engage a professional website designer. Such individuals advertise in local papers and Yellow Pages (look under Internet Services). They will normally quote you a set fee (starting at around £200) for designing your website and installing it on the web. You will have to pay a further sum to have your site regularly updated.

(6) Business Consultants and Advisers

There is a huge range of specialists who will offer advice on various aspects of your business. Probably the most relevant to the new small business are the advisory services set up and operated by government agencies in the hope of encouraging new business development and creating employment and wealth. One such is the Business Links network. There are around 240 of these centres in England, providing free or low-cost support, advice, services and business-related information. To find the address of your nearest, phone 0345 567765. Other sources of advice and information include local chambers of commerce and Training and Enterprise Councils (Learning and Skills Councils from April 2001).

Using Your Advisers

To make the best use of your professional advisers, bear in mind the following points:

(1) In the end it is still you who will have to make the actual decisions. For example, you must decide whether to sue a particular debtor – your solicitor can advise you on the procedures.

(2) Most professional advisers charge according to the amount of time they spend working for you. To make the most economic use of their services, therefore, you should do as much preparatory work as possible. With your accountant, for example, you should ensure that your books are properly completed and balanced before passing them over to him to produce your final accounts.

(3) Your professional advisers are also in business to make money. In choosing your advisers you should therefore apply the same care and judgement as when you are buying any other product or service. This includes getting estimates of fees and 'shopping around' before committing yourself.

With any adviser it is best to keep the relationship on a friendly but professional level, with each party having respect for the other's position. If you do not feel comfortable with an adviser, or do not feel you are getting the service you expected, then make arrangements to change your adviser.

Good advice is, however, well worth paying for, and often results in savings or extra income worth many times the fees charged. Advisers' fees, incurred for advice solely in connection with the business, are of course allowable as a tax deductible item of overhead expense.

23. EXPANDING YOUR HOME-BASED BUSINESS

Follow the advice in this book and, with just a little luck as well, your home-based business should soon be thriving. Initially you may not have enough work to keep you occupied the whole time, but within a few years – perhaps sooner – you may find yourself with more orders than you can fulfil (at least, to the standard you would wish). At this point you will face a tricky decision. Either:

A. Start turning down offers of work, and risk causing resentment and losing money, or

B. Take on someone to assist you, either an employee or one of the other options discussed later.

Deciding whether to expand your business can be tricky, and often the choice boils down to why you decided to become self-employed in the first place. If your main motive was to make money, the argument for expansion may be hard to resist. On the other hand, if you started your business primarily to fit in with your domestic circumstances or as an enjoyable sideline, you may prefer to continue as you are and forgo the financial benefits of expansion. In any event, it is important to be aware of the pros and cons.

The Advantages of Expanding Your Business

As a one-person business, your income potential is automatically limited by the number of hours you as an individual have available. Even if you decide to work 90 hours a week, every week (not recommended, for the sake of your health!), in the end this is all the time you have available. If there is more work than you can cope with in this time, the only way you will be able to complete it is if you have one or more people to help you. So long as the amount you earn from their efforts is more than the amount they cost, their contribution will add to your business profits. This may be best illustrated by an example.

EXAMPLE

Marco is a self-employed builder. In his first year he does a total of 1,470 hours of chargeable work at £15 an hour. This means that his gross income is 1,470 x 15 = £22,050. From this he has to deduct fixed costs of £5,000 (all his variable costs such as materials he charges to customers). This gives him a net profit before tax of £17,050.

As he has plenty of work in hand, at the start of his second year Marco takes on an assistant, Carol. He pays her £5 an hour, and charges customers for her work at £10 an hour. In his second year Marco's income from his own chargeable work to customers is again £22,050, but in addition he is able to charge customers for 1,600 hours of Carol's time at £10 an hour. This brings in another £16,000, giving him a total gross annual income of £38,050. Of course, Marco has to pay Carol a wage, which, as she works 35 hours a week with paid holidays, comes to 52 weeks x 35 hours x £5 = £9,100 a year.

Marco's fixed costs increase to £7,000 due to the additional expenses such as employer's national insurance he incurs by taking Carol on. Nevertheless, at the end of the year his net annual profit before tax is £38,050 (gross income) – £9,100 (Carol's wages) – £7,000 (overheads) = £21,950. In other words, employing Carol increases Marco's annual net profit by almost £5,000.

*   *   *

The above example illustrates the principle that employing people can make you money. There are, however, two important riders. One is that you must have sufficient work to occupy both yourself and your employees, or you risk paying them but not earning anything from them. And secondly, the amount you charge customers for your employees' time must more than cover the cost of their wages and any additional costs which employing them entails. The difference between what your employees cost you and what you can charge for their time is the contribution which employing staff makes towards paying for your overheads and ultimately adding to your profits.

One other point is that, although making more money is usually the main incentive for expansion, another may be to avoid disappointing customers and potential customers. As your business becomes established, your existing customers, seeing that you are a reliable supplier, may begin to place larger orders. Meanwhile, new customers will keep coming to you from different sources, including word-of-mouth recommendation. To cope with all this extra demand and avoid turning potential customers away (people whose custom you might welcome in a few months' time if business takes a downturn), you may well have to give serious consideration to expansion.

Drawbacks of Expansion

Expanding your business has many attractions, especially in financial terms. However, it does have one or two possible drawbacks, and it is important to take these into account when deciding how to proceed. The main drawbacks of expansion are loss of control, greater administrative demands and higher risk.

(1) Loss of Control

Expanding your business is likely to involve taking on staff or partners, and you will inevitably have to delegate some of your responsibilities to them. Some of the time it may be these people who are dealing with customers rather than yourself, and they may not always give as good a quality of service as you would like. As the business grows, there will be more people involved in it, and even if they are paid employees rather than equal partners, you will still need to pay some attention to their views. You will not have the same freedom of action that you may have had as a one-person business.

(2) Greater Administrative Demands

As the business grows the administrative demands inevitably increase. If you take on employees, for instance, dealing with their tax and national insurance contributions (as well as your own) will inevitably take up a proportion of your time. It may be possible to delegate some of these responsibilities to other staff or professional advisers, but you are still likely to find yourself spending more and more time doing this type of work. Of course, if you enjoy administration and management, this may not be a problem.

(3) Greater Risk

As the business expands the sums of money involved will become larger, and, so inevitably, will the risks. If you take on staff, you will need to ensure that there are sufficient orders to keep them all in work; if there are not, you will have to face the unpleasant prospect of laying them off.

It is quite likely that you will have to borrow money to finance your expansion. If the business subsequently fails, the debts you owe to banks, suppliers, staff and so on will be that much larger. Keeping such risks under control involves careful financial planning, and monitoring your business's actual performance against predictions. It may also involve changing to a different form of business organisation, such as a limited company.

Alternatives to Employing Staff

If you don't want to take on an employee, there are various other options you could consider, at least in the short term.

(1) Involve Your Partner

The obvious person to turn to for help initially is your partner or spouse. Even if they do not have your specific work-related skills, they may be able to assist with the administration, thus freeing you to spend more time on paid work for customers.

Paying your husband or wife a fee for their assistance can also have tax advantages, particularly if they do not have any other source of income. The reason for this is that the money you pay them can be set against their annual tax-free personal allowance. If you do this, however, the Inland Revenue may want to see proof that they do actually provide services to the business.

(2) Involve Other Members of Your Family

It may also be possible to involve other close family members, e.g. your parents or teenage children. Care may be needed here, however. Teenage children, especially if they are unemployed, may resent being pushed into a career they have no interest in. And parents may find it difficult to accept the role reversal which being your 'employee' entails. If, however, you have a good relationship with the relatives concerned and they seem genuinely eager to play a part, involving other members of the family in your business can offer many potential advantages.

(3) Use an Employment Agency

Particularly if you need help for short spells only, using a 'temp' from an agency can be an attractive option. The agency will take care of all the administration for you and simply invoice you for the temp's time. Of course, you will also have to pay the agency a fee for their service, and this can be quite substantial. Agencies can provide temporary staff in most office-related fields, e.g. clerical, word processing, book-keeping and so on. Some agencies (e.g. Manpower) can also supply labourers, drivers, assembly workers and other manual staff.

(4) Use an Office Services Bureau

Office services bureaux provide a wide range of office-related services for small businesses, including book-keeping, accounts, telephone answering, word processing, handling post, and so on. They can also perform tasks such as maintaining databases, producing address labels and filling envelopes for mailshots. You can call by in the morning with the day's assignments, and again in the evening to collect the finished work and any messages that have arrived for you. Offices services bureaux are listed in Yellow Pages under the headings Secretarial Services, Telephone Answering, and so on.

(5) Sub-contract Some of Your Work

Sub-contracting is common in certain trades and professions. Basically it involves passing over some aspects of a job to someone with similar (or complementary) skills. A builder, for example, may sub-contract some types of work (e.g. plastering or bricklaying) to other self-employed people who can do the job faster and/or better than he can, so that his own time can be used more efficiently on other matters. In this situation the builder would typically invoice the customer for the whole cost of the project, and pay the sub-contractor out of this.

Sub-contracting can be used in a wide range of spheres, including some with which it is not traditionally associated. The present author, for example, has successfully sub-contracted some parts of guidebooks he was commissioned to write to people living in the countries concerned who had better first-hand knowledge of these places than he did.

(6) Take on a Partner

Finally, you could take on someone else as a partner in your business. This can work very well if your partner has similar but complementary skills. For example, a 'stills' photographer might form a partnership with someone else who specialises in video-making, so that between them they can offer a full range of photographic services. Note that your partner need not work from the same premises as you. Each could continue to work from his/her own home, but using a common business name and administrative facilities. If you decide to go into partnership with someone, it is strongly advisable to have a formal partnership agreement drawn up by a solicitor. You should also speak to your accountant concerning the book-keeping and tax implications.

Final Thoughts

As your home-based business takes off, you are likely to find yourself needing good administrative and organisational skills, as well as the skills required to actually provide your product or service. This applies especially if you decide to expand by taking on staff and/or a partner. This will inevitably involve you in a greater degree of administration and management, and a greater burden of responsibility (see below). You will need to plan ahead, both on a long-term and short-term basis, to ensure that you use your working time and resources as efficiently as possible. You will also need to monitor your business's performance carefully to ensure that you are not in danger of over-reaching yourself.

Expanding your business can boost your income to far higher levels than you could ever achieve as a one-person operator, but it also imposes a greater burden of responsibility – not only on yourself, but on your family and any employees or partners. If you prefer to keep your home-based business small, therefore, you should not feel that this is an admission of failure. As stated earlier, the decision on whether or not to expand is a highly personal one, very much dependent on your own aims and ambitions in running a home-based business. If you are happy as a 'one-(wo)man-band' and willing to forgo the potentially much higher earnings you might achieve in an expanded business, then continuing as you are may well be the right decision for you.

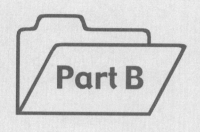

Part B

BUSINESS PROFILES

ALTERNATIVE/COMPLEMENTARY THERAPIES

While alternative therapies (also known as complementary therapies or medicines) are not new, in recent years they have grown in popularity, partly due to a growing roster of celebrity advocates such as Prince Charles. The term covers a wide range of therapeutic approaches, but one thing they all have in common is an emphasis on treating the whole person, not just a specific condition. Most practitioners place as great an emphasis on mental and spiritual wellbeing as they do on physical illness. Just a few of the better-known alternative therapies include:

Acupuncture: This is a form of Chinese traditional medicine. It involves the insertion of fine needles into one or more of about 365 acupuncture points on the surface of the body, each of which has a specific therapeutic function.

Aromatherapy: This branch of herbal medicine has become highly popular in recent years. Aromatherapists use over 200 different aromatic essences to treat a wide range of conditions. These 'essential oils' are normally administered through the skin by massage.

Homeopathy: This system of medicine was developed by the German physician Samuel Hahnemann (1755–1843). It operates on the principle that a substance which is toxic in large quantities can cure in smaller ones.

Phytotherapy (medical herbalism): Herbal remedies provide a gentle, drug-free way to restore health. Herbs are usually administered as an infusion (hot water poured over them), decoction (herbs are simmered in boiling water then strained) or tincture (herbs are immersed in a mixture of alcohol and water and taken diluted).

Reflexology: Reflexology works by applying pressure to particular points on the body surface, most commonly the feet. Reflexologists believe that different areas of the foot correspond with different areas of the body; so a problem with, say, the neck and shoulders can be treated by applying gentle pressure to the appropriate area of the foot.

Training courses in alternative therapies can be taken by almost anyone with an aptitude or interest. Unlike conventional ('allopathic') medicine, where qualification requires five years or more, many fields of alternative medicine do not require lengthy training. There are various exceptions to this, however. For example, to achieve a recognised qualification in homeopathy, students have to complete a rigorous training course of three or more years' duration.

At present most alternative therapies are not subject to official regulation; for example, anyone can set up in business as an aromatherapist or reflexologist without necessarily possessing any relevant skills or qualifications. In future, however, many of these specialisms are likely to become subject to legal regulation; and it is in any event important from both a personal and a business point of view not to skimp on the required training.

What do I need to get started?

If you have not done so already, you will need to complete a course of training in your chosen specialism. This should be a course approved by the Institute for Complementary Medicine (ICM) for membership of the British Register of Complementary Practitioners (see 'Where can I get more help?' below). For most courses no specific educational qualifications are needed, but you may be required to demonstrate certain personal characteristics such as empathy and good listening skills. Some forms of therapy such as Shiatsu (Japanese 'finger pressure therapy') require a degree of physical suppleness, while others such as Chiropractic (which involves manipulating joints) require some physical strength.

For many alternative therapies no special equipment is required. Acupuncturists will, of course, require the special needles used to treat patients, while other practitioners will need herbs, essential oils, medicines and so on. These are available from specialist suppliers, or in some cases from health food shops. You can work from a room in your own home, or alternatively visit your patients' homes. Some alternative therapists rent rooms above health food shops or in joint practices with other practitioners for part or all of the time.

Who will my customers be?

Your clients will come from all ages and backgrounds. Many will have long-standing conditions which have failed to respond to conventional treatment, while others may be suffering from a range of symptoms, perhaps brought on by stress. Some people may have serious illnesses which conventional medicine is unable to treat. In such cases your role may be to provide relief for symptoms and improve quality of life rather than (necessarily) offering a cure.

How much can I make?

Earnings are not usually the foremost consideration for people entering this field. Nevertheless, once you have established a regular clientele you should be able to earn a reasonable living. Most alternative therapists charge a set hourly rate, typically from £12 upwards. Many offer an initial consultation free of charge, to help establish whether or not the treatment they have to offer will be appropriate and beneficial for the person concerned.

Overheads in this occupation are generally low, especially if you work from a room at home. The main costs are likely to consist of advertising and any special materials/supplies (e.g. acupuncture needles, aromatherapy oils).

How can I sell my services?

In the beginning you will almost certainly have to advertise your services to attract clients. Yellow Pages have categories for a wide range of alternative therapies, including Acupuncture, Aromatherapy, Chiropractors, Homeopaths, Hypnotherapists, and so on. If there is not a category for your particular specialisation, you can also advertise under the categories Alternative Medicine/Therapies or Complementary Therapies.

Your local newspaper would be another good place to advertise. In addition, it would be worth having some attractive advertising cards designed and putting these up on supermarket notice boards and in local shop windows. Health food shops, clinics and doctors' surgeries would also be good places to leave a supply of advertising cards or leaflets.

As you become established you may find that much of your business arrives via word-of-mouth recommendations. People who have benefited from your services will be happy to recommend you to their friends and relatives. It is therefore well worth giving your clients a few business cards 'in case you know anyone else who might need my help'.

Where can I get more help?

The Council for Complementary and Alternative Medicine (CCAM) provides a forum for communication and co-operation between the professional bodies representing acupuncture, medical herbalism, homeopathy and osteopathy. The Council is committed to promoting high standards of training, qualification and treatment in complementary/alternative medicine.

The Council for Complementary and Alternative Medicine
Park House
206-208 Latimer Road
London
Wl0 6RE
Tel: 020 8968 3862

The Institute for Complementary Medicine (ICM) was formed in 1982 to provide the public with information on complementary medicine. The ICM also administers the British Register of Complementary Practitioners. You can obtain information from them on approved training courses in many forms of complementary medicine, including colour therapy, healing, seated acupressure massage, kinesiology, radionics and remedial massage, as well as most of the other therapies mentioned in this article.

The Institute for Complementary Medicine
PO Box 194
London
SE16 1QZ
Tel: 020 7237 5165
Web: www.icmedicine.co.uk

BABY-SITTING

Baby-sitting is an ideal occupation for those who do not mind being out late in the evenings, as it is always done in the baby or child's own home (unlike child-minding, which is done in the child-minder's home). To baby-sit very young children you will need some relevant experience; and many of the agencies which supply baby-sitters insist on their sitters having some form of childcare qualification (e.g. a nursery nurse's diploma), or experience as a primary school teacher.

There is no minimum legal age at which you may baby-sit, but most agencies require you to be over 18.

What do I need to get started?

The only essential requirements are a telephone and some customers! You do need to like children, and to have the ability to keep them in order when sitting older children. Otherwise you just need common sense. Ideally you should have your own transport, though if you do not have this it is normally accepted that one of the parents will take you home, or a taxi will be provided.

Who will my customers be?

Quite simply, your clients will be people with children who do not have handy friends or relatives to look after their children when they want to go out. Most baby-sitting jobs take place in the evening, though there are some situations, such as when a mother has to go for a hospital appointment, when a sitter may be needed during the day.

How much can I make?

You will not get rich in this occupation. Baby-sitters earn between £2.50 and £5 an hour for jobs which end before midnight, a couple of pounds an hour more after that.

If you go on to run a baby-sitting agency, your earnings will depend on how many sitters you can call upon and how many customers you can attract, but it is normal to add at least 50 per cent to the amount you pay the sitters. Most parents are happy to pay this extra cost as they do not have to telephone round to find a sitter at busy times, and because they know the sitters will have been checked and are reliable. You should ask all potential sitters for references and make a thorough job of checking these. You will also need to have insurance to cover both sitters and clients.

How can I sell my services?

As a sitter, you can join an agency which will provide you with jobs. This can be a good way to get started in this field. As well as (hopefully) providing you with a steady stream of work, an agency will provide a useful buffer between you and the parents of unruly children, and they will carry insurance to cover you in the unlikely event that anything goes drastically wrong.

As an independent sitter, you can put postcards in shop windows, advertise in the local papers, or prepare some flyers and pop them through likely doors in your neighbourhood. You could also leave a pile of flyers in local shops which sell baby and children's clothes, or ask to put a notice up in your local doctor's surgery. And pass the word around all your acquaintances who have children. You should also keep your eye on postcard advertisements for people seeking a baby-sitter.

Some social services departments maintain lists of sitters for children who are educationally sub-normal or have behaviour problems, but obviously they will require you to have appropriate experience and qualifications.

When running an agency, you can do all of the above, plus advertise in Yellow Pages and any newsletters published by local schools.

Where can I get more help?

There are no legal regulations for babysitting as there are for child-minding, and there is no central body for either babysitters themselves or babysitting agencies. However, many local education authorities run courses for teenage baby-sitters, and the Royal Society for the Prevention of Accidents publishes a number of useful leaflets (some of which are also available on their website).

Royal Society for the Prevention of Accidents (RoSPA)
Edgbaston Park
353 Bristol Road
Edgbaston
Birmingham
B5 7ST
Tel: 0121 248 2000
Web: www.rospa.co.uk

BEAUTICIAN/BEAUTY THERAPY

If you enjoy looking good and helping others do the same, this could be the ideal opportunity for you. You can work from your own home, in clients' homes, or (one or two days a week perhaps) in an upstairs room at a local hairdressing or beauty salon. If you decide to work from a room in your own home you are likely to need planning permission from your local authority.

Some authorities may also require you to register with them, depending on the range of services you intend to offer.

Beauticians offer a variety of beauty treatments, including depilatory waxing, eyebrow shaping, eyelash and eyebrow tinting, facials, manicures, pedicures, nail extensions, and general make-up advice and assistance. Beauty therapists traditionally offer a wider range of treatments, including some which are primarily concerned with promoting health and fitness rather than beauty as such: massage, toning and slimming treatments, exercise programmes, and so on. Some beauty therapists also offer electrolysis for the removal of unwanted body hair (specialist training is required for this). In recent years the distinction between beauticians and beauty therapists has become increasingly blurred, and nowadays the term beauty therapist is increasingly applied to anyone working in this field.

In theory, men can be beauty therapists as well as women, but in practice (for obvious reasons) the great majority are female. However, with modern men becoming increasingly concerned about good grooming and health, opportunities for men in this field look set to increase.

What do I need to get started?

To work as a beauty therapist you will need a pleasant personality and the ability to get on well with all types of people. There is no need for supermodel good looks, but you will need to be well-groomed, stylish and healthy-looking. Treatments inevitably involve close personal contact with clients, so it is important that you are comfortable with this. In particular, you must be able to cope with clients who may suffering from skin conditions or have a lower standard of personal hygiene than yourself.

It is not essential to possess qualifications, but in practice if you do not you are likely to be at a disadvantage. Of course, you may have qualifications already from your previous employment. Otherwise, courses are offered by a number of colleges and specialist beauty training institutions; for a list of providers, contact the Guild of Professional Beauty Therapists (details below). Beauty therapy courses usually take around six months to a year to complete. As well as the specialist skills involved, you will also be taught about health and hygiene, physiology and communication skills. Grants are not normally available for beauty courses, and the fees charged can be substantial, running to thousands of pounds in the case of some private colleges.

The materials and equipment you will need to set up as a beauty therapist depend on the range of treatments you intend to offer. As well as cosmetics, towels and so on, it may include electrical appliances for massage, slimming and toning, heat treatments, electrolysis and so on. The minimum initial expenditure is around £500, but could easily run into thousands.

Who will my customers be?

Your clients will be (mainly) women of all ages who wish to improve their looks and general wellbeing. You might also obtain work from local hair and beauty salons. Another possibility would be working as a freelance for a cosmetics company, giving demonstrations and running promotions in health clubs and similar institutions. You might also be able to get work as a freelance make-up artist for film, television and theatre productions.

How much can I make?

Rates vary according to the area and type of service. The best approach is to visit a number of local salons and check the prices they are charging for the services you intend to offer. Once you know the 'going rate' in your area, you can then set your own fees accordingly. As a general guideline, for basic beauty treatments you should charge your clients a minimum of £15 per hour. The cost of any materials (cosmetics, massage oils, etc.) will need to be added to this, or you could charge a higher hourly rate to cover the cost of materials as well.

How can I sell my services?

Local advertising is likely to work best in this field. Have some attractive, postcard-sized cards designed and put them up in newsagents' windows, supermarkets, leisure centres, doctors' surgeries and so on. Local health food shops and hairdressing salons would be good places to advertise as well (though if the latter already offer beauty treatments they are unlikely to accept advertising from a competitor). You could also try taking out ads in your local newspaper and Yellow Pages.

Where can I get more help?

The main organisation serving and representing beauty therapists in the UK is the Guild of Professional Beauty Therapists. They provide a range of services for their members, including professional indemnity insurance (essential in this occupation), legal and business advice, and the monthly journal Guild News. The Guild can also provide detail of organisations offering training in beauty therapy across the UK.

The Guild of Professional Beauty Therapists Ltd
Guild House
PO Box 310
Derby
DE23 9BR
Tel: 01332 771714
Web: www.beauty-guild.co.uk

BOOK-KEEPING

With more and more people setting up their own businesses, the demand for freelance book-keepers has never been greater. Keeping the books is one of those tasks many businessmen and women hate – yet it is essential to keep financial records, both for the taxman (income tax and VAT) and to see how well the business is doing. Many businesspeople are therefore more than happy to pay a freelance book-keeper to take care of this task for them, while they concentrate on doing what they do best – be this window cleaning or proofreading, childminding or desktop publishing.

Freelance book-keepers work mainly for self-employed individuals and small businesses. They ensure that all receipts and outgoings are correctly entered in the business's books (though most businesses today use computers for this purpose rather than the traditional account books or ledgers). They may also compile monthly management accounts, and handle matters such as VAT, wages, bank reconciliations (checking bank statements against the information in the business's books), and so on.

They may also be engaged on a short-term basis by larger firms, who may need assistance in preparing a report for the Inland Revenue or some other agency. Book-keepers do not, however, normally prepare a business's final (end-of-year) accounts, as this is the province of an accountant.

What do I need to get started?

Clearly you need an aptitude for working with figures (though with modern computers and calculators there is no need for you to be a mathematical wizard). You will need to be thorough and methodical. When using written books neat handwriting is important; though this is not, of course, an issue with computerised systems.

Although there is no legal requirement to possess qualifications before setting up in this field, in practice most clients will expect it. And, of course, if you are to do the job properly, it is desirable to have completed at least some formal training. It may be that you already possess book-keeping qualifications from a previous career. Alternatively, the International Association of Book-keepers (see below) offers courses at three different levels, Foundation, Intermediate and Advanced. The IAB also offers diplomas in computerised book-keeping, payroll administration and small business financial management.

Computer-based book-keeping is very much the norm today. Computerised systems can perform calculations quickly and easily, and allow information to be manipulated and presented in all sorts of ways. You can buy a basic home computer and printer for around £500, and this should be more than adequate for book-keeping purposes. Two of the most popular small business accounts packages for PCs are Intuit Quickbooks (01932 578500) and Sage Instant Accounting (0191 255 3000). Both these programs are widely available for under £100.

Who will my customers be?

Your main clients will be self-employed individuals and small businesses who need help with compiling their books. Larger businesses, as indicated above, may require your help in connection with special projects. Accountants may also sub-contract work to freelance book-keepers.

How much can I make?

As a self-employed book-keeper you can set your own fees. Your best option will be to charge an hourly rate. Fees charged vary considerably from one area to another, but when starting out somewhere between £10 and £30 an hour might be suitable. (To find the 'going rate' in your area, call a few local book-keeping services posing as a client and ask about their fees.) You can invoice clients every month or at the end of a particular assignment. Regular clients could be charged a fixed monthly fee. Depending on where you are based, running a part-time book-keeping business should bring in around £5,000 to £10,000 a year, while full-time earnings should be £15,000 to £30,000 or more.

How can I sell my services?

Try advertising in local papers and other publications aimed at businesses. It is also well worth taking out advertisements in Yellow Pages and Thomson's directory (if there is one covering your area). Contacting your local chamber of commerce or Business Link centre may also be worthwhile, as they should be able to put you in touch with new businesses who may require your services.

Existing businesses should also be approached. You could try a mailshot, phoning them up, or even calling in person. If they are not interested at the time, give them a business card or leaflet so they can contact you again in the future if their circumstances change. And don't forget to contact local accountancy firms – as mentioned, many of them sub-contract some of their work to freelance book-keepers, especially at busy times of the year such as approaching the end of January (the deadline for self-assessment tax returns to be submitted).

Finally, you could try approaching local office services agencies. Many of these require qualified book-keeping and accounts staff for short- and long-term contracts and even full-time jobs. Rates of pay are not the highest (the agency takes a big cut), but this can be a good way to gain experience when starting out, and you will also be eligible for benefits such as paid holidays. Look in Yellow Pages under the headings 'Secretarial Services' or 'Employment Agencies'.

Where can I get more help?

Most colleges run book-keeping and accounting courses, many of which can be taken as short courses or evening classes. A whole range of correspondence courses are also offered by the National Extension College (NEC). National Extension College courses are independently assessed by the Open and Distance Learning Quality Council to ensure that they meet the highest possible standards.

The National Extension College
18 Brooklands Avenue
Cambridge
CB2 2HN
Tel: 01223 450200
Web: www.nec.ac.uk

The main professional body in this field is the International Association of Book-keepers (IAB). Becoming an IAB member entitles you to a range of benefits, including a bimonthly magazine, subsidised courses and seminars, professional indemnity insurance schemes, and so on. IAB Members who have completed the Association's qualifying examinations and have at least two years' practical experience are entitled to use the letters MIAB (Member of the International Association of Book-keepers) or FIAB (Fellow) after their name.

The International Association of Book-keepers (IAB)
Burford House
44 London Road
Sevenoaks
Kent TN13 1AS
Tel: 01732 458080
Web: www.iab.org.uk

CAR CLEANING AND VALETING

In recent years car cleaning and valeting has been something of a growth area. Many people want to keep their cars in 'showroom condition', but lack the time, the inclination and (probably) the skills to do it themselves. They are therefore happy to pay a professional car valeter to do the job for them. If you want a healthy outdoor occupation and enjoy working with cars, this could therefore be a good opportunity for you.

At the most basic, you could offer a straightforward cleaning service. Armed with no more than a bucket, a sponge and a chammy leather, plus a bottle of wash-and-wax, you may be able to find a steady trade among householders willing to pay a few pounds for the convenience of having their car washed on the front drive. On the other hand, most areas nowadays have an automatic car wash nearby which offers much the same service; and you may also have to face accusations that you are stealing business from the local scouts! If you want a full-time business rather than merely a sideline, offering a full car valeting service is likely to be a much better bet.

Car valeting involves doing much more than a simple wash. A full valet might include all the following treatments: shampoo the vehicle; clean the wheels; wash the bodywork and wheel arches; de-grease and polish the door hinges; remove any stains and deposits; polish with long-lasting wax; shampoo the seats, carpets, mats and boot; clean and condition plastics, bumpers and dashboard; clean the windows inside and out; condition leather (if there is any); clean the engine bay and spare wheel compartment; remove minor scratches (if possible); and deodorise the vehicle. A full valet is a painstaking process likely to take at least an hour-and-a-half, perhaps longer if the vehicle is in a very dirty condition.

If your house has a suitable front or back yard, you could operate from here. This is, however, the type of business your neighbours could well take exception to, and planning permission – which you would need – could be hard to come by. A better option (discussed below) might be to operate a mobile valeting service.

What do I need to get started?

You need be willing to work outdoors and be reasonably physically fit. It goes without saying that you should enjoy working with cars. Car valeting is very much a customer service business, so it will help if you have a pleasant manner and are reasonably presentable. You must also be conscientious about providing your customers with the highest quality service – if a client suspects you of 'cutting corners', you are unlikely to ever obtain work from him in the future. However, the skills you will need are not difficult to acquire, and qualifications in this field are relatively unimportant.

If you intend to run a mobile valeting service, the equipment you will need is likely to include a small van (kept in pristine condition, of course!), a vacuum cleaner (preferably the wet-and-dry variety), car shampoo and wax, buckets, sponges, chammy leathers and so on. Preferably, the vehicle should include your own water and power supply, but this is not essential when first starting out. You will also need several sets of overalls, as the job can be mucky at times. Apart from the van, you should be able to get all the equipment and materials you need to set up in this profession for a few hundred pounds.

Who will my customers be?

Initially at least your main customers are likely to be private car owners. Once you have built up a group of such clients, an advantage of this particular occupation is that they will want you back at regular intervals to keep their pride and joy in tip-top condition.

Once your business is running successfully, you may also be able to obtain work from local companies who want someone to keep their vehicles in top condition. Potential customers here include car dealers (especially those selling second-hand cars), car hire companies, taxi firms and fleet managers in large companies. If you intend to branch out into corporate work, you will almost certainly have to consider taking on staff to assist you.

How much can I make?

In this field it is usual to charge a set fee according to the service being offered. For a full valet such as that described in the introduction, a typical fee would be in the region of £60. A more basic service ('standard' or 'mini' valet), not including a separate wax polish and engine wash, would normally cost around half this price. Overheads are minimal, comprising mainly the cost of cleaning chemicals and occasional replacement of equipment. Working full-time, it should be possible to clear £20,000 a year or more in this occupation.

How can I sell my services?

One approach used successfully by some valeting businesses is to produce a simple leaflet advertising the service and put it through letterboxes of homes in the local area. You could also try leaving your leaflet on the front windscreens of cars in the supermarket car park.

Another idea would be to approach local garages and ask if they are willing to promote your service to their customers – offer them a small fee for any introductions which result in work for you. Advertising cards in newsagents' windows are also worth trying, as is your local paper (most have a section among their classified advertisements for motoring-related services). Finally, don't neglect to advertise in Yellow Pages under Car & Commercial Vehicle Valeting.

Where can I get more help?

Training courses in car valeting are offered at many local colleges. They tend to be aimed mainly at people employed by garages and valeting companies, but there is no reason why a self-employed person could not enrol on them. Courses typically run one day a week, and lead to qualifications such as NVQ or SVQ Level 1 in vehicle valeting. For more information, contact the Motor Industry Training Council:

Motor Industry Training Council
201 Great Portland Street
London
W1N 6AB
Tel: 020 7436 6373
Web: www.mitc.co.uk

A number of car valeting companies have set up websites to advertise their services. One which is particularly worth visiting belongs to the Bath-based Cleancar Service (http://website.lineone.net/~cleancar). As well as listing the services they offer, this attractively designed site also includes an online car valeting manual including many practical tips.

CARPET AND UPHOLSTERY CLEANING

This business deals with the types of cleaning which are not generally covered by the ordinary domestic or office cleaner – items which need cleaning only at fairly long intervals. If you choose to restrict your activities to the domestic market you will have to seek new customers constantly, as you are unlikely to visit each home more than once a year. Adding 'disaster restoration' (cleaning up after fire or flood) to your repertoire will enable you to get work from insurance companies.

What do I need to get started?

This is a business that requires a fair amount of know-how to understand how best to tackle any given type of fabric and stain, and the right equipment and chemicals. You will also need a suitable vehicle to transport these materials, which will not easily fit into the average car. If you do not choose to invest in the necessary machinery immediately, most of it is available from hire shops, but the cost of hiring will obviously make a large dent in your takings. If buying, expect to pay around £600 for a basic cleaning machine.

There are numerous franchised operations such as Servicemaster, Safeclean and Rainbow International, which offer a full business package including all the necessary equipment and supplies of chemicals, plus full training and marketing support. These typically require an initial investment of well over £10,000.

Who will my customers be?

On the domestic side, your customers will be ordinary householders who want a spring clean, people who are putting their homes on the market, or people who have suffered a fire or some other domestic disaster. These will be almost entirely 'one-off' jobs. For a steady flow of work on domestic properties, you should approach letting agents or block landlords of good quality properties who will require each property under their care to be spring-cleaned between tenants. If you offer a disaster recovery service, you may be able to get steady work from insurance companies or loss adjusters.

On the commercial side, the best customers will be large office blocks, and hotel, pub and restaurant chains. Offices may have a workshop where you can clean furniture during ordinary working hours, but carpets will have to be cleaned overnight or at weekends, especially if you are using wet chemicals or those which require major ventilation. Hotels and pubs may call you in for a complete clean when they are closed for refurbishment (this can be a winter activity if you live in a holiday resort), or may want you to deal with individual rooms as and when they are vacant.

How much can I make?

Franchise operations say you should be turning over at least £50,000 after two years working full-time, and about 45 per cent of this will be profit. On a smaller scale and operating in the domestic market only, your earnings will depend on how many customers want the whole house cleaned. In this case, for an average three bedroom house, you should clear £80–£100 for a day's work. Smaller jobs, such as carpets only, will earn less overall, as you will spend time loading and unloading your equipment and travelling between jobs.

How can I sell my services?

For domestic jobs, leaflet drops and advertising in the local papers and Yellow Pages are the most effective and cheapest ways to advertise. Once you are up and running, you should get a lot of work from word-of-mouth recommendations.

For commercial jobs you will need more professional brochures and some convincing sales letters to send in mailshots to letting agents, facilities managers of office blocks and hotel housekeepers. You should also make a point of building up a network of contacts through your local chamber of commerce. Some franchise operations will assist you by forwarding enquiries generated by their national advertising.

Where can I get more help?

Both the organisations listed below offer training and advice on the latest developments in cleaning chemicals and their use.

British Institute of Cleaning Science
3 Moulton Court
Anglia Way
Moulton Park
Northampton
NN3 6JA
Tel: 01604 678710
Web: www.bics.org.uk

Cleaning and Support Services Association
Suite 301
New Loom House
101 Backchurch Lane
London
E1 1LU
Tel: 0207 403 2747

Franchise operators such as those mentioned in this article advertise regularly in the 'Business Opportunities' section of Exchange & Mart. For information about franchise opportunities in general, contact the British Franchise Association.

The British Franchise Association
Thames View
Newtown Road
Henley-on-Thames
Oxon
RG9 1HG
Tel: 01491 578050
Web: www.british-franchise.org.uk

CHILDMINDING

Childminders look after other people's children in their own home. With an ever-increasing number of women wanting or needing to go out to work, the service is in considerable demand. Childminding is by no means an easy option, but if you enjoy the company of children and are healthy, energetic, adaptable and not too house-proud, you may find this an enjoyable and fulfilling way of making a living.

Childminders do far more than simply watch over their charges. They provide a safe but stimulating environment, with plenty of opportunities for the children to learn through play. They also take them out from time to time, e.g. to a local park or playgroup. They provide meals as required, and supervise games and activities. Childminders must be registered with the local authority (see below), and are subject to an annual inspection.

In theory, men as well as women can be childminders. In practice, however, the overwhelming majority of childminders are female, and male childminders might have some problems overcoming popular stereotypes concerning their suitability for this type of work.

What do I need to get started?

To look after other people's children for money, you will need to register with your local social services' under-eights department and book a place on one of their childminders' pre-registration courses. The frequency and number of these courses will depend on the area you live in. A typical course will cover such areas as business record keeping, relationships with parents, planning activities for daycare, children's safety and behaviour, diet and nutrition, equal opportunities, and responding to emergencies.

Your home will also have to be inspected by a representative of the local authority to check that it meets the required safety standards. The exact requirements vary between authorities, but some of the things they will be looking for include stairgates, smoke alarms, covers on open electrical sockets, fire guards, safety glass or protective plastic film on patio doors, and general cleanliness and hygiene of kitchen, washing and toilet areas. You will be notified of any deficiencies and given time to make the necessary alterations.

As part of the registration procedure, you will be assessed on your attitude towards children, your knowledge of child development and your experience of caring for children. You will also be required to provide toys and equipment that meet the required British Safety standard where there is one. Though not compulsory, it is also highly desirable that you have completed a first aid for children course. You should also ensure you have adequate public liability insurance.

Who will my customers be?

Your clients will typically be working parents, including single parents, of pre-school children. In some cases it may be the grandparents who actually pay you. You could also offer your services to local businesses, who will then offer it to their employees. Businesses are gradually becoming more enlightened about the need to provide childcare support for their employees with young children, and a single contract with a local employer could provide a steady source of work for you.

How much can I make?

There are no set national pay scales for childminding, though in some areas childminders have grouped together and agreed on a uniform rate. Around £3 to £4 an hour is typical, but there can be wide variations. It is a good idea to ask around to find out what are the typical charges in your area. As a self-employed person you can set your own fees, but it will obviously be desirable if these are not too out-of-step with other childminders locally. You also need to consider whether the fees you charge will include food and drink, outings and so on, or whether parents will have to pay extra for these.

One other consideration is that you should have a policy on overtime/lateness charges. Most childminders work a standard day of 8 am to 6 pm to allow them a reasonable amount of time with their own families, but on occasion you may be asked to look after the child outside these hours (e.g. if a parent is working late). You should charge a higher rate than usual for this.

How can I sell my services?

First, check with your local authority to see if there is a local childminding association or childcare agency. You may have to pay a small fee to join, but they will then add you to their list of registered childminders and pass on your details to anyone who is looking for a childminder.

Other methods of advertising include your local newspaper, shops (many supermarkets have free notice boards for people providing a service in the local community), libraries, doctors' surgeries and playgroups. Another idea which is worth trying as more and more people get online is to set up a web page advertising your service (for a good example of this, see Lorraine's Childminding Services at www.simonbennett.freeserve.co.uk).

Finally, don't forget the power of word of mouth. If you have vacancies, ask your existing clients to mention this to any friends or neighbours with young children. It may be worth having some small advertising cards printed and handing these out, or even putting them through letterboxes in your local area.

Where can I get more help?

Two main organisations provide support and assistance for childminders, the Daycare Trust and the National Childminding Association. The Daycare Trust aims to promote the development of high quality childcare services, and provides telephone and written support for parents and childcare providers. They publish a helpful leaflet called *Start it up! Become a Registered Childminder.*

The Daycare Trust
380 Old Street
London EC1V 9LT
Tel. 020 7739 2866

The National Childminding Association is a membership organisation for childminders and others involved in providing daycare for young children. They offer an advice and information service and have a network of local groups.

The National Childminding Association
8 Masons Hill
Bromley
Kent
BR2 9EY
Tel. 020 8464 6164

Finally, if you have net access it is well worth taking a look at the Kids & Co. website at www.childcare-info.co.uk. This enterprising site is packed with information on setting up and working as a registered childminder – it even includes suggested activities, recipes, and so on!

CHILDREN'S ENTERTAINMENT

If you enjoy being with children and have the skills and personality to keep them amused for an hour or two, being a children's entertainer could be both fun and profitable for you. The main demand is for people who can provide entertainment at birthday parties for children typically between the ages of four and ten.

Most children's entertainers have a range of skills. They organise their 'shows' in a series of varied sessions to cope with young children's notoriously short attention spans. These might include joke-telling, magic, Punch & Judy, face painting, balloon modelling, juggling, stilt walking, children's discos, sing-songs, party games, competitions, and so on. Another popular activity at parties held in the summer is an inflatable such as a 'bouncy castle'. Some entertainers specialise in one particular field, most commonly magic (conjuring).

Audience participation is an important aspect of children's entertainment. To avoid any risk of boredom, the children themselves need to be involved in some way, e.g. by helping with tricks, dressing up, or simply holding things. Entertainers need to be especially watchful that the birthday boy or girl does not feel left out and (if at all possible) wins the best prizes!

What do I need to get started?

You will need a fairly outgoing personality and the ability to get on well with children (not everyone can cope with a roomful of near-hysterical seven-year-olds). You must also be able to reassure anxious parents with charm and tact.

So far as the actual entertainment is concerned, it will help if you possess a range of skills such as those listed above. Many of these, however, can be acquired relatively easily, to a basic level at least. If you intend to specialise in an area such as magic, you will of course need to spend more time honing your skills. Some degree of aptitude is probably essential to succeed as a specialist magician.

The cost of setting up as a children's entertainer is fairly minimal. You are likely to need one or more costumes (not only to amuse the children but to protect your normal clothing from flying jelly and ice cream). You will need the appropriate props and equipment, and a supply of sweets and small toys to give away as prizes. Finally, you will require some sort of transportation to get you and your costumes and equipment to and from the venues.

Who will my customers be?

Your clients are most likely to be the parents of young children, mainly from reasonably prosperous, middle-class households. You may also be able to obtain work from playgroups, summer play schemes and schools. Specialist magicians may also (if they wish) market their services to adult audiences, for example to provide the cabaret at a restaurant or the evening entertainment at a business meeting or convention.

How much can I make?

Children's entertainers can charge up to £100 an hour for a show. Magicians may be able to charge much more than this, especially if performing to a large audience. In theory this gives this occupation very high earning potential; but in practice most clients will only want you at the weekend, limiting the number of bookings you are likely to be able to accept in any given period. Of course, this does mean that children's entertainment can be an ideal second or part-time occupation.

Overheads in this field are low, consisting mainly of the cost of transportation and 'consumables' such as sweets, toys and balloons. Periodically you will also need to replace your equipment and costumes, and buy new tricks, props and so on.

How can I sell my services?

Begin with an advertisement in Yellow Pages under 'Entertainers' – many people working in this field find this an excellent source of bookings. Other good places to advertise include local entertainment guides and directories, and your local newspaper.

Probably the best method of advertising is word-of-mouth, so be sure to encourage children (and their parents) to recommend you to all their friends. Repeat business is also a possibility, either from the child's brothers and sisters, or the same child the following year. In any event it is a good idea to have some cards printed and leave a supply of these with your client, both for future reference and to give to friends and neighbours. Another idea would be to prepare party bags for the children to take away with them. As well as toys, sweets, and so on, these would also (of course) include your advertising card.

Other good places to advertise include newsagents' windows and local supermarkets, as well as libraries, clinics and playgroups. In addition, if you are computer-literate you could try setting up a web page to advertise your service (for an example of what can be done, see www.clownsareus.co.uk). Finally, you could try registering with one or more local entertainment agencies.

Where can I get more help?

There is no shortage of books available to help you learn basic children's entertainment skills. Some adult education centres offer courses in circus skills (juggling, stilt-walking, unicycle riding, etc.). A number of companies sell conjuring books and equipment by mail order or via the internet. Details of one such company are given below.

The Magic Company
PO Box 488
Southampton
SO17 2XW
Tel: 023 8063 5701
Web: www.magic.co.uk

COMMISSION SELLING

Selling isn't everyone's cup of tea, but if you can do it you need never be short of earning opportunities. As a commission seller, you will be self-employed working on behalf of one or more companies selling their products and/or services. For each sale you make, a percentage of the order value will go to you as commission.

There are two main types of commission selling. The first is where you act as an agent for a company such as Betterware or Kleeneze, delivering their catalogue to homes in your area, then calling a few days later to take orders. The second is where you are trained to sell your company's products direct to customers in their homes. This is often referred to as direct selling. Products in this category range from home improvements such as curtains and blinds to personal care items such as cosmetics and diet plans.

What do I need to get started?

You need to enjoy meeting people and persuading them to buy your products. Where direct sales are concerned, you should be able to handle the rejection that comes when someone you've spent several hours pitching to turns you down.

You need a product to sell. The Direct Sales Association (see below) produces a free booklet listing all its members. This will give you a good idea of the range of products available for this type of selling. Be wary, however, of advertisements which promise enormous earnings; in particular, beware of advertisements which state 'OTE' beside the earnings figure. This means 'On Target Earnings', and these are frequently based on wildly optimistic sales levels that are rarely if ever achieved. Many companies say you can 'easily' earn £20,000 a year plus, but this is rarely achievable unless you work at least five full days and evenings a week.

You will receive training in both selling techniques and the merits of the actual products, either direct from the company or from your local area manager or supervisor. Where the product is complicated, this training may take several days.

Who will my customers be?

For household items such as Betterware, the customers will be householders in your allocated district. Betterware reckons its agents need about 1,000 households to make the exercise worthwhile.

For direct sold products customers will also be private householders, but their names and addresses will be provided to you by the company head office or local sales office. They in turn obtain these from national advertising or sometimes by telesales canvassing, and wherever possible you should confirm the appointments before you go to them. Some telesales canvassers are paid for each appointment they make, and they may therefore make appointments with people who are not really interested in buying – which you won't find out until you have wasted a lot of time and travelling expenses. For the same reason, you should have the right to refuse any appointments which are too far from your home or you will soon find you have spent more in petrol than you have earned.

How much can I make?

This varies according to the organisation and the type of product. For direct sold home improvement products and services, a 20 per cent commission is the norm; for other products it may be as much as 30 per cent.

For catalogue-delivery and order-taking operations, it is said that working ten hours a week should bring in about £100 of commission. There is no reason why you should not take agencies with more than one company at a time (as long as the products are not the same) and thus increase your chances of sales without having to increase your delivery/collection time.

There is normally some provision for successful salespeople to rise through the ranks into supervisory positions, when you will then be organising the salespeople for a large area. This does, however, require a much larger time commitment and may even be a salaried full-time job.

Some direct sales companies operate multi-level marketing (MLM) programmes. These involve salespeople recruiting other sellers, and then getting a small commission from sales achieved by these people as well as themselves. There is nothing necessarily wrong with this, as long as you do not fall foul of one of the less reputable MLM organisations which require you to make a payment to join their scheme on the basis that you can then earn more money by recruiting others. This practice is not only unethical, it is illegal.

Where can I get more help?

The Direct Selling Association produces a free booklet which lists all its members. This will give you a good idea of the products sold by this method, as well as providing the necessary contact details. This information is also available via the DSA website.

The Direct Selling Association
29 Floral Street
London
WC2 9DP
Tel: 020 7497 1234
Web: www.dsa.org.uk

If commission selling appeals to you, see also the article later in the book on Party Plan Selling.

COMPUTER INSTALLATION AND MAINTENANCE

Over five million computers are sold every year in the UK, many of them to people who have little or no prior knowledge of computing. An opportunity has therefore opened up for people with a good practical knowledge of computers to offer an installation and maintenance service. There is in fact a range of related services you could offer:

Computer installation: Many people buying a new computer system are rather daunted by the thought of setting it all up. Parts have to be identified and connected correctly, manuals negotiated, software installed, and so on. In a well-populated urban area it would be possible to run a successful business offering this service alone.

Repairs: Modern computers are generally quite reliable, but breakdowns do occur. The most common causes are a sudden power surge or accidental damage (e.g. a cup of coffee being spilt on the keyboard!). Many problems are solved simply by swapping one or two components, meaning experienced individuals can often perform this type of task quite quickly (and profitably).

Upgrades: The time may also come when people want their computers to be upgraded – with more memory, for example, or a faster processor. They may want additional features installed, e.g. a DVD drive, or they may require help in configuring some new software.

Cleaning: It may not sound very glamorous, but computer cleaning is an important and specialised task. Cleaning kits and materials are available from specialist computer shops. Getting a regular computer cleaning contract from one or two local businesses could provide a steady source of income.

Consultancy and problem solving: This is a huge field. At one end of the scale are people considering buying a computer for the first time, perhaps for their children's education, who want independent advice on what they should obtain. At the other extreme are businesses seeking advice on how they should upgrade their computer systems or set up an internal network. The latter type of work can be highly paid so long as you have the necessary skills and experience.

Offering a remote backup service: This is a more specialised service. Many businesses keep a range of important information on their computers which it would be highly inconvenient (not to mention costly) to lose. A remote backup provider offers a service whereby the client's data is saved regularly on another computer via a modem and phone line. This means it can be quickly restored if the client's own computer is damaged, stolen or breaks down.

What do I need to get started?

You must have a good working knowledge of computers and be comfortable with opening them up in order to repair and upgrade them. You will need an understanding of the various components (hard disk, motherboard, memory, CD-ROM drive, etc.) and the way they are connected. You will also need the practical skills to fit a new processor, additional memory chips, a DVD drive, and so on.

In addition you will need good communication skills, both on the phone and face-to-face. At times you will have to be patient and tactful, e.g. when dealing with a client who knows a little about computers but not as much as he thinks he does. Qualifications are not essential in this field, but you will certainly need some relevant practical experience. Courses are readily available at local colleges and adult education centres, and also from specialist agencies such as ICS (see below).

You do not, strictly speaking, require a computer of your own to enter this field, though one will undoubtedly be useful for practising your skills and testing solutions to tricky problems. It is also very helpful to have internet access, as the net can be a valuable source of computer-related information and resources. You may well have a computer already, but if not you could buy a basic machine for around £500 (then practise your skills by upgrading it!). You will need a specialist computer toolkit, with a range of screwdrivers, pliers, chip extractors, soldering iron and so on. Finally, you will require some form of transport, as much of the work will be done in your clients' homes or business premises.

Who will my customers be?

Your clients will be mainly small businesses and private individuals who need help with their computers. Older people in particular, who may not have grown up with computers, often appreciate assistance in getting their new machine up and running; and they may also like to have someone local they can turn to for advice if any problems occur. Businesses, similarly, may lack anyone with specialist knowledge of computers, and will be keen to find someone offering a prompt and reliable service when the need arises.

How much can I make?

For installing someone's new home computer and providing basic instruction to get them up and running, you could charge a fee of £25 (based on around one hour's work in total). For other services you could charge an hourly fee of £15 to £25 for private individuals, £25 to £50 (or more) for businesses. Your overheads should be modest, mainly consisting of transport costs in visiting your clients.

How can I sell my services?

The ideal solution is to negotiate an arrangement with a local computer retailer, whereby your service is referred every time someone buys a computer. You might even be able to arrange for your fee to be included in the retail price of the computer, so that the store can advertise that installation is included. A number of large computer stores currently offer such deals, so if there are any near you it would be worth contacting them to ask if they need additional help to carry out installations in clients' homes.

You could also try advertising in local papers, and with cards in newsagents' windows, supermarket notice boards and so on. If your service includes repairs and maintenance as well as installation, an advertisement in Yellow Pages would certainly be worth trying. Finally, when you are installing new computers in clients' homes or business premises, don't forget to leave your card with them in case they ever need your help in the future.

Where can I get more help?

There is no shortage of books covering the skills required in this occupation. One comprehensive general guide is 'Upgrading and Repairing PCs' by Scott Mueller (Que). A number of computer-related distance learning courses are offered by International Correspondence Schools (ICS), a division of the publishers Harcourt. Their range includes a computer repair course.

ICS
Freepost 882
Clydeway Skypark
8 Elliott Place
Glasgow
G3 8BR
Tel: 0500 121 211

COMPUTER PROGRAMMING

Computer programmers make their living writing the step-by-step instructions computers use to perform their tasks. Relatively few freelances write machine code (the deepest level of instructions used by computers for their internal operations). Most home-based freelances are applications programmers. They help their clients customise standard 'off-the-shelf' programs so that they meet the specific needs of the business concerned. Most freelances have a particular area in which they specialise, e.g. accounts packages or databases. Some freelances possess specialist knowledge of one or more computer languages, e.g. C++ or Visual Basic.

The computer industry is booming at present as businesses become aware of the many benefits computers can provide (not to mention the need to avoid falling behind their competitors). If you have skills in this field – and especially if you live in a well-populated urban area – you should have little difficulty in finding potential clients.

What do I need to get started?

Programmers need a logical mind, with the ability to break down a complex task into its component parts. They also require patience and perseverance, as creating a complex program can be a painstaking and time-consuming process.

Training and qualifications are likely to be essential. If you are considering going into this field the chances are you will have some relevant experience already, but courses are also readily available from local colleges and specialist training agencies such as Computeach (see below). Adult education centres also run courses, but be careful – in some cases, due to budgetary constraints, the computers they use are old or even obsolete. Skills acquired on such machines may therefore be of limited practical value to potential clients.

So far as equipment is concerned, your number one requirement will, of course, be a computer. This should be as modern and powerful as possible, so that you can run all the latest software. You are also likely to need a printer and possibly a modem (if the computer does not have one installed already) to connect with the internet. In addition you will need a range of reference books and manuals in your specialist subjects. Your basic start-up costs, not including the price of any specialist software, are likely to be in the region of £2,000.

Who will my customers be?

Your clients will be mainly small businesses who need help in setting up and configuring a new computer application. This could be an accounts package, a customer database, or perhaps an internal computer network. You may also be able to obtain work from larger companies who need specialist assistance with a particular project. You might also obtain part-time or temporary work via specialist IT recruitment and computer training agencies.

How much can I make?

Earnings depend very much on the services you offer and your level of skill. As the end of 1999 approached some freelance programmers were asking (and getting) £1,000 a day or more for ensuring that their clients' computers would not succumb to 'the millennium bug'. This situation is unlikely to arise again in the near future, but £200–£300 a day is quite standard. Overheads in this field should be modest, mainly comprising transport costs when visiting clients and occasional updating of hardware and software.

How can I sell my services?

It is worth advertising in local business directories, and possibly in Yellow Pages, but most freelances find that the majority of their clients come via word-of-mouth recommendations. One good starting point would be your previous employers (assuming you left them on good terms). It is also worth making contact with other local professionals such as business consultants and accountants, as they may well have clients who need your specialist assistance.

Another good source of referrals is your local computer shop. Many of their customers will have bought computers quite recently and may require your help to get them to perform the tasks they purchased them for. Creating your own internet web page would obviously be a good idea. Finally, you could try offering to write a regular column for your local paper about the benefits of computers for businesses. You should not expect to be paid for this, but it could be an excellent way of drawing attention to your services.

Where can I get more help?

One well-established provider of distance learning courses in programming and related skills is Computeach International. They offer a wide range of courses, including programming, systems analysis, networking, database management and so on.

Computeach International
PO Box 51
University House
Dudley
West Midlands
DY3 2AG
Tel: 01384 458515
Web: www.computeach.co.uk

The leading organisation for people working in the computer industry in the UK is the British Computer Society. Membership is available at various levels based on experience and successfully completing the Society's examinations. Members receive a range of benefits, including discounts on books and computers, meetings and special events, a bi-monthly newsletter, and so on.

The British Computer Society
1 Sanford Street
Swindon
Wiltshire
SN1 1HJ
Tel: 01793 417424
Web: www.bcs.org.uk

COMPUTER TRAINING

In recent years computers have begun appearing everywhere: in homes, in schools, in business and in government. The pace of change has been so fast that many people have found they need help getting up to speed with the new technology. An opportunity has therefore opened up for freelance computer trainers who can run courses and provide instruction on a range of subjects, including:

• Introduction to computers
• Word processing
• Desktop publishing
• The internet

- Accounts packages
- Databases
- Presentation software.

Freelance computer trainers provide instruction for both small groups and individuals. They design and run training sessions and courses, typically of one to three days' duration. Courses may be provided to introduce people to computers and specific computer applications, or to improve their existing skills. Trainers prepare a training plan, create handouts and other materials such as overhead projector slides, and deliver the actual training.

Training sessions for individuals are generally delivered at the student's home, probably using his or her own computer. Another approach is to book a suitably equipped room in a school, college or adult education centre, and advertise courses direct to the public. You may also be able to obtain work from companies and other large organisations, in which case the client will normally arrange the training room and facilities.

What do I need to get started?

While you do not need to be a computer 'expert', you will need to be confident about working with computers and possess a reasonable level of knowledge concerning the subjects in which you intend to offer training. Just as important, however, is an interest in (and aptitude for) teaching. You will need good communication skills, to explain to students how they can achieve the desired results from computers and help them overcome any problems they may experience. As with all teaching and training, you will require patience and the ability to get on with people of all ages and backgrounds.

Qualifications are not essential in this field, though anything computer-related will obviously be helpful in demonstrating your credentials. For some types of work (e.g. running training sessions for companies) some type of qualification will usually be expected. Many software manufacturers run special courses on their products, and you should certainly consider taking these if you intend to offer training on the software concerned. You might also consider studying for an adult education qualification, for example the Further and Adult Education Teachers Certificate (C&G 7307) which can be taken at many local colleges. Members of the Institute of IT Trainers (see below) can apply for certification of their skills and the right to use designatory letters such as AIITT (Associate of the Institute of IT Trainers).

You will require a computer in this occupation, though this will be used mainly for preparing handouts and visual aids and trying out educational software. Most actual teaching will be done using your client's computer (in the case of individuals) or in a suitably equipped classroom. Your basic set-up should cost you around £1,000 to £2,000. In addition, you may want to obtain specialised equipment such as an LCD projector which will enable you to project a computer's monitor display onto a larger screen or the wall.

Who will my customers be?

Your main clients will be private individuals and small business owners and managers who need help in mastering computers or specific computer applications. Larger businesses and other organisations (e.g. local government) also engage freelance trainers to prepare and run courses for their staff as the need arises. Specialist computer training agencies may also be a source of work. Finally, you could offer your services to local schools, colleges and adult education centres.

How much can I make?

If you are providing training for an individual, the most you are likely to be able to charge is around £15 to £20 per hour. If you decide to organise and run your own classes, your earnings will be potentially much higher. For example, a class of twenty people each paying you £50 for a one-day training session would bring in £1,000. From this you might need to deduct £200 for room hire and incidentals, leaving you with a handy £800 net profit. If you are running courses for businesses, you would normally quote a set fee: this would not be less than £300 for a day or £200 a half-day. Finally, if you obtain work in adult education or a college you will normally be paid an hourly rate, typically £15–£20 an hour. In educational institutions you are very likely to be treated as an employee for the time you are teaching, and (unusually for self-employed people) will have tax and national insurance deducted at source.

How can I sell my services?

If you plan to offer training sessions on a specific application (e.g. Pegasus Accounts), it is important to obtain certified or licensed trainer status from the company concerned. This will generally involve taking a short course and passing an examination. The company will then pass on to you any enquiries they receive about training providers in your area.

The manufacturer or supplier should also be able to give you details of local user groups; again, these should prove a good source of referrals. It is also worth contacting professionals in other related fields such as accountants or business consultants, as they may well have clients who would benefit from your training services. Don't forget, also, your local computer shop. Many of their customers will have bought computers or programs quite recently and may need help in mastering them. Establishing a good relationship with your local computer shop can generate a steady stream of referrals.

If you decide to organise and run your own training sessions, you will need to advertise them using leaflets, newspaper advertising, and so on. You can also write to local colleges, adult education centres and so on to see if they need part-time teachers or tutors. The spring, when the programme for the next academic year is being planned, is often the best time to get in touch.

Where can I get more help?

The Institute of IT Training is the UK's leading organisation serving and representing computer trainers. Members receive a range of benefits including professional recognition, a library and resource centre, a free subscription to the Institute's magazine IT Training, and networking opportunities through local and regional groups.

The Institute of IT Training
Institute House
University of Warwick Science Park
Coventry
CV4 7EZ
Tel: 024 7641 8128
Web: www.iitt.org.uk

CRAFT WORK

At a time when most high street shops stock only cheap, mass-produced items, many of which are imported from the Far East, genuine hand-made products are becoming more and more popular and are fetching a premium price. To find out exactly what items sell best, you need to visit some craft fairs – items on sale will include patchwork quilts, knitted garments, turned wood items, candles, musical instruments, jewellery, decorated eggshells, ceramics, toys, wickerwork, carvings and many more.

Another aspect of craft work is that of restoration, and this can include anything from restoring antique toys and musical instruments to stained-glass windows.

What do I need to get started?

Since the field is so varied, the only common feature is the ability to produce good quality work. Quality is the key to this business, as really good work attracts a premium price which does actually give you a proper reward for the time and effort you put in. If you have artistic ability as well as manual dexterity, and can thus produce items which are original as well as being attractive, you will do even better than someone simply turning out 'standard' items.

Who will my customers be?

Your customers will be people looking for unusual and attractive items, either as special gifts (e.g. for birthday, anniversary or retirement presents) or to adorn their own homes. If you find your product is popular, you may be able to sell it through shops and other outlets such as mail-order companies.

How much can I make?

Since this field is so varied typical earnings are difficult to specify, but you should aim to earn at least a living wage after paying for your raw materials and marketing expenses. If your product proves popular, you may be able to move on to employing other staff, and thus earn rather more.

One problem with making craft items to sell is that unless you are able to find some shops who want a regular supply, your income will be erratic. Many weeks may pass while you build up your stock for the next craft fair, and a high proportion of sales occurring in the run-up to Christmas.

How can I sell my services?

If selling to gift shops, you will need to make up samples and do the rounds of the likeliest shops seeking orders, having first done your costings carefully. You will find that many will only accept your products on a 'sale or return' basis, and the prices they offer you may be very low when set against all the time and effort you've put in.

Craft fairs are a much better way to sell handcrafted items, so long as they are not too expensive (items costing under £10 generally sell best). You will need to book stands at appropriate fairs well in advance, and will require a good supply of stock for each one. An alternative, or additional, way to make money from craft work is to supply kits or the raw materials for other people to make up items, rather than actually producing them yourself.

For high value items, craft services and restoration work, you will do better to advertise in appropriate publications. For instance, if you are an ornamental stone mason, *Country Life* could be your ideal advertising medium. Finally, don't forget that local papers like to run stories about successful craftsmen and women in their area. If you win an award or a prestigious contract, therefore, take a few moments to write a press release and send it to the local media. The resulting coverage could well generate a range of enquiries from potential clients.

Where can I get more help?

There are numerous magazines on each type of craft work, and many book publishers who produce books on crafts. One of the best known of these is the Guild of Master Craftsmen; they also offer membership and assistance to craft workers. Don't forget, either, your local library, which should have a good selection of crafts books, including some which are out of print. A recently published book called 'Secrets of the Craft Business' includes information on how to sell craft products through agents, and lists sources of craft materials at wholesale prices. It is not available from bookshops, but can be purchased for £20 from Turning Point, Cornerways, Gorran, Cornwall, PL26 6LR.

The Crafts Council publishes 'Running A Workshop', a 250 page book providing detailed information on starting and running a crafts business. Subjects covered include researching the market, type of business, tax and national insurance, photographing work, selling to craft galleries, selling by commission, exhibiting, selling abroad, copyright, promotion and publicity, and health and safety. The price is £7.50 plus £2.00 post and packing. Order by phone on 020 7806 2558 or via the Crafts Council website (see below).

Crafts businesses often grow from a hobby, and for those who are serious about turning their hobby into a business there are grants available from the Crafts Council, local Training and Enterprise Councils (to be replaced by Learning and Skills Councils) and the Rural Development Commission. For those under thirty, the

Prince's Youth Business Trust also offers grants and low interest loans.

The Crafts Council
44a Pentonville Road
London
N1 9BY
Tel: 020 7278 7700
Web: www.craftscouncil.org.uk

Rural Development Commission
Tel: 020 7276 6969 for local office details

The Prince's Youth Business Trust
Tel: 020 7321 6500 for local office details

The Guild of Master Craftsmen
86 High Street
Lewes
East Sussex
BN7 1XN
Tel: 01273 477374

CURTAINS AND LOOSE COVERS

Although both curtains and loose covers are widely available in the shops, good quality versions are not so easy to come by. Neither, if you are not that way inclined (and many people are not), is the ability to know what will suit any given home and its occupants, and this is where you can come in. Many people prefer to have their home re-curtained without the hassle of having to measure up themselves or worry about rings or ruflette tape. They also like to have curtains which suit their style of living and personality, and loose covers to match. All of this is less easy for the average person to achieve than just going along with the current fashion.

Customers are prepared to pay a good price for this service, but in return they do demand top-quality workmanship.

What do I need to get started?

The most important things you need are the expertise to make all types of curtain and loose cover, plus an excellent knowledge of what fabrics are currently available (and where to find matches for older fabrics). You need to be able to work fast and accurately, having first taken precise measurements. You also need a fair store of tact, as many of your customers will have unrealistic ideas of what can be achieved, and they may also present you with quantities of unsuitable fabrics which they want you to use.

Once you are established, it helps if you carry your own fabric samples, and you may be able to do a deal with some suppliers to get discounts on their fabrics. And of course, unless you are using out-workers to make up your products, you will need a good sewing machine with all the appropriate attachments, as well as other tools and equipment for cutting, piercing and ironing, and a large worktable to lay things out on.

You will certainly need some transport to reach your customers' homes or offices, and to deliver the finished products.

Who will my customers be?

Many of your clients will be private householders, especially young professionals who do not have the time or the inclination to traipse around the shops choosing their own soft furnishings. There is also a possibility of curtain work from large firms of builders who want their show homes 'dressed', and from businesses who want to adorn their office windows with something better than Venetian blinds.

You may also find work through, or for, firms of upholsterers and (possibly) antique dealers.

How much can I make?

In general, you should price your labour at between £5 and £10 per hour. Experience will tell you how long it will take to make up any given type of curtain or loose cover. Set your prices to cover this plus the cost of materials (if you are supplying them), and add an amount for the initial consultation and measurements, remembering that not every consultation will result in an order. If customers ask you to leave your measurements and fabric recommendations with them while they 'think about it', you should charge them up front for this service, as they are quite likely to take these and get the job done elsewhere.

You can make extra money by bulk-buying such items as lining fabrics, threads and fittings (ruflette tape, curtain rings and so on) and charging your customers the retail price for them. If you make a point of buying all your supplies and main fabrics from one outlet, you should also be able to obtain volume discounts or bonuses from them.

How can I sell my services?

The main method is by placing advertisements in your local papers and Yellow Pages. Once you are established, you will find much of your work comes from personal recommendations.

As well as interior designers and upholsterers, you may be able to obtain some work through fabric shops or even dry cleaners. Leave batches of business cards or brochures with them.

Where can I get more help?

There are many magazines for home-makers and interior designers which will provide invaluable information, both in their editorial and advertisement sections, and of course there will be many books in your local library to help you with technical details.

There are also City & Guilds courses available in upholstery and soft furnishings throughout the country.

Guild of Master Craftsmen
166 High Street
Lewes
Sussex
BN7 1XU
Tel: 01273 478449

Association of Master Upholsterers and Soft Furnishers
102a Commercial Street
Newport
South Wales
NP9 1LU
Tel: 01633 215454

DESKTOP PUBLISHING

Modern technology has made it possible for individuals to design and produce highly professional-looking documents on computer. Desktop publishing, as this is known, eliminates many of the stages required in the normal publishing process: paste-up and typesetting, for example. What's more, the advanced software (programs) now available mean that you no longer require years of training and experience to get presentable results.

There is a huge market for desktop publishing services among businesses and other organisations large and small. The range of documents you may be asked to produce is equally varied, spanning logos and letterheads, business cards, press advertisements, leaflets and brochures, posters, newsletters, reports, price lists, posters and presentation materials of all kinds. In today's highly competitive marketplace, crudely typed and photocopied documents are no longer acceptable. Printed materials of all kinds are expected to look good and be produced quickly.

With the wide range of work on offer, some desktop publishers choose to specialise in a particular field, e.g. newsletters. Others enjoy working on a variety of different projects. Whichever path you choose, running your own home-based desktop publishing business can be both creative and fulfilling, though sometimes (with tight deadlines the norm) quite highly pressurised.

What do I need to get started?

Qualifications are not essential when starting out, but you will need good general computer skills and the ability to use ancillary technology such as scanners. A thorough knowledge of the desktop publishing software you will be using is essential. You will require skills in design and typography, and the ability to write and edit other people's writing. You will also need proofreading skills, and should know (or learn) the standard BS marks, as these may be used by your clients when 'marking up' proofs.

Many jobs have to be completed to a tight deadline, so you will need to be well organised and conscientious; you must be prepared to work through the night if necessary if a client needs a particular job finished for the next day. You will need good communication skills, both to sell your services and to draw out from clients what exactly they require (visual concepts are notoriously hard to put into words). Patience can also be a necessity, as clients may change their minds several times before they are satisfied.

So far as equipment is concerned, you will need a good modern computer: either a Macintosh or an IBM-compatible. At one time Macintosh computers were *de rigueur* for people in the design field, but nowadays there is very little to choose. Macintoshes have a reputation for being more 'user-friendly', but IBM-compatibles – by far the bigger sellers – have a wider range of software available for them and are likely to become even more dominant in the future.

Other requirements include a high quality laser printer and scanner (for scanning artwork and text into your computer). You will also need desktop publishing software. Your choice will be to some extent dictated by the type of work in which you intend to specialise. However, you are likely to need a page design program (Microsoft Publisher, Aldus Pagemaker, Quark Express), a word processor (Microsoft Word, Corel WordPerfect, Lotus Word Pro), and a drawing program (Adobe Illustrator, Corel Draw).

Who will my customers be?

Businesses of all types and sizes are potential clients. A local factory may need you to produce a price list or monthly newsletter; shops may want you to prepare attractive-looking handbills and point-of-sale material; and restaurants may require your services to produce eye-catching press advertisements and menus. Other potential clients include charities and other organisations such as churches, political groups and parent-teacher associations. Even private individuals may require your services on occasion, e.g. to produce wedding invitations or personal stationary. Finally, other home-based businesses are also likely to be in the market for your services, e.g. to design an attractive logo and letterhead for them.

How much can I make?

A good way to find out the 'going rate' in your area is to go to your local print shop and ask them to quote for designing some business stationary for you. The chances are you will be surprised by how expensive it is. Of course, the print shop is likely to have higher overheads than you (e.g. the chances are they will have to pay business rates, rent, staff costs and so on), but even so you should use their rates as a general guide to the fees you should be asking.

There are three main ways for charging for desktop publishing services: by the hour, by the page or by the job. The minimum rate you should consider is £15 an hour, while £25 plus may be more realistic. You should charge more for colour work than black-and-white. If charging by the page, typical prices vary between £15 and £30, again with more for colour. In practice clients will normally ask you to quote a price for each job, so you should use these rates to guide you in setting your prices rather than quoting them directly to your client.

The initial cost of setting up as a desktop publisher can be relatively high (though prices have fallen in recent years), but once you have bought the necessary equipment and software your day-to-day running costs should be fairly low. A full-time home-based desktop publishing business can expect to bring in at least £15,000 a year, rising to £30,000 or more if you gain a good reputation within your speciality.

How can I sell my services?

Start by preparing a leaflet advertising your services (ensure it is your best work – in this business above all others you cannot afford to send out second-rate advertising material) and deliver it to businesses in your local area – by post, by hand, or by means of a leafletting service. Another option would be to advertise in the business-to-business section of your local paper. It is also well worth getting a listing in your local Yellow Pages and Thomson's Directory (if one is published for your area).

Another idea is to contact local printers to offer your services. Though most will have a member of staff who can do basic desktop publishing, they may well need someone to provide extra cover during busy periods and holidays. In addition, if you have specialist skills and/or equipment, they may be able to refer some business in your direction. Although printers are your competitors to some extent, on many occasions your roles will be complementary (e.g. you may have to take your finished artwork to a printer to have copies made on their litho machine). It is therefore in your interests (and theirs) to develop a good working relationship.

Where can I get more help?

If you wish to study for a qualification in this field, enquire at your local FE college regarding part-time courses. Distance learning (correspondence) courses in desktop publishing and related fields are available from various providers. One is the National Extension College (NEC), which offers courses in desktop publishing, design and editing, as well as a range of home-study courses on computing. National Extension College courses are independently assessed by the Open and Distance Learning Quality Council to ensure they meet the highest possible standards. NVQs and other qualifications may be available.

The National Extension College
18 Brooklands Avenue
Cambridge
CB2 2HN
Tel: 01223 450200
Web: www.nec.ac.uk

DIY AND ODD-JOBBING

There are many little jobs which need doing around the modern home, from replacing tap washers to putting up shelves, not to mention the nasty ones like cleaning out drains and gutters. While many people are willing and able to do these jobs for themselves, others (including many older people) are not, and are happy to pay someone else to get them done.

Although this is usually thought of as a man's business, there is no reason why a competent woman should not do it. Many women, especially the elderly, are unsure of inviting men into their homes but would be happy to engage a female DIYer.

The more tasks you can tackle, the more work you will get, and you might even like to offer an all-in service. For instance, spending a half-day in someone's home and doing all those little jobs that aren't worth a special visit, such as rewiring plugs, dealing with dripping taps, or replacing a cupboard hinge.

There are some tasks which you should not do unless you have the proper qualifications, such as rewiring a house, and some which you are forbidden by law from doing without the relevant qualification, such as fixing gas appliances.

What do I need to get started?

The most important thing you need is the expertise to do a good job in a reasonable length of time.

You will need a well-stocked toolkit including such items as hammers and screwdrivers, spirit levels and rulers, chisels and saws, an electric drill with a range of attachments and so on, plus plenty of consumable items such as nails, screws, clips and washers. You will also need at least one ladder, possibly a portable scaffolding tower, and definitely a good vacuum cleaner and other means of cleaning up after you. All of this means you will also need a capacious car or van to carry all this equipment. Everything else you might need, such as drain rods or specialised power tools, can be hired until such time as you feel the need to buy your own.

Unless you have someone else at home to take messages, you will also need a telephone answering machine to deal with calls from potential customers which come while you are out working. Another possibility would be a mobile phone.

Who will my customers be?

Many will be private householders, especially young professionals who do not have the time or inclination to do their own odd jobs, or elderly people who can no longer cope with them.

Private landlords with multiple homes to let often need someone to perform odd jobs and general maintenance, and it is well worth approaching firms of letting agents for this work.

How much can I make?

In general, you should aim for an hourly rate of between £8 and £12. Experience will tell you how long it will take to do any given job, and you should set your prices to cover your time plus the cost of materials and disposable items. If doing a lot of small jobs for different people, don't forget to include the time spent travelling between jobs in your costings.

You can make extra money by bulk-buying such consumables as light bulbs, screws, nails, sandpaper and so on, and charging your customers the retail price for them. If you make a point of buying all your supplies from one outlet, you should be able to obtain volume discounts or bonuses from them. Where your customers want you to buy a lot of specialised and expensive materials to do particular jobs, it is not unreasonable to ask them for part-payment up-front to fund this.

How can I sell my services?

The main method is by placing advertisements in your local papers and Yellow Pages, and by placing cards in newsagents' windows and making leaflet drops in likely areas. Another good place to put advertising cards is in pensioners' clubs and 'pop-in parlours'. Once you are established, you will find much of your work comes from personal recommendations.

Where can I get more help?

There are numerous books and magazines covering DIY tasks around the home. College and adult education classes are widely available in subjects ranging from bricklaying to electrical wiring, plastering to interior decorating. A number of internet sites also offer step-by-step advice on a range of DIY tasks (see, for example, www.diyfixit.co.uk).

There are no professional bodies which deal with such a disparate set of skills as odd-jobbing, but you might find it worth joining the Guild of Master Craftsmen for the respectability it will give you and the reassurance it will give your customers.

Guild of Master Craftsmen
166 High Street
Lewes
Sussex
BN7 1XU
Tel: 01273 478449

DRIVING INSTRUCTION

With over 3/4 million people reaching the age of seventeen each year and so becoming eligible to drive, there is never any shortage of work for qualified driving instructors. If you enjoy driving and don't mind sitting in a car for hours on end, becoming an instructor could be a satisfying and rewarding business for you. The work involves bringing students from complete beginner stage up to a standard where they can pass the national driving test. Some instructors also offer more advanced tuition, e.g. for the RoSPA or Institute of Advanced Motorists' tests.

As a driving instructor, you can either run your own business or work for a school such as BSM which employs self-employed instructors on a franchised basis. In the latter case you will receive marketing and administrative support from the school, and in most cases use of a vehicle, in exchange for a weekly franchise fee. BSM engage both full-time and part-time instructors.

What do I need to get started?

You will need to be a safe, confident driver. Good communication skills are essential, as is the ability to remain calm under pressure and act decisively when the occasion demands (e.g. your pupil is just about to turn the wrong way into a one-way street!). You must also be willing to work in the evenings and weekends, as these are the only times when some people in full-time employment can take lessons.

To work as a paid driving instructor in the UK you will need to qualify as a Driving Standards Agency Approved Driving Instructor (ADI). This involves passing three examinations. In order to register as a trainee instructor you will have to meet the following requirements:

• You must have held a full driving licence for at least four years
• You must have no unspent criminal convictions
• You must be able to read a standard car numberplate at a distance of 27.5 metres.

The DSA examinations are in three parts and you have to pass them all within a two-year period. Part One is a written test of 100 multiple choice questions on the Highway Code and general driving knowledge. Part Two is a practical test of your driving ability on various types of road (urban, country and motorway). And Part Three is a test of your ability as an instructor. The examinations are demanding, and it is highly advisable to take a course of instruction before attempting them. The total cost of taking a course and completing the three tests is likely to be in the region of £1,000.

To provide driving tuition you will, of course, need a suitable vehicle. By law this must have dual controls so that you can intervene quickly if an accident seems imminent. Your car must be very well maintained (regular spot checks are made on driving school cars by DSA officials). A new dual control car is likely to set you back £8,000 or more. If you work for a company such as BSM a car will normally be provided as part of the franchise arrangement, and the school will also provide administrative support. Otherwise you will also need someone at home (or in an office) to take bookings and enquiries and handle the paperwork for you while you are out on the road.

Who will my customers be?

Your customers will be people of all ages and backgrounds (though with a large proportion of young people) who wish to learn to drive. Some will have an aptitude for driving, others not, but all will expect to pass the test with your help. You may also be able to obtain work from individuals who wish to take the IAM or RoSPA advanced driving tests, or from companies who want the driving skills of potential employees evaluated before they take them on. The armed services engage self-employed driving instructors to provide intensive tuition for some new recruits to get them through the test as quickly as possible.

How much can I make?

Typical fees are £16 for a one-hour lesson, £18 in Greater London. Working full-time you could expect to earn a gross income of around £600 a week. From this you would need to deduct overheads such as insurance, petrol, depreciation on your car and so on, leaving you with a net income of around £350 a week (about £17,000 a year). If you work for a school such as BSM, most of the overheads will be covered by your franchise fee, but the net cost is likely to work out about the same.

How can I sell my services?

If you do not work for BSM or a similar school you will need to advertise. Yellow Pages should be your first port of call, along with Thomson's local directory (if there is one covering your area). If you live in a town with a large student population, you could try advertising in the students union building or in the college/university newspaper. Offering a student discount (around 10% say) should attract a steady flow of enquiries from potential pupils.

Where can I get more help?

The Driving Standards Agency has overall responsibility for driving tests and driving instruction in the UK. People wishing to learn more about becoming an instructor are advised to obtain a copy of the ADI Starter Pack (ADI 14) which tells you everything you need to know before starting instructor training. The pack – for which a small fee is payable – includes the necessary documents to apply for registration.

Driving Standards Agency
Stanley House
56 Talbot Street
Nottingham
NG1 5GU
Tel: 0115 901 2500
Web: www.driving-tests.co.uk

The UK's largest driving school, with around 2,000 self-employed driving instructors on its books, is BSM. They also offer training courses for the DSA examinations, and ongoing professional development and support for instructors.

BSM
RAC House
Forest Road
Feltham
Middlesex
TW13 7RR

Tel: 020 8917 2500
Web: www.bsm.co.uk

Finally, the Driving Instructors Association (DIA) represents over 10,000 professional driving instructors in the UK. The DIA helps instructors with their businesses, and provides a wide range of information and services for its members.

The Driving Instructors' Association
Safety House
Beddington Farm Road
Croydon
CR0 4XZ
Tel: 020 8665 5151

EVENT PLANNING/ORGANISING

This is a business which can cover anything from organising a son or daughter's 18th birthday party up to major corporate hospitality events with several hundred guests. For private customers, the event will be associated with a birthday, anniversary, wedding or some other celebration such as passing final exams. For corporate customers, the event might also be an anniversary (e.g. of the company's founding). It could just as well be a new product launch, a corporate hospitality event such as taking a group of valued clients to the races at Ascot, a sales conference, an annual general meeting, an incentive event for successful salespeople or a prize jaunt for competition winners. Your customers will be people or businesses who have neither the inclination nor the time to do their own organising. For corporate customers, it often costs less to use an event planner than to get their own staff to do the necessary work.

This can be a seasonal business, so it is wise to offer planning for a wide range of events to keep you busy throughout the year.

What do I need to get started?

Basically you need to be a very organised person, capable of co-ordinating several different aspects of each event. You need to have good people skills, as your customers and their guests may well get into a panic when it looks as though things are not going to go smoothly. You need to have considerable experience of the type of events you will be planning, as this is the only way you will know what needs to be done when, and what might go wrong. One way of getting this experience initially is by volunteering to organise events for an employer, a friend's company, a church or other group.

In addition to this you will need a good range of contacts and suppliers to whom you can sub-contract the various aspects of each event (catering, flowers, photography, entertainment, etc.). And finally, you will need some good advertising brochures and – for corporate customers especially – a standard contract so that there can be no recriminations about who was meant to do what.

Who will my customers be?

This depends on the type of event you will be planning and where you operate. In the domestic market, your customers will be ordinary people who want to arrange a party or other celebration. In the corporate market, your clients will be businesses and other organisations, which could include charities, professional associations, clubs and societies, schools and colleges, and the military.

How much can I make?

For a simple party lasting a few hours and involving a few dozen people, you should make £60–£80. For a major anniversary or celebration event involving 6–8 hours' organisation, you should expect to net at least £200. You will make more out of corporate events, as most companies expect to pay a reasonable fee for professional services. In general your money comes out of the 'per head' amount which you charge your customers; the more elements there are to the event, the greater this should be. In general the best paying events are those from which your clients also expect to make a profit.

It is not unreasonable to charge extra for weddings. These are the most stressful of all events and involve more elements than most, especially if you provide a full service with cars, photographs, flowers and honeymoon travel. For elements which are not dependent on the numbers of guests attending, such as honeymoon travel, you should get a commission from the travel agent or other provider. You will, however, have to make it clear in advance that you expect this.

How can I sell my services?

For local domestic events, start by advertising in Yellow Pages and the local papers, and by placing batches of cards with the people who will provide the various services at the events. Many customers will start to organise their own event, only to realise that it involves more work than they expected. They will then pick up your card at the florist's or balloon shop and ring you out of desperation. Once you are up and running, much of your business will come from word-of-mouth recommendations. You should also ensure that your cards are liberally sprinkled about the events themselves for guests to pick up. For a wider customer base, advertise in the appropriate magazines for your specialities; for instance, *Brides* magazine if your speciality is weddings.

You will get some corporate customers from Yellow Pages and other advertising, but you will also need to cultivate contacts through your local chamber of commerce, and do mail-shots to likely organisations.

Where can I get more help?

There are no organisations or franchises available to help the domestic event planner, but for major corporate events you might want to join the Corporate Hospitality and Event Association. Benefits of membership include discounts, meetings, free publicity and social gatherings.

Corporate Hospitality and Event Association Limited
Arena House
66-68 Pentonville Road
London
N1 9HS
Tel: 020 7278 0288
Web: www.eventmanager.co.uk/cha.htm

A distance learning course in event organising is available from Strad Media Limited. In ten lessons this covers most aspects of event organising, including music and theatrical promotions.

Strad Media Limited
8 Trinity Enterprise Centre
Furness Business Park
Barrow-in-Furness
LA14 2PN
Tel: 08707 404011

FOOD PREPARATION AND SALE

There are many possibilities in the food and catering business. They include specialising in wedding cakes; cooking for dinner parties, cocktail parties or directors' lunches, either in your own kitchen or your customer's; and selling home-made cakes and preserves on a market stall. Most of the well-known specialist jam and preserve companies started this way and grew to the stage where they operate from small factories and sell their products directly to retailers. In general it is best to concentrate on some sort of speciality such as cordon bleu cookery, canapés or finger food for parties, wedding/birthday cakes, or the new growth areas of vegetarian and organic food.

What do I need to get started?

Although it is obvious that you need to be a good cook to prepare food, the techniques used for ordinary household cookery are not adequate for commercial food preparation on any large scale. The techniques you need can be learnt at adult education classes, and these will also bring you up to date on the current hygiene regulations.

You do not necessarily need to be a cordon bleu cook, but if you are catering for dinner parties you will require a wide repertoire of dishes to suit modern tastes. It is usual to offer a list of dishes you can prepare, rather than attempt to tackle unfamiliar dishes suggested by your customers.

You will also need good cooking and food preparation and storage equipment: cooker, refrigerators, food processor and mixers, a large collection of saucepans and bowls, an equally large collection of serving dishes, and a number of good knives. If you are cooking in other people's kitchens, it is wise to mark all your equipment so that it can be quickly (and unarguably) recognised.

If you intend to prepare food for sale on your own premises, you must comply with the Food and Drugs Act, the food hygiene regulations and the trading standards regulations (these cover labelling and weights and measures). To find out about these, start with your local council's environmental health department and trading standards departments. They will want to inspect your kitchen to see that it is suitable and that your hygiene standards are up to scratch. They may require certain improvements to be made before authorising you to prepare food for sale to the public.

Obviously to safeguard your customers' health you must be rigid in your hygiene standards when you prepare food on their premises, and in this case it is wise to stick as closely as you can to the requirements for preparing food on your own premises. For example, you should have separate knives and chopping boards for different types of food to prevent cross-contamination, and clean overalls and hair coverings for yourself.

Also, in these days of allergies, it is sensible to offer customers a standard form to fill in listing any allergies which might restrict your choice of ingredients. And, with food poisoning scares also frequent, it is wise to insure yourself against such claims. It might not be you who caused a guest's illness, but it will cost you a lot to defend yourself in court proving this.

Who will my customers be?

This depends largely on the type of food business you run. For small catering jobs such as private parties, your clients will be individuals who entertain at home frequently. For special occasion products such as wedding cakes, although the end-users will be private individuals, your direct customer could be a wedding or event organiser, or the various venues used for weddings and parties. For regular small catering jobs such as directors' lunches, clients will be local companies. Other customers for items cooked on your own premises on a regular basis could be local wine bars or pubs who want a supply of bar snacks.

For items which you make and sell such as jams and preserves, customers could be either members of the general public or businesses which cater to them such as delicatessens or food shops.

How much can I make?

Again, this depends on the type of business you run. For small dinner parties or lunches, you should aim to make £8–£10 a head on top of your costs. For 'finger food' parties it will be less per head, but there will be more heads involved. Home-made produce should give a profit of at least 40 per cent on the cost of production.

How can I sell my services?

For private customers, advertisements in local papers are a good place to start, especially at the times of year when people tend to have parties. An advertisement in Yellow Pages under 'Caterers' and/or 'Wedding Services' should also pay dividends. It might also be worth circulating local businesses with a request that your card or brochure be placed on their company notice board (offering a small discount to employees of the organisation concerned will improve the effectiveness of this ploy). Once you are up and running, you should also get a lot of customers from personal recommendations.

For catering jobs for small businesses, you will need a brochure and a mailshot to bring your services to their attention. Send this to the personnel department.

To sell made up dishes such as quiches or pies to local delicatessens, pubs and wine bars, start with telephone calls and offer to provide some free samples for trial.

For small items such as cakes and jams, take a stall at your local Farmers' or Women's Institute markets.

Where can I get more help?

There are numerous trade magazines for the food industry (ask your newsagent for a list and to order them for you) such as *The*

Grocer, *Good Food Retailing* and *Food Industry News*. These will give you a good idea of what is happening in the industry and will show you where there might be gaps you can fill.

MAFF (the Ministry of Agriculture, Fisheries and Food) issues several useful booklets aimed at people working in the food industry, including 'Success with a small food business' and 'The Food Safety Act and you'. They also publish the 'Foodsense' series of booklets aimed at consumers on subjects such as food hygiene, labelling, additives and so on. The Department of Health also issues booklets on food hazards, food hygiene regulations and temperature control regulations. If these are not available from your local council, apply directly to the addresses below.

If you want to make cakes, jams, pickles or other preserves for sale on a market stall, ask your local branch of the Women's Institute for their guidelines.

Cookery & Food Association
1 Victoria Parade
by 331 Sandycombe Road
Richmond
Surrey
TW9 3NB
Tel: 020 8948 3870

MAFF Publications
Admail 6000
London SW1A 2XX
Tel: 0645 556000
Web: www.maff.gov.uk

Department of Health
PO Box 777
London
SE1 6XH
Tel: 020 7210 4850
Web: www.doh.gov.uk

GARDENING

If your garden grows better than that of any of your neighbours, you might consider using your 'green fingers' as the basis for a profitable business. Chances are that if you're a keen gardener you already have most of the equipment you need, so all you will require is some method for transporting this and you're in business. Another attraction of gardening is that, once you have built up a group of clients, they will want you back at regular intervals to keep everything looking spick and span.

There are various types of gardening service you could operate. At the most basic, you could simply offer a lawn mowing service; many older people and busy couples appreciate being relieved of this routine task. Alternatively, or in addition, you could offer a garden upkeep service. This would include such tasks as weeding, planting (and plant selection), pruning, sowing, digging, sweeping and tidying, and so on. There is also a steady demand in suburban areas for people who can make a neat job of trimming hedges, conifers and other small trees.

If you are more ambitious, you could also consider offering a garden design and landscaping service. This type of work is better paid and can be highly creative and fulfilling. However, you will need a good knowledge of garden design and planting, and some artistic skills or aptitudes. See Where Can I Get More Help? for information on courses you can take. If you decide to offer a landscaping service you will almost certainly need to employ other people to provide labour.

One drawback of gardening is that it is a seasonal activity. It is impossible to work in very bad weather, and clients will generally not expect to see you in the depths of winter. Because of this, many gardeners have another source of income to help see them through the darker months, e.g. 'odd-jobbing' or general building work.

What do I need to get started?

You need be willing to work outdoors in all weathers and be reasonably physically fit. Gardening typically involves a lot of bending, so don't even consider this opportunity if you have a bad back! You will also need to be willing to spend every day performing a high proportion of routine, repetitive tasks such as pruning, planting and digging. Gardening is a customer service business, so it will help if you have a pleasant manner and are reasonably presentable.

Most clients with large gardens will have equipment you can borrow, but you are likely to require more. Good quality electric and petrol lawn mowers are likely to be high on your list of requirements, and you may also need to obtain a wheelbarrow, shears, secateurs, pruning saw and so on. Power tools such as strimmers and shredders can also save you a lot of time and effort for some jobs. You will need some means of transporting your equipment: a small van, perhaps, or an estate car.

Who will my customers be?

Your main customers are likely to be private householders. Gardening is one of those tasks people do not always have the time or the inclination to perform themselves, but nearly everyone wants to have an attractive garden. Prosperous suburban areas with a high proportion of busy 'professional' couples probably offer the best prospects. By contrast, areas with a high proportion of rented or council property are unlikely to provide much in the way of work.

As you gain experience you may also wish to consider offering your services to local companies. A growing number of businesses, especially those based in out-of-town locations, have their own grounds; and to impress clients and other visitors they like to have these landscaped with attractive flower beds, trees, water features and so on. You may offer your services to assist with design and planting and with providing regular upkeep. If you decide to go down this path you are likely to have to take on staff, and perhaps obtain professional qualifications.

How much can I make?

Gardening is not a get-rich-quick business. If you are simply providing a lawn mowing and/or garden upkeep service, you are unlikely to be able to charge much more than £5 per hour. Overheads are small, however, mainly fuel for your car or van and the occasional replacement of worn-out tools. If you offer a garden design and landscaping service you can charge much higher rates, from £10 an hour upwards. The top garden designers and landscapers can virtually set their own fees.

How can I sell my services?

Probably the best approach is to call door-to-door, concentrating on houses with large gardens which do not look as well-tended as they could be. Ask the householder if they need any help with their garden, and give them a copy of your business card or leaflet (if no-one is in, drop this through the letterbox).

You could also put advertising cards in newsagents' windows and on supermarket notice boards. The local newspaper is well worth trying (many have a column in their classified sections for gardening services) and you could also take out an ad in Yellow Pages. Another idea is to offer to write a gardening column for your local paper. You should not necessarily expect to be paid a fee for this, but it will provide invaluable free publicity for your gardening service.

Where can I get more help?

A wide range of open learning courses in gardening and garden design is available from the Horticultural Correspondence College. Founded 70 years ago, the HCC is accredited by the Open & Distance Learning Quality Council. The satisfactory completion of all courses leads to the award of the HCC Certificate. Courses are also available to prepare students for external examinations such as the Royal Horticultural Society's General Examination in Horticulture.

The Horticultural Correspondence College
16 Notton
Lacock
Chippenham
Wilts
SN15 2NF
Tel: 01249 730326
Web: www.btinternet.com/~hc.college/

The professional association for people working in this field is the Institute of Horticulture. The Institute provides a range of services for its members, who include garden designers, landscape contractors, private and local authority gardeners, and so on. Different grades of membership are available depending on experience and qualifications.

The Institute of Horticulture
14/15 Belgrave Square
London
SW1X 8PS
Tel: 020 7245 6943
Web: www.horticulture.demon.co.uk

HOME AND OFFICE CLEANING

Cleaning other people's homes, or offices and shops, is one of the easier businesses to get into. There has always been, and will always be, a big demand for people to do this work. It is also, if you decide you don't like it, easy to get out of, as you won't have to spend a lot on equipment or supplies. The work is not highly paid, but if you go on to establish a cleaning business, with your employees doing the actual cleaning, your earnings can be much higher.

As well as regular cleaning, you could also offer a spring-cleaning or 'just moved into a new home' service. These tasks can be combined with furniture, carpet and curtain cleaning services, which you can either do yourself (hire the equipment as and when you need it) or by working with specialist cleaners who provide these services but do not do 'ordinary' cleaning.

What do I need to get started?

As a cleaner you require little more than the time to do the work and, of course, the know-how to do it properly. Domestic cleaning is usually done during the day, but office and shop cleaning has to be done outside normal business hours, either in the evening or the early morning.

Experienced cleaners often prefer to supply their own cleaning materials and equipment (vacuum cleaners, brushes and so on), as they get to know what really works and what does not. Commercial cleaning materials are often more powerful. Although they have to be bought in bulk and thus require some outlay at the beginning, they work out cheaper in the long run than the materials you can buy in the average supermarket.

If you decide to offer cleaning services to companies, you will be expected to be a properly set-up business and invoice monthly. Unless your business grows to such an extent that you have hundreds of cleaners, it is wise to restrict your area to that which you can easily visit yourself during the day, as it is essential to supervise staff closely. You will also need to understand the provisions of the Offices, Shops and Railway Premises Act which apply to such areas as toilets. You are usually expected to provide all equipment and materials.

Who will my customers be?

For domestic cleaning jobs, your clients will be people who do not have the time or the inclination to do their own cleaning, or perhaps older people who can't physically tackle the work themselves. Some may be moneyed and have no time for cleaning or think it is beneath them. These people may need careful handling, especially if they have precious objects in their homes.

For commercial jobs, your customers will be local offices and shops.

How much can I make?

As a cleaner you will earn about £5 an hour, more in the centre of big cities or if dealing with remote houses in the country where it takes you time and a vehicle to get to work. If you supply your own equipment and materials you can add another £2–£3 an hour.

As an agency which supplies cleaners you should add 50% to the cost of the cleaners, unless you also supply the materials and equipment, in which you should charge double. You will earn about £3 an hour for each cleaner, so obviously the more cleaners you have working for you, the more you can earn. However, until you are certain your staff are reliable, you will have to be prepared to go and do the physical work yourself, so your earnings may again be restricted to the number of hours you can work. Against these earnings, you will have to pay out for insurance to cover breakages or other damage caused by your staff, plus the costs of advertising.

There are a number of cleaning franchises which you can buy into, such as Molly Maid, Merry Maids or Poppies for domestic cleaning, Dublcheck for commercial cleaning, and VIP Bin Cleaning or Wheelie Clean if you fancy cleaning wheelie bins. All of these require you to purchase your franchise and then offer training, ongoing support and, in some cases, access to their national accounts – companies with premises throughout the country.

How can I sell my services?

As a cleaner, the easiest way to advertise is by cards in shop windows, on supermarket notice boards or in local paper small ads. You may even find people looking for a cleaner the same way. Once you have started, you will be bound to get many word-of-mouth recommendations.

For business customers, you will need to get some brochures printed for mailshots, and also to advertise in Yellow Pages. Join your local chamber of commerce and attend functions and local business exhibitions to meet potential customers.

Where can I get more help?

The British Institute of Cleaning Science and the Cleaning and Support Services Association can provide advice and assistance on cleaning and cleaning materials. The National Federation of Master Window and General Cleaners provides information on all aspects of cleaning; they also stock a wide range of professional cleaning equipment, available to members at trade prices. Finally, the British Franchise Association can provide information on the various franchise opportunities in this field.

British Institute of Cleaning Science
3 Moulton Court
Anglia Way
Moulton Park
Northampton
NN3 6JA
Tel: 01604 678710
Web: www.bics.org.uk

Cleaning and Support Services Association
Suite 301
New Loom House
101 Backchurch Lane
London
E1 1LU
Tel: 020 7403 2747

National Federation of Master Window and General Cleaners
Summerfield House
Harrogate Road
Reddish
Stockport
Cheshire
SK5 6HH
Tel: 0161 432 8754
Web: www.nfmwgc.com

The British Franchise Association
Freepost: RG1500
Henley-on-Thames
Oxon
RG9 1HG
Tel: 01491 578049
Web: www.british-franchise.org.uk

HOUSE-SITTING AGENCY

A combination of high boarding costs for pets, rising crime rates and a general reluctance among householders to leave their homes empty when away on holiday or on business has led to a great demand for house-sitters. These are people who move into a home while the owners are away to look after the place, tend the garden and care for any pets. Sitters don't themselves earn a great deal, and most are retired people or at least middle-aged (though sitters for agencies specialising in larger animals such as horses can be as young as 25). If you want to earn a reasonable income in this business you will do much better to run an agency providing sitters rather than acting as one yourself.

What do I need to get started?

Clearly you need to know what home or animal sitting is about, so it is advisable to start by joining one of the existing agencies to gain experience of the actual job. Although not all assignments involve animals, most do, so you will need a rapport for at least the usual pets such as cats, dogs, cage-birds and smaller animals such as rabbits and mice.

To start your agency you will need the usual office equipment and sufficient capital to pay the premiums for public and employer's liability and professional indemnity insurance, plus the cost of advertising and other printed items. You will need a good quality brochure and an agreement for sitters which includes your 'rule-book'. The rule-book must cover such things as the time permitted away from the customer's home each day (normally no more than three hours, during daylight only) and what sitters can and cannot do while living in the customer's home (no smoking, no heavy drinking, no visitors, etc.).

And, of course, you will need some sitters. You should ask them for, and thoroughly check, at least two references. Where specialised services are involved, you will need an additional reference or paper qualification which proves they have the relevant experience and knowledge. You will then need to make your assessment of their suitability at an interview. It is best to do this in their own home, as this will give you a better idea of their personalities than meeting them in your office or some public place. A person who does not look after his or her own home is unlikely to care properly for the home of a client. It is normal for sitters to be non-smokers, and they should be asked to read and sign a copy of your sitters' rule book.

Who will my customers be?

Potential clients include anyone who has a nice home, who is a keen gardener, or who has pets or larger animals. Some will be retired people who take a lot of holidays, while others may be young professionals who travel on business. They will not necessarily be wealthy, as the cost of home-sitting can compare quite favourably with that of boarding fees for a couple of dogs. You may choose to specialise in providing sitters for large animals, or in sitters who can care for unusual plants, in which case your customers will be enthusiasts in these fields.

How much can I make?

The cost of home-sitting is fairly standard, starting at around £30 per day, with additional amounts for jobs which involve looking after large animals. Between half and two-thirds of this goes to the sitters and you (as owner of the agency) keep the rest. Arrangements vary according to the agency. Some actually employ the sitters, while others take their share as a booking fee and the self-employed sitters collect the balance at the end of the assignment. It follows that you will earn about £50 for each week's sitting assignment. As few as two customers each week will earn you £5,000 a year, so your earnings will be restricted only by the numbers of sitters you can find and the number of customers you can attract. Assuming that your sitters do a good job you will get a lot of repeat business. This is not a seasonal business, as people take holidays or travel on business throughout the year.

How can I sell my services?

Agencies who specialise in pet-sitting report good results from liaising with local vets. For customers further afield, advertise in magazines aimed at owners of the appropriate animals (e.g. *Horse and Rider*), some of which have special 'holiday' issues in the early spring. The same applies to other specialities; for instance, if you intend to specialise in garden care the most appropriate magazines are the Royal Horticultural Society's journal *The Garden*, or the newsletter of the Hardy Plant Society. Otherwise you are most likely to succeed by advertising in magazines such as *Country Life* or *Country Living*. *The Lady* is, apparently, a good source of potential sitters but not of paying customers. The same applies to advertising on the internet. Yellow Pages is also a good source of customers. Two existing agencies are listed below; as a means of gaining experience, you may wish to contact them to offer your services.

The Home Service Ltd
Cedar House
Ferry Road
Sudbourne
Woodbridge
Suffolk
IP12 2BS
Tel: 0800 074 6642
Web: www.housesitters.co.uk

Animal Aunts
Smugglers
Green Lane
Rogate
Petersfield
Hampshire
GU13 5DA
Tel: 01730 821529

INDEXING

Some indexers work in-house in publishing houses, libraries and other organisations, but the majority are home-based freelances. The work involves preparing indexes not only for books but for magazines and journals (single issues or volumes), audio tapes, films, computer disks and other information sources.

Indexes must be arranged logically and systematically. They are usually (though not invariably) in alphabetical order. A good index greatly increases the usefulness of the information source concerned by making it quick and simple for readers/users to find any item of information they may require.

An indexer generally starts by familiarising herself with the material concerned. She then develops a list of keywords and phrases which will appear in the index, and decides how these will be arranged. Entries normally appear in alphabetical order, but in some cases it may be more helpful for readers if they are 'nested' under a particular heading. Thus, the index of a book about freelance writing might have as a main entry 'short stories' and under this a series of items including marketing, plotting, competitions, and so on.

What do I need to get started?

To succeed in this field you must have an interest in language and an eye for detail. You must be able to spell accurately and have a good grasp of grammar and punctuation. You will need to be thorough and conscientious, and able to organise your own time effectively.

You will also require a good educational background; the Society of Indexers reports that most of its members are graduates. The majority of successful indexers are subject specialists in one or more fields, and work mainly or exclusively within these. Thus, one indexer might work primarily on mathematical books, another on medical reference texts, and a third on music and ancient history.

Indexing requires prolonged concentration, so you will need somewhere quiet to work. You will also require a good dictionary and specialist reference books appropriate to your chosen field. Most indexers nowadays rely on a computer with specialist software to take care of routine processes such as finding and listing references to a specific term, while they themselves concentrate on the wording of the index. Increasingly, publishers require indexes to be supplied on disk. An answering machine, fax and email facilities will also help publishers contact you promptly.

Who will my customers be?

Your main clients will be publishers of non-fiction and reference books (novels and short story collections seldom include indexes!). Increasingly, also, you may find opportunities with specialist electronic publishers, e.g. for reference works appearing on CD-ROM. You may also be able to obtain work from authors directly. Publishers often expect authors to provide indexes for their books, but many have neither the time nor the inclination (nor, indeed, the skills) to do this, and are pleased to be able to pass the task over to a specialist.

How much can I make?

For simple indexing or adapting an existing index, the NUJ (National Union of Journalists) 'Freelance Fees Guide 1999/2000' recommends a minimum rate of £13.80 an hour, rising to £16.00 an hour for standard indexing. The NUJ recommends that an extra £1.60 an hour at least should be added to these rates if the work is done on a computer screen.

Experienced indexers can (and should) charge higher rates for more complex work or demanding schedules.

How can I sell my services?

Start by writing to publishing houses offering your services. Concentrate on those publishers who produce books within your field (or fields) of specialist knowledge. A list of UK and (some) overseas publishers, together with their main subject areas, can be found in 'The Writers' and Artists' Yearbook' (A & C Black) or 'The Writer's Handbook' (Macmillan). In your letter don't forget to mention any relevant qualifications and experience, both in indexing and your subject specialism/s.

To get work from writers, you could try advertising in journals such as *The Author* and *Writers News*. Members of the Society of Indexers (see below) who are suitably qualified can apply to be listed in the Society's directory 'Indexers Available', which is published annually and distributed to publishers. Publishers looking for indexers for particular jobs can obtain details of registered indexers from the Society.

Where can I get more help?

The main organisation serving and representing indexers in the UK (and overseas) is the Society of Indexers. This non-profit-making organisation was set up to promote high standards in indexing. Members pay £40 a year, and for this receive the Society's journal *The Indexer* and its quarterly newsletter *Sidelights*. They can also attend regular meetings, conferences and courses.

The Society of Indexers
Globe Centre
Penistone Road
Sheffield
S6 3AE
Tel: 0114 281 3060
Web: www.socind.demon.co.uk

The Society of Indexers also offers an open learning course. This consists of five units as follows: Unit A – documents, authors, users and indexers; Unit B – choice and form of entries; Unit C – arrangement and presentation of indexes; Unit D – information sources and reference tools; Unit E – the business of indexing. Each Unit requires about 45–50 hours of study, and each has its own related formal test. Successful completion of all five tests leads to the award of Accredited Indexer of the Society. After gaining some commercial experience, an accredited indexer can then apply for registration. This involves compiling an index of some complexity and taking a short test paper.

INTERIOR DESIGN

Interior design is one of the growth areas of the new millennium. With the high cost of buying and selling property, more and more people are deciding to redecorate or re-model their homes instead (a trend reflected in the huge popularity of TV series such as Changing Rooms). Many people decide to tackle the work themselves, but around one in seven gets help from an interior designer. In addition, a growing number of businesses want their premises to be given the 'designer touch'. All this adds up to good news for people with the aptitude and skills to become freelance interior designers.

The work of an interior designer generally begins with a meeting to discuss the client's requirements and measure and assess the space available. The designer then spends some time developing a design which incorporates such elements as colour scheme, carpets, curtains, textiles, blinds, shelving, paint finishes, furniture, loose covers, and so on. He or she expresses these ideas to the client in the form of plans and sketches. Once approval has been obtained, the designer may then supervise the implementation of the design, engaging painters and decorators, carpet-fitters, builders and other craftsmen as required. Designers may also perform some of the actual physical work themselves.

What do I need to get started?

You will need good colour vision and a sense of how colours and textures can be combined to produce pleasing effects. You will need to stay up to date with the latest fashion trends, whilst understanding the main 'classical' styles and keeping a sense of balance and proportion. Good communication skills are also required, both to understand your clients' needs and to explain to them your proposed solutions. If you will be taking responsibility for implementing your designs as well, you will require organisational and management skills when engaging and supervising decorators and other contractors.

Many interior designers nowadays work with computers, so some aptitude for this will be helpful. Modern computer-aided design software such as Autocad enables you to experiment with different ideas and present your designs to clients with three-dimensional realism. A computer is not essential for this occupation, but if you do decide to obtain one you should expect to spend at least £2,000 on a good modern set-up including a colour printer and design software. Other requirements will include a drawing board, artists' pens and pencils, measuring equipment, and so on.

Who will my customers be?

Especially when starting out, your main customers are likely to be private householders. Prosperous suburban areas with a high proportion of busy 'professional' couples probably offer the best prospects. Areas with a high proportion of rented or council property are unlikely to provide much in the way of business.

You may also be successful in obtaining work from local companies. Your most likely clients include shops, pubs, restaurants, showrooms and offices. Another possible source of work is new house builders; these companies often engage freelance interior designers to provide the finishing touches to their show homes and sales offices.

How much can I make?

Interior designers charge for their work in various ways. Some charge a flat fee for each project, while others quote an hourly rate, typically ranging from £20 to £100 or more. Others add a service charge of around twenty percent to items such as carpets and curtains which they buy for their clients. Still others charge their clients the full retail price for such items which they are able to obtain at trade prices and keep the difference as their fee (thus giving the client their services at a price no higher than they would have paid for the materials anyway). However you decide to charge, it is important that this is clearly understood and agreed by your client, and it should be formalised in a contract or letter of agreement.

A successful full-time interior designer can expect to earn at least £30,000 a year. This business can also be run on a part-time basis, when the annual earnings will of course be reduced proportionately. The overheads in this field are modest, comprising mainly transport costs when visiting clients and suppliers.

How can I sell my services?

Your first step should be an advertisement in Yellow Pages and in Thomson's local directory if there is one serving your region. Look under the headings 'Interior Designers' and 'Design Consultants' to see how others advertise, and see if you can do better! You could also try an ad in your local paper; but you may find you get better results advertising in one of the more up-market colour magazines distributed free of charge in many areas.

Another idea would be to prepare a leaflet or brochure advertising your service and have this delivered to local homes and businesses. If you decide to try this, be prepared to invest in a well-designed, glossy production, preferably including photos of completed projects. Another approach adopted by a growing number of interior designers is to create a website advertising your services. For a good example of what can be done, see the website of Juniper House Interior Design at www.juniperhouse-interiors.co.uk.

Where can I get more help?

A range of courses in interior design is available from the KLC School of Design. Founded twenty years ago, the KLC School is accredited by the Open & Distance Learning Quality Council. Part-time, full-time and distance learning courses are available.

KLC School of Design
Unit 503
The Chambers
Chelsea Harbour
London
SW10 0XF
Tel: 020 7376 7400
Web: www.klc.co.uk

The main professional association for people working in this field is the Interior Decorators and Designers Association (IDDA). The Association provides a range of services for its members. It also offers a free matching service for potential clients looking for a designer in their area. Different grades of membership are available depending on experience and qualifications.

Interior Decorators and Designers Association
1–4 Chelsea Harbour Design Centre
Lots Road
London
SW10 OXE
Tel: 020 7245 6943
Web: www.idda.co.uk

INTRODUCTION AGENCY

Introduction agencies provide a popular means for unattached people to meet others of like mind. At one time agencies suffered from a certain stigma, but with soaring divorce rates and the increasing isolation of modern life, their role in society has become increasingly accepted. Running an introduction agency today can be a profitable and highly fulfilling home-based business.

Agencies fall into three broad categories. The first type uses computers to match members, generally on the basis of a questionnaire which they fill in. Clients are given printouts of around six other members with whom they may be compatible, and left to make contact for themselves. The second type circulates lists of members, including brief details of their age, background, interests, etc. These are sent on a regular (say, monthly) basis, and again members are left to make contact with other members themselves. And the third type arranges personal introductions. In this case, new members are normally interviewed by the agency owner (or a member of their staff) and assessed for compatibility with other people on the agency's books. Some agencies combine two or more of these services, perhaps offering a basic computer dating service and a more personalised (and expensive) 'gold service' with introductions arranged in person.

A problem facing anyone starting a new agency is the need to build up the membership base as quickly as possible, so that anyone joining has a large pool of potential introductions. One solution is to join a franchised organisation such as Elite Introductions. In exchange for a fee, you can run your own introduction agency under the Elite banner, receiving advice and practical support from their head office. You will also have access to a computer database containing details of all members of local Elite franchises throughout the country. This means that, initially, many of your introductions may be to people registered with other (near-by) branches of the Élite network. Élite Introductions can be contacted on 0121 323 3637, or see their website at www.eliteintroductions.com.

Another alternative for quickly generating a pool of compatible people is to focus on a particular client group. There is a huge range of possibilities here. For example, you could set up an agency serving vegetarians, over-50s, board game enthusiasts, science fiction fans, gardeners, teachers, Roman Catholics, skateboarders, etc. To reach your target clientele, it is then simply a matter of advertising in the journals and magazines they are most likely to read.

What do I need to get started?

An introduction agency is very much a people business. You don't need any particular educational or vocational qualifications, but you will need to enjoy talking to men and women and working out what makes them tick. A good telephone manner is important, as most people's first contact with you will be over the phone. You will also need to be well organised and efficient.

You will need some method for deciding who is likely to be compatible with whom. In general, people prefer to meet people with similar backgrounds and interests to themselves. Many couples, however, have personalities which are to some extent complementary; their relationships appear to work because each gets something different from the other. In any event, it is well worth reading some introductory books on this subject, and perhaps taking a part-time course in social psychology.

Finally, if you intend to use a computer to match people, you will need the appropriate equipment and software. Computer programming skills (or a knowledgeable friend/partner) will be a great help here, but failing this there are various 'off-the-peg' matchmaking programs you can buy, and you can generally adapt these to meet your particular circumstances. One possible choice is EROS (Electronic Romantic Operative Software) from Drew Software International. If you have internet access, you can download a shareware (try-before-you-buy) version of this program from www.drewsoft.com/eros.htm.

Who will my customers be?

Your clients will be people looking for companionship of various sorts. Many will be looking for a long-term relationship, perhaps including marriage. Others simply want to meet new people and have a good time (however they define this) without too many strings attached. Still others are seeking friendship. All, however, will be hoping to meet other people with whom they are, broadly speaking, compatible. Potential clients are not just young people; indeed, many agencies find that the majority of their members are people in their 30s and 40s who may be newly divorced or separated and perhaps having difficulty making contact with other unattached people in their age group.

How much can I make?

The amount you can earn in this business depends very much on the type of agency you run and how successful you are in attracting clients. The UK's biggest computer dating agency, Dateline, charges £150 a year for basic membership, plus an extra £5 for further lists of introductions after the first one. Other agencies which arrange introductions personally charge much more: £1,000 plus in some cases. As a rough guide, an individual running a small one-person business can expect to earn around £15,000 to £25,000 a year in fees, rising to £40,000 or more if their agency really takes off. Your major operating expenses will be advertising, publicity materials and stationery.

How can I sell my services?

Most agencies start by advertising in local newspapers. Many areas have more than one such paper, and it may be necessary to try several to find the one that brings in the best response. You could also try putting advertising cards in newsagents' windows. One successful agency regularly uses the Royal Mail's Household Delivery Service (see Help From the Post Office in Part A) to have its publicity material delivered to every home in a particular area. Although this means many people receiving the information will not be in the market for the service, it is possible to target specific areas. Concentrating on those likely to have a high proportion of single people (inner city zones with many multi-occupied properties, for example) could well be a fruitful policy.

It is also worth pointing out that an introduction agency has a certain novelty value which you may be able to exploit to get free publicity. This applies especially if you are aiming at a very specific clientele. Mark Shone, an Elvis Presley fan, set up an agency specifically to bring fans of the singer together. His agency has received extensive (free) coverage in the local press and on regional TV programmes. You can visit the agency's website at www.always-elvis.co.uk, or contact them on 01543 670370.

Where can I get more help?

The main organisation representing introduction agencies in the UK is the Association of British Introduction Agencies (ABIA). To join you will have to pay an annual fee and adhere to the Association's code of practice. One benefit of joining ABIA is that your agency will be included on the list sent to people who contact ABIA requesting details of its member agencies. You will also be able to state that your agency is an ABIA member on your publicity materials, thus reassuring potential members that you take seriously your responsibility to provide a good service.

The Association of British Introduction Agencies
25 Abingdon Road
London
W8 6AH
Tel: 020 7937 2800

LAUNDRY SERVICE

Although many clothes and pieces of domestic linen are supposed to be drip-dry and non-iron, there is nothing so pleasant as crisply ironed sheets and shirts – as long as you don't have to iron them yourself. So, at least, think many modern householders. Which is why ironing and laundry service businesses are on the increase, and why there is still plenty of room for new ones to start up.

There are three possibilities here. You can either go to your customer's own home and deal with their laundry there, get them to drop it off at your premises and collect it again later, or offer a collection and delivery service as well. You can just do the ironing part, but doing the washing as well does put a stop to arguments about how items have come to be stained.

What do I need to get started?

Initially you will need no more than a decent domestic washing machine, tumble drier and steam iron. Of course, you will also need a good ironing board, with attachments for sleeves and collars, and a spacious clothes rack to air ironed garments thoroughly before they are folded. As your business grows you may need additional washing machines and driers. If you find you are doing a lot of large items such as sheets and tablecloths, you will need a proper commercial roller iron.

You will also need some sort of box and labelling system to keep each customer's belongings separate, and some smaller bags for individual items like shirts. If you are to make up a washing-machine-load of items belonging to more than one customer, you will need some net bags to keep each set of items separate. You, and anyone you employ, will need to look clean and tidy, so some sort of simple uniform would be a good idea.

Who will my customers be?

Most of your customers will be single men or other professionals who need a steady supply of smart shirts for work and leisure wear. Others will be householders who want the luxury of crisp bed and table linen, or busy mums who don't have time to iron for their families.

There is some scope for doing the laundry for small local restaurants or hotels, but most of these use commercial linen services.

How much can I make?

Depending on where you are located, you can charge about £1 to wash and iron a single cotton shirt or lady's blouse. Larger but straightforward items like sheets and tablecloths come at about the same price. Alternatively, you can charge by a mixed washing-basket full – about £15 per basket (assuming that it is not a basket containing more than fifteen shirts). You should make an additional charge for using special softeners in the wash or starching. Don't forget to check with customers whether they have any allergies which could be affected by the washing powders or starches you use.

With delicate or tricky fabrics such as silk, you assess the charge when you see the items, but in general you can charge up to twice as much as you would for the equivalent item in cotton or linen.

And you can also make a charge for collection and delivery, based on the distance and the number of items involved. For instance, if you have a to make a special twelve-mile round trip to collect and deliver twelve shirts, you might charge £2, but if you only have to drive three miles to collect a batch of 50 items, you might not charge at all.

How can I sell my services?

As well as the usual advertisements in the local newspapers, cards in newsagents' windows and an entry in Yellow Pages, plus domestic leaflet drops, you might try offering your service on a group basis to places where the workers have to wear uniform shirts, such as police or fire stations.

Where can I get more help?

The Textile Services Association offers an information service to laundries and other related businesses.

The Textile Services Association
7 Churchill Court
58 Station Road
North Harrow
Middlesex
HA2 7SA
Tel: 020 8863 7755

LEAFLET AND NEWSPAPER DISTRIBUTION

If you want a business which provides exercise and fresh air, and are not too concerned about amassing a fortune, leaflet and newspaper distribution could be the opportunity for you.

In recent years there has been a huge growth in the number of items stuffed through letterboxes. Leaflets are particularly popular with local businesses as a means of bringing their products and services to the attention of potential customers. As well as shops and supermarkets, businesses regularly using this method of advertising include estate agents, restaurants, doctors and dentists, travel agents, health clubs, taxi firms, tourist attractions, garden centres and a wide range of other service businesses. Most areas are also served by one or more free newspapers, and someone has to deliver each issue, week in, week out. This can therefore be another regular and reliable source of income.

Although distribution work in itself is not highly paid, if you become a team leader supervising others the rewards are greater.

You might also decide to set up your own leaflet distribution agency, employing other people to do the actual letterbox-stuffing, in which case the potential earnings are greater still.

What do I need to get started?

The requirements to get started in this field are minimal. Clearly you will need to be reasonably fit and enjoy walking. You must also be prepared to work outdoors in all weathers – during the day, the evenings and at weekends. Potential clients will also want to see that you are trustworthy and reliable.

This is an ideal business for those with little or no starting capital. No special equipment is needed beyond a shoulder bag to carry your deliveries (and even this will often be provided by your client). Some form of transportation will be useful for getting to different delivery areas, but a bicycle or even public transport should suffice. If you wish to become a team leader or set up your own distribution agency, however, a car or van is likely to be essential.

Who will my customers be?

Your main customers are likely to be local businesses. Specialist leaflet distribution agencies are potential clients as well; in addition to delivery staff, they also require supervisors and back-checkers (people who make random checks in areas covered to ensure that the householder has indeed received the item in question). Free newspapers engage large numbers of delivery staff and team leaders.

How much can I make?

Rates for leaflet and newspaper distributors can be anything from £3.50 to £6.00 an hour. Fees may also be expressed as a rate per thousand items delivered, in which case they typically range from £25 to £50 per 1,000. Most people should be able to deliver around 100 to 200 leaflets in an hour.

Rates of pay are higher for team leaders, who supervise (and in some cases recruit) other distribution staff and provide transportation to take them to the area where deliveries are required. If you decide to start your own distribution agency, your earnings will (of course) be the difference between what you pay your staff and the rate you charge your clients, less any overheads.

How can I sell my services?

Write to (or phone) businesses in your area, especially those you know advertise regularly by this method. If they do not handle the actual leaflet distribution themselves, they should be willing to put you in touch with the agency concerned. You could also try applying directly to agencies (look in Yellow Pages under the headings 'Leaflet Distributors' and 'Circular and Sample Distributors'). Free papers frequently advertise for delivery staff and team leaders – look in the latest issue for details, or contact the paper directly and ask if they have any vacancies in your area.

If you decide to set up your own leaflet distribution agency, you will need to advertise in Yellow Pages and other local business directories. You could also write directly to local businesses and other potential clients. If you decide to go down this path, you will need to be prepared to spend time (and money) recruiting and managing delivery staff.

Where can I get more help?

The best way to learn about this business is to do it, perhaps initially working for a local business or free newspaper. If you have internet access you can see how some established distribution agencies operate by looking at their websites. West London Promotions provide a distribution service for leaflets, circulars and catalogues in the West London area and parts of Surrey and Middlesex. Their website is at www.westlondonpromotions.co.uk. Another company offering nationwide coverage (in association with the Royal Mail and local free papers) is National Letterbox Marketing; their website is at www.nlm.hertford.co.uk.

LIFE COACHING

A comparatively new profession which began in the USA, life coaching involves helping people achieve success in their personal and professional lives. This sometimes entails face-to-face meetings, but in many cases is done by a series of regular phone calls. Life coaching is not a form of therapy or counselling, but rather a method of personal development. Coaches help people first to understand what they want from life, and then direct and support them as they formulate and follow a plan to achieve their goals. As a coach, your role is to listen without judging, and perhaps offer some new perspectives which will help your clients focus their thinking.

What do I need to get started?

As a life coach, you need to be a good listener, a good communicator, and possess a positive, forward-looking personality. Unlike therapy or counselling, which seek answers from past events, life coaching concentrates very much on planning for the future.

You do not need an expensive office, as most of your client contact will be by telephone. Your clients will want to be able to get through when they call you, so you may want to install a second line (and/or use a BT service such as Call Waiting). You will need some business cards and brochures; and since your clients will be paying a substantial amount for your services, these must be of good quality and properly printed. Computer-generated clip art will not do.

You will also need some training in coaching techniques. Courses in life coaching are quite expensive, and you may prefer to get a flavour first by attending a one-day personal development event. Many of the speakers at these events are themselves life coaches.

For full training in life coaching in the UK, you can either take the two-year internet and 'teleclass' course offered by the American organisation 'Coach University', which costs US$3,495 (about £2,200), or attend the shorter intensive courses offered by the British Coaching Academy, which cost £1,900 plus VAT. (These training costs are, of course, tax-deductible business expenses.)

Another form of training relevant to this profession is NLP – Neuro-Linguistic Programming. This involves listening to the precise words people use to gain an insight into their personalities, accompanied by the careful choice of your own words to make your comments and suggestions more meaningful to them. The cost of training depends on how much you do, as you rise through the ranks until you become a Master Practitioner.

Who will my clients be?

Your clients can be almost anyone, from older people seeking a change of direction in their lives to younger people who want someone to help them formulate a career or business plan. What they will all have in common is a desire to get more out of life, and a feeling that they need an independent ally who can help them recognise and set their goals and encourage them along the road to success.

Typical clients might be middle-class, middle-aged 'empty nesters' who seek a new outlet for their energies, newly qualified professionals who want someone to talk to about career and life decisions, self-employed business people who are facing major decisions which they cannot discuss with anyone else, or even show-business personalities.

You can, of course, choose to specialise in one particular type of client, and your choice will be determined by your own background. For instance, if you want to deal mainly with lawyers, you will need some experience of that profession so you understand what they are talking about.

How much can I make?

A typical client will talk to you for four half-hour sessions each month, and for this they will pay from £50 to £150 per month. You will need more than half an hour of your time for each client, as you will want to make notes on the conversation as it takes place and prepare for each call in advance. But even so, when you build your practice up to a full-time level, talking to eight or ten clients each day, you can earn from £100 to £300 a day. With some high-profile clients such as show-business personalities, you can easily earn a lot more.

You can also earn substantial fees as a speaker at one-day personal development seminars, or go on to train other coaches.

How can I sell my services?

Once you are established, you will find a high percentage of your clients come as a result of recommendations from existing or previous clients. When you start up, you will need to advertise. For specific professions, advertise in the appropriate professional journals, such as *The Lawyer* or *Accountancy Age*. For more general clients, the best medium is the quality newspapers, especially those published on Saturday or Sunday.

If you do your training with The British Coaching Academy, they offer an ongoing support service that helps find clients for you through their national advertising. This service normally costs £595 per year, but is free for your first year after training.

Where can I get more help?

There is no professional body for life coaches, but the following can offer information and training.

Coach University can be found on the internet at www.coachuniversity.com

The British Coaching Academy
109 Victory House
Somers Road North
Portsmouth
PO1 1PJ
Tel: 0800 783 4823
Web: www.britishcoachingacademy.com

The British Coaching Academy also publishes a monthly newsletter called *Life Coaching* from the same address.

The NLP Academy
35–37 East Street
Bromley
Kent
BR1 1QQ
Tel: 020 8402 1120

MAIL ORDER

Mail order is really a method of trading rather than a business in its own right. A huge range of goods can be sold in this way, from designer tee shirts to garden tools, computer software to birthday cakes! Because in this type of business all transactions are done via the post, there are huge savings on premises, staff and so on. Many thousands of mail order businesses are run very successfully by individuals from their own homes.

Products most suitable for sale by mail order are those which cannot easily be bought locally (e.g. novelty items, speciality foods, items for collectors and hobbyists, and so on). Some other products also sell well by mail order, e.g. goods for the elderly/infirm, and goods of a personal nature which people may be embarrassed to ask for in a shop. One of the best mail order sellers is information. This can take various forms, including books, magazines, cassettes, computer software and even correspondence courses. Items which, generally speaking, do not sell well by mail order are heavy, bulky products (too expensive to post), fragile items, awkwardly shaped items, and items which are readily available through shops and other outlets.

You can obtain products to sell from a variety of sources. These include manufacturers, importers, surplus and liquidation sales, auctions, publishers and specialist mail order product wholesalers. The best way of contacting potential suppliers is through trade shows and magazines (e.g. *Exchange & Mart*). You can also create products yourself, e.g. by creating craft items or writing and reproducing information reports and booklets.

What do I need to get started?

To succeed in this business you will need to have – or develop – a good knowledge of marketing, advertising and selecting/devising suitable products. It will help a lot if you have the skills to produce effective press and direct mail advertisements – but if this is not your strong point you may be able to hire others to do this for you. You must be willing to tackle a wide range of tasks, from negotiating with a newspaper's advertising department to fulfilling your customers' orders.

The equipment needed when starting out in this field is minimal. A franking machine can save you a lot of time and effort when sending mailshots and despatching packages and parcels. A personal computer is also very useful (arguably essential) for tasks such as preparing leaflets, brochures and press advertisements. A computer will also be a necessity if you wish to advertise your products via the internet. For a basic set-up, including a colour printer and scanner (for incorporating photos of your goods), you should expect to pay in the region of £2,000.

Who will my customers be?

One of the great attractions of running a mail order business is that the entire world is a potential marketplace (this applies especially if you advertise via the internet). Your customers will be people who have developed a trust in mail order and want or need a product they cannot obtain otherwise. A very important category of customer will be people who have bought from you previously (see How can I sell my services? below).

How much can I make?

A rule of thumb used by many mail order dealers is to charge the customer three times the amount the product actually cost them to buy or make. You need to allow a third of your final sale price for advertising and other overheads, leaving the final third for profit.

The amount you can actually earn in a year depends on a number of factors, notably your sales volume, the mark-up on each item, and the amount you spend on advertising and so on. However, an efficient mail order operation should generate a net annual income of £20,000 to £50,000 or more.

How can I sell my services?

Advertising in specialist magazines is often the most cost-effective approach. For example, a mail order dealer in football memorabilia might advertise in magazines aimed at sports enthusiasts and collectors. In many cases a simple classified ad will be all that is required.

Another popular approach is to buy mailing lists from a specialist list broker and use them in targeted mailshots. Lists are available for a huge range of consumer categories, from hypochondriacs to business opportunity seekers, gamblers to millionaires!

Because of the high cost of advertising, most mail order dealers do not really expect to make much profit on their first sale. Rather, they hope that the buyer will be pleased with his purchase and continue to buy from them in the future. Most successful mail order businesses have a backbone of loyal customers who come back to them time and time again. For this reason, it is important to have a range of products you can offer your customers, and keep on extending this.

Where can I get more help?

A wide range of books is available about mail order trading. One 'classic' in this field is 'How to Get Rich in Mail Order' by Melvin Powers (Wilshire Book Company, USA). There are also specialist distance learning courses. One such is the Mail Order Home Study Masterclass from Streetwise Publications. This covers choosing a suitable product, using the power of advertising, the importance of market testing, expanding your business, and so on.

Streetwise Publications Limited
Riverside House
Claire Court
Rawmarsh Road
Rotherham
South Yorkshire
S60 1RU
Tel: 01709 820033

If you wish to obtain lists for targeted mailshots, the addresses of a number of list brokers can be obtained from the Direct Marketing Association (DMA). The information is also available via their website.

Direct Marketing Association
Haymarket House
1 Oxendon Street
London
SW1Y 4EE
Tel: 020 7321 2525
Web: www.dma.org.uk.

MODELLING

You don't have to be Naomi Campbell to make money as a model. All types of people are needed, including tall people, short people, fat people, 'ordinary' people, and even ugly people! There are also agencies needing people to model specific parts of their anatomy (mainly the hands and feet). You can earn good money from modelling, even on a part-time basis, and it can also be great fun, giving you the chance to rub shoulders with famous film and TV stars. The main types of opportunity available include the following.

High fashion modelling: This involves modelling the latest designer fashions, including cosmetics and jewellery. The rate of pay is the highest of all forms of modelling, but the requirements for acceptance are also very demanding.

Modelling for publications: This involves modelling for non-advertisement sections in (mainly) glossy magazines. The physical requirements are less stringent than for high fashion modelling, but the pay rate is considerably less.

Advertising modelling: This involves modelling for advertisements in a wide range of media, including newspapers and magazines, posters, brochures and so on. Rates of pay vary, but are generally good.

Glamour modelling: In this type of modelling the aim is for the model herself to look attractive and/or sexy (compared with high fashion modelling, where the model's role is to display the clothes to best effect). An elegant lady in an evening dress, the eye-catching face of a beautiful girl, a shapely woman in casual dress, swimwear or lingerie can all become subjects for glamour photography. Most nude photography also falls into this category.

Catalogue modelling: This is a steady source of income for many part-time models. Mail order clothing companies in particular need models to show off their latest ranges to good effect. This is not the highest paid work, but it can provide a regular, reliable source of income for those with the looks required.

Runway modelling: This involves modelling standard-sized clothes at trade shows and conventions, department stores, hotels, exhibitions and so on. Many model agencies specialise in this 'bread-and-butter' form of modelling.

Speciality and character modelling: As mentioned above, this covers a huge range of opportunities for people who have a particularly strong or distinctive feature to their appearance. There is also a demand for 'character models' who epitomise a certain 'look' – kindly, aggressive, gentle, etc.

Finally, it is worth adding that there is also considerable demand for models with acting skills and experience, for work in films, television programmes and commercials. This is another area of work which can prove highly lucrative.

What do I need to get started?

You don't need to be stunningly good-looking to obtain work as a model, but you do need some feature which will make you of interest to an agency (and, by extension, to their clients). The work itself is not difficult but it can be repetitive, making patience and a good sense of humour an asset. Shooting for a TV commercial, for example, may go on for a week or more, with many re-takes until the director is satisfied they have the perfect shot. This does of course mean you can expect a substantial cheque at the end of the job.

To get into this field, the one essential thing you must have is a portfolio. This is a selection of photographs of yourself which you will present to agencies and potential bookers in the hope of getting work. Your photographs must be professionally taken, and are likely to cost you several hundred pounds. This is, however, an essential investment if you hope to pursue even a part-time modelling career. Other than that, your business-related expenses will include cosmetics and fashionable clothing (the good news is that you can set the cost of these against income for tax purposes!). It is also helpful to have your own transport so that you can easily to get to auditions and photo-shoots.

Who will my customers be?

In the first instance your customers will be model agencies. These are the businesses whom potential bookers turn to when they require a model for a particular purpose. There are hundreds of model agencies across the UK: look in Yellow Pages for details of your local ones, or you can get a list from the Association of Model Agents (see Where can I get more help? below). Bookers may include film and TV companies, design houses, advertising and public relations agencies, magazines, catalogue companies, and so on.

How much can I make?

Rates vary but are generally good, ranging from £400 to £2,000 or more per day. The model agency takes a proportion of this – typically around 25% – but for this they handle all the paperwork and administration on your behalf and market your services to their clients. Except for the very top names, modelling work can be intermittent, which means that you may need to combine this occupation with some other source of income to tide you over the barren periods.

How can I sell my services?

Your first step will be to 'sell' yourself to a model agency, and to achieve this, as stated above, you will need an attractive portfolio (some agencies will not even agree to see you unless you have one of these). The US-based website E-Model (www.e-model.net) suggests that a new model's portfolio should comprise no more than three to five pictures, including a head shot, a full-length shot showing the proportions of your body, a fashion shot, and an action shot. You will need to keep your portfolio up-to-date, to reflect your current 'look' and the latest fashions.

Where can I get more help?

The Association of Model Agents represents the leading model agencies in the UK. They will send you a list of their member agencies on request.

The Association of Model Agents
122 Brompton Road
London
SW3 1JD
Tel: 020 7584 6466

If you wish to try your luck as a specialist model, the London-based agencies Ordinary People and Ugly are worth contacting. Ordinary People specialises in character models, including people who simply look 'average' – the man or woman in the street, as it were. Ugly, despite its name, represents not only models who fit that description, but also those who are unusually tall, short, fat, thin and so on.

Ordinary People
8 Camden Road
London
NW1 9DP
Tel: 020 7267 4141

Ugly Model Agency
256 Edgware Road
London
W2 1DS
Tel: 020 7402 5564

PAINTING AND DECORATING

Most people today expect to live in a nicely decorated home. Many are prepared to do their own painting and decorating, but a high proportion are happy to pay someone else to do the work. Even those who are prepared to do their own interior decorating will get a professional to repaint the outside of their house, and you may therefore find that much of your work is exteriors. It is, however, unwise to limit yourself to exteriors, as this work is very seasonal and dependent on good weather.

What do I need to get started?

The most important thing you need is the expertise to do a good job in a reasonable length of time. You also need a fair store of tact, as some of your customers will have unworkable ideas of what they want, and may also produce unsuitable materials which they want you to use. Once you are established, it helps if you carry your own paper and paint samples. You may be able to do a deal with some suppliers to get discounts.

As well as obvious consumable supplies like paint and brushes, you will also need some basic equipment, including a set of ladders, a paper-cutting table, and possibly a steam paper stripper and electric paint strippers (though these can be hired when you start up). If you also intend to do exterior painting, you will need a portable scaffolding tower. You will require a good vacuum cleaner and other means of cleaning up behind you as you work. You will also need a telephone answering machine (and/or mobile phone) to deal with calls from potential customers which come when you are out working.

Who will my customers be?

Many will be private householders, especially young professionals who do not have the time or inclination to do their own decorating, or the elderly who can no longer cope with it. Private landlords often have a policy of redecorating homes when each set of tenants leaves, and it is well worth approaching firms of letting agents for this work. There is also a possibility of decorating work from large firms of builders.

Young professional couples may want special paint finishes such as rag-rolling or marbling; the elderly, in contrast, are likely to want a simple, traditional job with basic finishes.

How much can I make?

In general, you should work on the basis of an hourly rate of between £8 and £12. Experience will tell you how long it will take to do any given job, and you should set your prices to cover this, plus the cost of materials and consumable items. You can charge a little more for fashionable special paint finishes such as marbling or stencilling.

You can make extra money by bulk-buying such items as lining paper, undercoat and consumables (brushes, rollers, etc.) and charging your customers the retail price for them. If you make a point of buying all your supplies from one outlet, you should also be able to obtain volume discounts or bonuses from them. Where your customers want you to buy a lot of specialised and expensive materials, it is not unreasonable to ask them for a payment up-front to fund this.

How can I sell my services?

The main method is by placing advertisements in your local papers and Yellow Pages and also by placing cards in newsagents' windows and making leaflet drops in likely areas. Another good place to put advertising cards is in pensioners' clubs. Once you are established, you will find much of your work comes from personal recommendations.

You may be able to obtain some work from interior designers, or from other small businesses such as carpenters or odd-jobbers. The latter are often asked if they know anyone who does decorating.

Where can I get more help?

There are several trade associations covering this business. As well as providing leaflets with advice on starting and running your decorating business, they also negotiate with suppliers to provide discounts for their members. Membership has the additional benefit of providing you with the respectability which will reassure potential customers.

There are City & Guilds courses available in painting and decorating throughout the country.

British Decorators Association
32 Coton Road
Nuneaton
Warwickshire
CV11 5TW
Tel: 01203 353776

Web: www.british-decorators.co.uk
Guild of Master Craftsmen
166 High Street
Lewes
Sussex
BN7 1XU
Tel: 01273 478449

UK Trades Confederation
Braintree House,
Braintree Road
Ruislip
Middlesex
HA4 0EJ
Tel: 020 8842 4442
Web: www.uktc.org

PARTY PLAN SELLING

This is a business where you demonstrate and then sell goods to small groups of people in a private home, taking a commission on every sale. The homeowner is called the hostess (they are almost always female) and the other people are her neighbours and friends. The hostess invites her guests to a 'party' at which she provides tea and coffee (or in some cases wine) and snacks to provide the party atmosphere. In return for hosting the party, the homeowner receives a gift from the parent company. The thinking behind party plan selling is that it allows the guests plenty of time to handle and try the products in a relaxed atmosphere, which they can't always do satisfactorily in a shop.

Probably the best-known example of party plan selling is Tupperware, the kitchen equipment manufacturer, but there are many others, including companies selling books, photograph albums, fashion jewellery and accessories, 'adult' products, diet and health foods, skin care and cosmetics, and even energy products and services (gas and electricity).

What do I need to get started?

First, you need some friends and acquaintances who will host parties for you. Once you have done a few parties, you should find that many of the guests will be prepared to host parties at their homes as well. There is also, of course, nothing to stop you organising some parties at your own home.

Then you need a range of products to sell, and you should choose one which appeals to you personally. The whole essence of this business is that your enthusiasm for the products encourages the guests to buy, and this will not work if you do not truly believe in them. You should, ideally, choose products which cannot be bought elsewhere, such as Tupperware or Avon cosmetics, and a company which has a wide range of products. Otherwise you will soon find you have reached saturation point for sales in your area.

It is wise to choose a company where your situation is that of an order-taker rather than a supplier who has to purchase quantities of the products and then sell them on. If you do choose the latter, you should ensure the company will accept returns of unsold stock and give you a full refund for them if you want to finish. Ideally your chosen company should be a member of the Direct Sales Association, which has a code of conduct that covers such relationships with salespeople.

Some companies ask you to pay for your basic demonstration kit. This can cost from £30 to £60, but samples of products newly introduced after that should be supplied free. Some companies whose products are health supplements or diet plans will expect you to use their products for a period before starting to sell them. All the companies which produce jewellery, cosmetics or fashion accessories will expect you to wear their products when demonstrating them.

You will receive training in both selling techniques and the merits of the actual products, either directly from the company or from your local supervisor.

Who will my customers be?

Your clients will be ordinary members of the public who are invited to the parties. In most cases the great majority will be female. Occasionally they will pass your phone number to their friends who will telephone you for supplies of the products.

How much can I make?

Commissions vary from product to product but are usually around the 30% level. Most of the main companies say you should be able to earn £5,000 a year working a few evenings a week, and £20,000 a year or more if you work full-time. There are often incentive schemes with cash bonuses or foreign holidays for the most successful salespeople.

There is normally some provision for successful salespeople to rise through the ranks into supervisory positions, when you will then be organising the salespeople for a large area. This does, however, require a much larger time commitment and may even be a salaried full-time job.

Some companies in this field operate multi-level marketing (MLM) programmes. These involve salespeople recruiting other sellers, and then getting a small commission from sales achieved by these people as well as themselves. There is nothing necessarily wrong with this, as long as you do not fall foul of one of the less reputable MLM organisations which require you to make a payment to join their scheme on the basis that you can then earn more money by recruiting others. This practice is not only unethical, it is illegal.

Where can I get more help?

The Direct Selling Association produces a free booklet which lists all its members, with a note of which ones operate using party plan. This will give you a good idea of the range of products sold by this method, as well as providing the necessary contact details. This information is also available via the DSA website.

The Direct Selling Association
29 Floral Street
London
WC2 9DP
Tel: 020 7497 1234
Web: www.dsa.org.uk

See also the article earlier in this book about Commission Selling.

PERSONAL FITNESS TRAINER

If you are physically fit yourself and would enjoy helping others achieve a similar condition, this could be the ideal opportunity for you. Personal fitness trainers design workout routines for individuals and small groups. They guide their clients through these routines three or four times a week, either in their own homes or in a gym. As well as exercise plans, trainers also advise and assist clients with other aspects of their lifestyle, most notably their diet. For many clients the main aim is to lose weight, and diet and exercise both play a very important part in this.

What do I need to get started?

To work as a personal fitness trainer you will need to be fit and healthy-looking. The work involves building close personal relationships with your clients, so you will need a pleasant personality and the ability to get on well with all types of people. You will also need motivational skills to encourage your clients to exert themselves to achieve greater benefits, whilst always being aware of the need to avoid going beyond safe limits. As well as practical exercise routines, you will need a good knowledge of exercise theory and nutrition.

It is not essential to possess qualifications, but in practice if you do not you are likely to be at a disadvantage. The main recognised qualification for fitness instructors is the NVQ (or SVQ) level 2 in Coaching, Teaching and Instructing Exercise and Fitness. Courses are also available at NVQ/SVQ level 1 in instruction in movement to music, gymnasium, step, aerobics, aqua exercise, circuit training and weight training. Full details relating to training as a fitness instructor are contained in the information sheet 'Qualifications for Fitness Instructors', available from Sport England (see below).

The cost of setting up as a personal fitness trainer is minimal. If you want to work with your clients in a commercial gym you will need to be a member yourself, but if this occupation appeals to you the chances are you will belong to a gym already. You will not need much in the way of equipment, as clients normally provide this themselves. Some personal fitness trainers even sell fitness equipment to their clients, thus providing them with an additional source of income.

Who will my customers be?

Your clients will be men and women, mainly in their thirties and forties, who wish to lose weight and improve their appearance and general well-being. Many will be in occupations which are well paid but sedentary. This means they may get little exercise, and they may also suffer from stress and a poor diet.

How much can I make?

The fees you can ask depend upon the 'going rate' in your area and your personal reputation, but most personal trainers charge in the region of £30 to £50 an hour. Trainers typically provide three one-hour sessions a week, giving a weekly return of around

£120 per client. Working with just seven clients on this basis would give you a gross income of over £40,000 a year. There is, however, invariably a high dropout rate among clients, so you will need to be marketing your services constantly to make up for individuals who fall by the wayside. Your overheads should be minimal, comprising mainly transport costs in visiting clients' homes.

How can I sell my services?

Gyms and health clubs are good places to advertise, but be sure to discuss your plans with the management first. You could also try doctors' surgeries, slimming classes and local Weight Watchers groups. This is, however, one field where word-of-mouth and personal recommendations are often the single most important source of new clients. Have some attractive-looking business cards and leaflets printed up, therefore, and distribute these as widely as possible.

Another good way of attracting business is to run fitness demonstrations and classes, and offer to give talks about fitness at clubs, business conventions, women's groups, and so on. You could also offer to write a column of fitness tips for your local newspaper. You should not expect to be paid for this, but it can be a very good way of building awareness of your service and attracting enquiries from potential clients.

Where can I get more help?

The main organisation serving and representing personal trainers in the UK is the Association of Personal Trainers (APT). Membership of the APT is graded according to qualifications and relevant experience. The categories are APT Master Personal Trainer, APT Associate Personal Trainer and APT Student Trainer. The APT also acts as an agency, putting potential clients in touch with personal trainers nationwide.

Association of Personal Trainers
Suite 2, 8 Bedford Court
Covent Garden
London
WC2E 9OU
Tel: 020 7836 1102

A wide range of information about sport and fitness training is available from Sport England. They also publish the information sheet 'Qualifications for Fitness Instructors'. This is available free of charge on their website.

Sport England Information Centre
16 Upper Woburn Place
London
WC1H 0QP
Tel: 020 7273 1500
Web: www.english.sports.gov.uk

PET BOARDING

Many people who like animals find themselves looking after their friends' or neighbours' animals at holiday times. It is a small step from here to thinking of turning a favour into a business, but one that should be considered carefully before actually taking that step and doing it.

First, there are onerous regulations with which you must comply, including the Pet Boarding Establishments Act, the Diseases of Animals (Approved Disinfectants) Order, various other health and safety requirements from your local council and, of course, planning permission, which is not easy to obtain.

Second, to obtain the essential licence from your local council, you will have to build and maintain kennels or catteries which comply with all these regulations, and these involve a considerable capital outlay (about £1,000 per cat unit, more like £2,000 per dog unit). As well as the kennels or cat cabins themselves, you will have to lay non-porous concrete bases and provide such refinements as 'sneeze barriers', lighting, heating and insulation, and possibly even cooling ventilation for very hot weather. You will also need to consider fire precautions and install satisfactory fire-fighting equipment.

Interestingly, at the present time, all of these regulations apply only to cats and dogs (although this is likely to change in the future). So if you do not want to get involved in any of this official stuff, you might think instead of boarding small animals such as rabbits, hamsters, guinea pigs or cage birds.

What do I need to get started?

To board cats or dogs, you need to comply with all the regulations mentioned above, and you will have to obtain planning permission. You will need suitable accommodation for the animals you propose to house – cats and dogs in particular need reasonable-sized pens or cages, together with a larger area where they can be exercised (in the case of dogs) or stretch their legs (in the case of cats). To board cage birds, you will need some form of secure housing where you can put the birds' cages or stands (in the case of larger birds such as parrots).

It is essential that you have a good knowledge of the animals themselves, and the ability to recognise when they need veterinary attention. You also need some printed forms for your customers to sign, with your terms and conditions on them – these should cover not only your 'open' hours, but also what happens if people do not return for their animals at the proper time. Although this is often mentioned, it actually rarely happens (it is more likely with dogs than cats). Your terms should also require that owners produce up-to-date vaccination certificates when they deliver each animal.

You will also need storage space and a separate refrigerator for the animals' food, and a hygienic method of disposing of droppings and other waste material such as soiled cat litter. Different councils deal with this in different departments – it might be the cleansing department, or the environmental health department, or they might refer you to a private contractor. Whichever it is, large quantities of waste should not be disposed of in an ordinary domestic dustbin. In the unhappy, but not rare event, of a pet dying while in your care, you will need a freezer to preserve the body until the owners return.

Finally, once you get big enough to board large numbers of animals, you will need some kennel-hands to assist. One person is generally reckoned to be able to handle up to forty cats or twenty dogs (which take more time as they have to be exercised). This does not, however, mean that one person alone can cope with that many animals, even if this is only on a part-time basis. You must never leave your premises unattended while customers' animals are there.

Who will my customers be?

For small animals such as rabbits and guinea pigs, clients will be mainly families with young children, and your business will be almost entirely linked to school holidays.

For all other animals and birds, your clients will include a wide range of families and individuals. Summer will be your busiest time, but there will be a steady stream of animals whose owners prefer to take their holidays out of season.

Larger establishments may be able to obtain lucrative (and non-seasonal) contracts with their local social services department, which has an obligation to look after the pets of elderly or sick people under their care.

How much can I make?

You will not make a lot of money from small animals or cage birds, as many people are able to get their neighbours to look after them. If the owners bring food and bedding, you can charge about £2.50 per day for a single animal/bird and about £4 for two sharing. If you have to supply the food, obviously you add the cost to this. For larger birds, and those which need fresh fruit, you can charge anything up to £8 a day (and perhaps more for parrots which do not behave themselves!).

For cats, the going rate is about £5 per day (£8 for two cats sharing) and you can expect a profit of about 7 per cent of turnover.

For dogs, your charges will depend on the size of the dog. For small dogs, the going rate is about £7.50 per day, rising to £10 for medium to large breeds such as Labradors. With larger dogs such as St Bernard's or Great Danes, you set a rate depending on the amount of food it requires. For difficult dogs, you also set a rate for the individual. As dogs need considerably more attention, you will make more like 20–50 per cent of turnover, the difference being whether or not you have to pay kennel staff.

How can I sell my services?

For private owners, start with advertisements in the local paper and Yellow Pages, plus cards in the windows of pet shops and at your local veterinary surgeries.

For social services departments, try a mailshot to the offices of as many departments as are within easy reach of your premises. They will like you best if you offer a collection service.

Where can I get more help?

The Feline Advisory Bureau offers a detailed booklet called 'Starting a Boarding Cattery', and also general assistance. There is no similar organisation for dogs, although the Kennel Club may be able to point you in the right direction. There is, however, a book called 'Running Your Own Boarding Kennels', published by Kogan Page.

Otherwise, buy some of the many magazines published for pet owners and study the advertisements for animal housing, feed and bedding supplies.

The Feline Advisory Bureau
'Taeselbury'
High Street
Tisbury
Wiltshire
SP3 6LD
Tel: 01747 871872
Web: www.fabcats.org

PHOTOGRAPHY

There are two sorts of photography for money. The first is where you are commissioned to produce prints of your work which you sell to the people in the pictures or the owners of the items portrayed. The subjects could be wedding pictures, studio portraits, or even photographs of people's houses, cars or animals. This type of photography is known as social photography.

The other sort of photography is where your work ends up in newspapers, magazines, on the internet, or perhaps as posters or postcards. Newspapers generally require black-and-white prints, whilst most magazine and other publishers prefer colour transparencies (or, increasingly these days, digital images). What you sell is the right to reproduce the picture, not the ownership of the picture itself, which remains yours. You can sell this right for any given picture many times over.

Whichever type of photography most appeals to you, it is best to have a speciality. This is partly because you will learn what sort of pictures sell best and how to take them, and partly because most people, whether private individuals or professional editors, prefer to use a specialist photographer.

What do I need to get started?

All photographers need three things, the most important of which is the ability to 'see a good picture' – in other words, to know how to frame what you are portraying to produce the best possible result. You do not need to be a brilliant photographic artist, merely to produce good workmanlike pictures. It is also important to be organised and reliable.

Finally, you must have a good camera with a selection of lenses (wide angle, zoom, close-up, etc.) and a tripod to ensure your camera remains steady. You do not need a great deal of gadgetry, or even an expensive 'medium format' camera such as a Hasselblad – most professional photographers today use a 35mm single lens reflex (SLR) camera with automatic focusing (but the facility to focus manually if desired).

Social photographers need a studio where their subjects can pose, or some portable lights to use in their subjects' homes, plus a trade-price supply of frames and albums.

All photographers need access to a good processing laboratory, plus a trade-price supply of presentation envelopes, captioning and copyright labels, and film. If you are computer-literate, and want work from equally computer-literate editors, you might invest in the software to copy your pictures onto a CD-ROM. Not all editors are computer-literate, however, and at the time of writing relatively few magazine and book printers have the facilities to reproduce pictures from digital cameras – so before investing in digital equipment, you should check that you can actually sell the images it produces.

Who will my customers be?

For social photography, your customers will be private individuals and organisations such as schools which organise group photography sessions. If you do a lot of wedding work, as well as the families of the bride and groom, you might get some work through event organisers or the venues used for weddings.

For journalistic photography, your customers will be the publishers of the magazines, newspapers and books in which your work is used, but your contact will be either the picture editor, the features editor or the (general) editor. You can also, if you produce sufficient pictures on a regular basis, sell your work to publishers via picture libraries. Libraries will want an initial batch of several hundred photographs, and further equally large batches at regular intervals.

How much can I make?

For social photography you get paid in two ways. First, you charge a flat fee for taking the photographs and producing proof prints. This fee should reflect the cost of your time, your travelling costs, and the cost of the film you use, plus a small amount for wear and tear on your equipment. Second – and this is where the real money comes from – you sell prints of your work, for which you charge five or six times what the prints cost you from your processing laboratory, plus the recommended retail price of the frames or albums. There is no reason why you should charge any less than the local high street studios, so check their prices before setting your own.

For photographs which are reproduced in books, magazines and newspapers, there is a set of standard fees which are dependent on several factors. These include the size and location of the reproduction (quarter, half or full page, inside or cover) and the circulation of the book or magazine. You get more for international circulation than UK circulation only. However, since what you are selling is the right to use the picture once only, you should be able to sell a good picture over and over again. The absolute minimum you should get is £25 for a single use of a colour transparency. If you sell your work through a picture library, they will pay you about half of what they get for the use of the picture, which again is for a single use only.

How can I sell my services?

For social photography, advertise in the local papers and Yellow Pages. If you specialise in pictures of animals or some other subject area, place advertisements in publications serving people with an interest in the topic concerned. You should also put your cards in newsagents' windows and (in the case of animal photography) pet shop windows, vets' surgeries and so on.

For magazine or bookwork, if you are not selling via a picture library you will have to approach editors yourself and ask if you can visit their offices to show them a selection of your work. Some will be happy to look at samples on a CD-ROM, but others will want to see the quality of the actual transparencies you produce. Before doing this for any given publisher, buy a copy of their publication and make sure that what you have to offer is the sort of thing they currently use.

Picture libraries will also want to see samples of your work before they agree to take you on. As with publishers, there are general picture libraries and those which specialise in particular subjects, such as gardens or wildlife. All can be located through the 'Writers' and Artists' Handbook' or 'The Freelance Photographers' Handbook', which are on sale in good bookshops.

Where can I get more help?

The Bureau of Freelance Photographers offers considerable help to its members, including a monthly newsletter which includes market information, an advisory service and special offers of equipment at discount prices. It also publishes the annual 'Freelance Photographers Handbook', which is available in bookshops to non-members. The Handbook gives details of many magazines and newspapers which use freelance photographers' work, and also lists a wide range of photographic suppliers and services.

The Bureau of Freelance Photographers
Focus House
497 Green Lanes
London
N13 4BP
Tel: 020 8882 3315
Web: www.thebfp.co.uk

PICTURE FRAMING

Picture framers enhance paintings, drawings, photographs and similar items by mounting them in an attractive, well-made frame. Picture framing is a craft-based service for which there is a steady demand. If you enjoy – and have an aptitude for – woodwork and art, this could be the ideal home-based business for you.

What do I need to get started?

You will need an eye for colour and proportion in order to select a frame to display a picture to best effect. You will also have to be good with your hands and possess the necessary carpentry skills. Patience is another essential requirement, as picture framing is a precise task demanding care and concentration.

Training and qualifications are not essential, but it is certainly a good idea to take a course if one is available (see Where can I get more help? below). Given reasonable aptitude, however, you can learn the necessary skills by reading books (e.g. 'How to Make Your Own Picture Frames' by Hal Rogers and Ed Reinhardt), seeking part-time work in a local picture-framing shop, and practising on your own frames.

You will need a reasonable-sized room or perhaps a garage to work in. The equipment required will include a worktable and shelving to store wood, glass, paintings and so on. Tools required include a mitre saw (essential for cutting corners accurately), clamps, rulers, knives, staple guns, a T-square, and a selection of hammers of different weights. Good tools can be expensive, but without them you will be unable to produce frames of a saleable standard.

Finally, you will require a selection of materials, including glass, hardboard and mouldings. To offer your clients a choice of sizes and types of frame (gold, plain wood, plastic, antique finish, metal, and so on), you will need to keep a good selection of materials in stock. Your total expenditure on tools and materials is likely to be at least £2,000.

Who will my customers be?

Potential clients include antique shops, art dealers, museums, professional artists, craft shops, photographers, artists' groups, architects and designers, advertising agencies, and other local firms and organisations. You can also offer your services directly to the general public. Some framers enjoy working with the public, while others prefer to work for businesses. In most areas you will be able to choose which method you personally prefer.

How much can I make?

Picture framers usually aim for a rate of £20 to £50 an hour. They price per frame, taking into account the size, materials used and complexity of the task. A frame that requires thirty minutes work at £30 an hour means £15 in labour. Add to this the cost of materials (at retail prices, which are usually at least double the wholesale cost) to establish the frame's price. Depending on your client, you may be able to charge a higher price based on the perceived value of the frame. A full-time picture framing service should bring in £20,000 to £40,000 a year for the owner. This business can also be run very successfully on a part-time basis.

How can I sell my services?

If you wish to work for businesses, the best approach may be to write to potential clients directly. Prepare a leaflet describing your services, including photographs of frames you have made, and send this with an accompanying letter. You could also try advertising in the local press and specialist publications aimed at artists and other potential client groups.

You could also try selling your services to the general public. The difficulty here is that most people have no need for a picture framer most of the time, so simply advertising in the local press is unlikely to be cost-effective. A better approach may be to advertise in Yellow Pages. Look under 'Picture Framers and Frame Makers' to see how others advertise their services, and see if you can do better!

Finally, don't neglect to attend local art shows and crafts fairs. You could try booking a stall and having a selection of your work on display, but at the very least you should leave a supply of your leaflets and/or business cards in a prominent position. Ensure, also, that all your satisfied clients receive a few cards or leaflets, as they may well have colleagues, friends or neighbours who could be interested in your services.

Where can I get more help?

Part-time courses in picture framing are run at many local colleges and adult education centres. One institution offering short residential courses is Higham Hall College in the English Lakelands.

Higham Hall College
Bassenthwaite Lake
Cockermouth
Cumbria
CA13 9SH
Tel: 017687 76276
Web: www.higham-hall.org.uk

A wide selection of picture-framing materials, including wood, plastic and MDF mouldings, tools, adhesives, clips and hangers are available from the Picture Framing Warehouse. They will send you their catalogue free on request (also available via the website).

Picture Framing Warehouse
12 Heather Avenue
Abbeymead
Gloucester
GL4 5UX
Tel: 01452 610055
Web: www.picture-framing.co.uk

PRIVATE INVESTIGATION

If you're looking for a slightly offbeat opportunity which nevertheless offers good profit potential, private investigation might be just the business for you. The range of assignments taken on by private investigators is surprisingly wide. Just some of the tasks they perform include:

- Tracing missing persons
- Surveillance
- Debt collecting and repossession
- Insurance investigations
- 'Vetting' employees and potential employees
- Counter-espionage
- Personal protection (bodyguard) work
- Process serving (delivering legal documents)
- Statement taking and reporting
- Store detective work.

Of course, not all investigators perform all these tasks, and (especially if you live in a well-populated urban area) it is quite possible to specialise in one or more fields which interest you the most.

Working as a private investigator undoubtedly has a certain glamour attached to it. However, while some aspects of the job can be exciting, others may be mundane, even boring. In a surveillance case, for example, you may have to spend hours sitting in a car opposite an empty house waiting for the residents to return home. Although films, books and TV shows sometimes suggest otherwise, investigators have no special legal powers. Though they must sometimes work at the limits of the law, they have just the same legal responsibilities (and rights) as anyone else.

What do I need to get started?

In the UK at least, no special licence is required to operate as a private investigator. You should have good eyesight (aided by glasses or contact lenses if necessary) and the ability to communicate with people from all backgrounds. Certain personal characteristics are desirable, including assertiveness and persistence. A methodical approach is also important, and you will require a good knowledge of the law as it applies to investigators (though this can be acquired by reading and taking courses). Maturity and common sense are essential, and older people who have 'seen a bit of life' often do better in this profession than younger, less streetwise individuals. A growing number of private investigators are women, and many are highly successful.

The equipment you need will depend very much on the range of services you intend to offer. At the most basic, you can get started with just a phone and a typewriter. A computer with word processing facilities will be extremely useful for producing reports and preparing invoices, quotations, and so on. Internet access is also desirable, especially if you intend to offer a tracing service (much useful information can be accessed quickly and cheaply via the net). Other equipment you may need includes still and video cameras, counter-surveillance scanners, walkie-talkies, tape recorders, binoculars and so on. However, rather than buying these all in advance, you should be able to obtain them as and when the need arises.

Who will my customers be?

Despite the popular image, the majority of the average PI's clients are not private individuals but businesses. The latter may include banks and building societies, insurance and finance companies, personal loan and debt collection companies, administrators and receivers, and businesses of all types and sizes.

Much work comes from solicitors and barristers who are unable – through lack of time or ability – to do the work themselves. For example, solicitors rarely send their own staff to serve legal papers: it is potentially dangerous, too costly, and has to be done properly. Many government organisations use private investigators at times, including the VAT section of the Department of Customs and Excise, and many health and local education authorities.

Most investigators prefer business clients to private ones, as they present more opportunities for regular work, and there is less likely to be any difficulty in obtaining payment.

How much can I make?

Earnings can be high in this field, sometimes very high, depending on the kind of work you specialise in and your ability to attract clients. Payment falls within two main categories: by the hour, or a set fee for specific tasks. Sometimes, particularly in debt collection, the investigator earns a percentage of money recovered (typically around 20%). Expenses should be charged separately, including mileage, correspondence, films, processing, and so on.

Typical earnings are from £15 an hour upwards, depending on the duties involved and the risks associated with a particular task. Many operators earn much more than this. Higher fees should be set for evening and weekend work.

How can I sell my services?

As with many businesses, you should consider advertising in Yellow Pages and Thomson's local directory (if there is one covering your area). Take a look under the heading 'Detective Agencies' in Yellow Pages to see how other PIs advertise their services. You should be prepared to spend some money on a good quality display advertisement, as people will want to see a bit about the services you offer before they pick up the phone. A simple name and address listing is unlikely to prove productive.

Another idea worth trying is a mailshot to potential clients such as solicitors and local companies. In addition, as you become established you may find that other methods which do not involve paid-for advertising can be very effective in bringing in business. These include personal recommendations, business cards (given out freely to friends, acquaintances, clients and so on), referrals, and regular assignments from past, satisfied clients.

Where can I get more help?

A comprehensive open learning course in private investigation is available from Streetwise Publications. This is written by a team of real-life PIs, and covers most areas with the exception of personal protection (bodyguard) work.

Streetwise Publications
Riverside House
Claire Court
Rotherham
S60 1RU
Tel: 01709 360166

The two leading UK organisations for private investigators are the Institute of Professional Investigators (IPI) and the Association of British Investigators (ABI). The IPI offers Membership and Fellowship status for applicants with appropriate qualifications and experience. They also run vocational training courses. The ABI offers a range of useful publications, including 'The Process Servers' Guide', 'Directory of Registers and Records', and 'Countering Industrial Espionage'. They also publish a journal, *The New Investigator*.

The Institute of Professional Investigators
Suite 353, Glenfield Park Business Centre,
Blakewater Road
Blackburn
Lancashire
BB1 5QH
Tel: 01254 680072

The Association of British Investigators
ABI House
10 Bonner Hill Road
Kingston-on-Thames
Surrey
KT1 3PE
Tel: 020 8546 3368
Web: www.uklegal.com/abi

PROOFREADING AND COPY EDITING

If you frequently find yourself noticing grammatical mistakes in books, magazines and newspapers, proofreading and/or copy editing could be the business opportunity for you.

Proofreaders perform a final check on the text of books and other written documents before they are sent to be printed. They mark up any errors they find using a standard set of proofreading marks (either BS 5261 part 2 or the older BS 1219). These corrections are then incorporated by the typesetter before the book goes to print.

Proofreaders may be asked to work in one of two ways. They may be sent the author's original typescript with the copy editor's corrections marked on it, along with a copy of the proofs. In this case they are required to check that the typesetter has carried out all the editor's instructions and not inserted any errors of his own. This task is known as reading against copy. Alternatively, the proofreader may simply be sent a set of proofs and be asked to read through them checking for any errors (e.g. spelling, punctuation or factual mistakes). This is known as performing a straight (or blind) reading.

Copy editors are involved at an earlier stage of the publishing process. They work with the author's original typescript. As well as correcting spelling and punctuation mistakes, their task also includes correcting grammatical errors, eliminating bias or possible libel, and generally polishing the text so that it reads well and conforms to the publisher's house style. Copy editing is a more creative task than proofreading, and also more demanding. Many freelances start off as proofreaders and perhaps graduate to copy editing later.

What do I need to get started?

To begin with, you must have an interest in language and a love of good writing. A good grasp of grammar, spelling and punctuation is essential, though you can take courses if you are not as strong in this area as you ought to be.

You will also need to learn the standard proofreading marks. These are reproduced in a range of writing and proofreading/editing guides, e.g. 'The Writers' and Artists' Yearbook' (A & C Black) and 'Copy Editing' by Judith Butcher (Cambridge University Press). You should also have a good modern dictionary to check spellings and usage, and – for copy editing at least – a thesaurus and style guide such as the 'Guide to Written English' (Cassell).

You can get by as a proofreader without a computer (though one will still be useful for correspondence, accounts and so on). If you intend to offer a copy editing service as well, however, a computer will be a necessity. More and more publishers are insisting that writers submit their work in electronic form, either on floppy disk or via e-mail. As a copy editor you will be expected to transfer this to your own computer and perform the editing on that. Nowadays it is possible to buy a basic home computer and printer for around £500.

Who will my customers be?

Your main clients will be book, magazine and newspaper publishers. You may also obtain work from businesses looking for someone to edit and proofread their brochures, newsletters, annual reports and so on. Writers and aspiring writers may also require your services – in the case of the latter, they may be hoping you can bring their work up to a publishable standard. Other potential customers include design houses, advertising and public relations agencies, printers and typesetters.

How much can I make?

For freelance proofreading, the NUJ (National Union of Journalists) 'Freelance Fees Guide 1999/2000' recommends a minimum rate of £13.80 an hour. For basic copy editing the guide recommends a minimum of £16.00 an hour, rising to £16.50 an hour for more involved sub-editing and rewriting, and £20.00 an hour for project management. The NUJ recommends that an extra £1.60 an hour at least should be added to these rates if the work is done on a computer screen. In practice you may not always be able to get NUJ rates when you are starting out. Equally, however, you may be able to negotiate rates above the NUJ minimum as you gain experience.

How can I sell my services?

You could start by sending a mailshot to publishing houses offering your services. A good selection can be found in 'The Writers' and Artists' Yearbook', mentioned above, or 'The Writer's Handbook' (Macmillan). This is a highly competitive sphere, however, so it may be best to focus on those publishers who are active in areas where you have some specialist knowledge. If you are a keen birdwatcher, for example, you might decide to target specifically those publishers who produce ornithological titles. When you write, don't forget to mention any relevant qualifications and experience.

Local businesses and advertising/PR agencies are also well worth mailing. In addition, you could try advertising your services in publications likely to be read by potential clients. Several proofreaders advertise regularly in journals such as *The Author* and *Writers News*, and this can be a good way to attract business from writers. You could also try advertising in local business magazines and directories.

Where can I get more help?

There are various correspondence courses you can take in proofreading and copy editing. Two well established commercial providers are Chapterhouse and Maple Publishing. The former offer a range of introductory courses in proofreading, editing and improving your English, while the latter offer a comprehensive proofreading and editing course.

Chapterhouse
1 Southernhay West
Exeter
EX1 1JG
Tel: 01392 499488

Maple Publishing
Studio 11, Windmill Place
Windmill Lane
Southall
Middlesex
UB2 4NJ
Tel: 020 8813 9868

More advanced courses are offered by the Publishing Training Centre. These include 'Basic Editing: a Practical Course', written by Nicola Harris. This comes in two parts, part one being the teaching materials and part two a set of practical exercises. You can buy the material and study it yourself; or, for an additional fee, take it as a correspondence course with tuition from an experienced editor.

The Publishing Training Centre
45 East Hill
London
SW18 2QZ
Tel: 020 8874 2718
Web: www.train4publishing.co.uk/bookhouse

The professional organisation for freelance proofreaders and editors in the UK (and overseas) is the Society of Freelance Editors and Proofreaders (SFEP). Members receive a regular newsletter and discounts on training courses and publications. They are also entitled to a listing in the organisation's annual Directory.

Society of Freelance Editors and Proofreaders
Mermaid House
1 Mermaid Court
London
SE1 1HR
Tel: 020 7403 5141
Web: www.sfep.org.uk

RENTING ROOMS OR PROPERTY

If you have a spare room in your house, you can turn it into a money-spinning business by renting it out to a lodger. The good news is that the government lets you earn up to £4,250 a year (about £82 a week) in rental income free of all tax under its 'Rent a Room' scheme. If your rental income exceeds this figure, you can opt to pay tax on the balance over £4,250 or pay tax on your net profits after all expenses are deducted. You can choose which of these two options to take every year, depending which is the more financially advantageous for you.

A more lucrative alternative to renting a room is offering bed-and-breakfast. This obviously has most potential in seaside and other tourist areas, though there is also likely to be some demand near major exhibition and conference facilities. If your home is large enough you could even consider turning it into a guest house or hotel, offering evening meals and other facilities such as a bar and games room. This is likely to involve making structural alterations to your property, however, and the legal requirements are more stringent, requiring the assistance of a solicitor.

What do I need to get started?

Clearly you will need a home that lends itself to this use. Most landlords specifically forbid sub-letting, so you will need to own the property outright or be in the process of purchasing it with a mortgage. The room in question should be of a reasonable size, with easy access to a bathroom. It will also be in everyone's interest if your lodger can get to and from the room without having to go through your own private accommodation.

Planning permission is not generally required if you intend to rent out a single room, but you will need to inform your household insurance company and may be required to pay a higher premium. If you have a mortgage, check the attitude of the lender to your taking in lodgers – some are relaxed about it, but others may object. If you decide to take in a number of tenants there are additional requirements you will need to fulfil. You will have to comply with fire regulations, and will probably have to apply to your local planning department for permission for a change of use. This applies with even more force if you decide to set up as a B&B or guesthouse.

Who will my customers be?

Most people who are new to this business start off in a small way, perhaps taking in single lodgers on a short-term basis: students, apprentices, industrial personnel on special projects or training courses, holiday-makers, and so on. As you become more experienced you may wish to consider taking on longer-term tenants. In many parts of the country there is a desperate need for reasonably priced rented accommodation for people who, for one reason or other, are unable (or unwilling) to buy a home themselves. These include unemployed people and people in low-paid jobs. Whether you wish to take in such tenants is a decision only you can make. On the plus side, many will have their rent paid to you automatically via Housing Benefit. On the minus side, some may possess anti-social tendencies, so you will need to choose carefully.

How much can I make?

Rents vary considerably according to the facilities you are offering and the area concerned. It is therefore essential to check round other establishments and find out the going rate. If you intend to offer accommodation to students, a quick call to the local college or university's accommodation office should be sufficient to find out typical charges. For guidance on bed-and-breakfast rates, contact your regional tourist board (see below). Under the Rent a Room scheme, as mentioned, you can earn up to £4,250 a year without having to pay any tax, though obviously you will need to set aside a certain amount of this money for repairs and so on.

How can I sell my services?

Get in touch with the personnel or accommodation office in any nearby establishments where people are likely to come on a temporary basis: universities and colleges, factories, computer firms, hospitals, teacher training institutions, language schools, theatres and art centres, and so on. A representative from the organisation may wish to meet you and inspect the accommodation you are offering. This can work to your advantage, however, as you will have someone within the organisation to refer to if there are any problems or disagreements between you and your lodger. You could also try advertising in your local paper and in newsagents' windows.

If you plan to offer bed-and-breakfast accommodation, your regional tourist board should be able to assist you with marketing your service. Most have a registration scheme for B&Bs and guesthouses within their regions. These generally involve registering with the tourist authority and providing full details of the accommodation on offer. You will also be required to pay a fee which covers an entry in at least one tourist guide for the area and the opportunity to be listed or advertise in other regional or national publications. As part of the registration requirements you will have to submit to regular inspections.

Where can I get more help?

Full information on the Rent a Room scheme is available from the Inland Revenue in their leaflet IR87 'Letting and Your Home'. This can be obtained from any Inland Revenue tax or enquiry office, and it can also be viewed on their website at www.inlandrevenue.gov.uk. More general advice on renting out a room (or rooms) in your home can be obtained from the Department of the Environment, Transport and the Regions (DETR). Their free publications include 'Letting Rooms in Your Home', a question-and-answer guide to the rights and responsibilities of landlords and tenants, and 'Letting Your Home is Now Easier and Safer', which includes information on the latest changes that simplify the procedures for letting rooms and property.

DETR Free Literature
PO Box 236
Wetherby
West Yorkshire
LS23 7NB
Tel: 0870 1226 236
Web: www.detr.gov.uk/pubs/index.htm

More information about setting up a B&B can be obtained from books such as 'Open Your Own Bed and Breakfast' by Barbara Notarius, Frederick G. Harmon and Gail Sforza Brewer (John Wiley & Sons) and from regional tourist authorities. A list of all the regional tourist authorities (including those for Wales, Scotland and Northern Ireland), including links to their websites, can be found on the net at www.englishtourism.org.uk/who/partner.htm. This information can also be obtained by post from the British Tourist Authority.

British Tourist Authority
Thames Tower
Black's Road
Hammersmith
London
W6 EL
Tel: 020 8563 3164
Web: www.bta.org.uk

SLOT MACHINE ROUND

Most pubs, clubs and other leisure facilities nowadays possess at least one slot machine, and in general they do a steady trade. You might be surprised to learn that many of these machines are not owned by the pubs or clubs themselves, but by individual, often home-based, entrepreneurs. They call regularly to collect the takings and perform routine maintenance, and either pay the owners of the premises a fee or split the takings with them.

In the past this could be a difficult business to get into, requiring a combination of negotiating skills to arrange locations and technical skills to install, maintain and repair the machines. However, several companies now offer this as a complete business package. As well as supplying machines, they will arrange sites for them in pubs and clubs in your local area, and provide training and technical support as needed.

What do I need to get started?

No special skills are required to operate a slot machine round, though you should at least be capable of performing basic cleaning and maintenance tasks (e.g. replacing 'blown' bulbs). The necessary training for this is normally provided by the companies offering this business opportunity, as part of their total business package. Any necessary repairs to your machines will normally be performed by specialist technicians.

You will also, of course, need to buy the machines. Apparently the best ones for people new to this business are quiz machines, otherwise known as SWP (skill with prizes). With this type of machine the law allows you to share all takings 50/50 with the owner of the premises. All you have to do is go round once a week, empty the machines, perform any necessary maintenance and count your 'winnings'. Popular quiz machines include Monopoly, The Crystal Maze, Cluedo and Tele Addicts.

Generally with these machines the player is asked a series of questions and has to pick the correct answer from a range of alternatives. You can buy a basic three-machine package for prices starting at about £4,000, with up to £20,000 for a package of sixteen machines. These prices cover the cost of the machines, training, siting and ongoing support.

You will also need operating licences for each of your machines. These can be purchased from Customs and Excise. The current cost is £24.75 per month, which can be paid by direct debit. Apart from the petrol costs involved in travelling from site to site, this should be your only regular overhead.

Who will my customers be?

Ultimately your customers will be the individuals who play your machines. These are people from all walks of life, though predominantly young and male. In the first instance your clients will be the owners of the premises in which your machines are sited – pubs, clubs, shops and so on. In effect these people will be taking a share of the profits from your machines in exchange for allowing you to site them in their premises. While they will not be paying you directly, it is still very important to keep them happy with your service.

How much can I make?

A slot machine round is not a get-rich-quick scheme. As a rule of thumb, it will take about twelve months to recover your initial investment. After that, however, your share of each machine's takings will be almost entirely profit. A part-time business with three machines can be expected to bring in £4,000 or so a year, while a round of sixteen machines should give you an annual income of at least £20,000.

How can I sell my services?

If you purchase your machines through one of the companies providing this as a complete business package you will not have to sell your services to pubs and so on, as this is done for you by the companies' own sales staff. Once the machines are in place, they will do all the actual 'selling' for you (modern electronic machines draw attention to themselves through flashing lights, music, sound effects and so on). However, if a venue proves less profitable than you hoped, you can always ask to have your machine re-sited.

Where can I get more help?

Two well-established companies in this field are Winfall Leisure and the Nationwide Machine Company. Both offer a complete business package including machines with sites pre-arranged, training and ongoing support. Modern machines are designed to last for a number of years, but when they finally become outdated or worn-out, the companies will accept them in part-exchange for newer models.

Winfall Leisure Limited
Frederick House
Gors Road
Towyn
Abergele
Clwyd
LL22 9LS
Tel: 01745 334294

Nationwide Machine Services Limited
Westwood House
Regent Road
Manchester M5
Tel: 0161 872 4200

TEACHING ENGLISH AS A FOREIGN LANGUAGE (TEFL)

With factors such as the opening up of Eastern Europe and the growing pre-eminence of English as the worldwide language of commerce, the demand for qualified teachers of English as a foreign language has never been greater.

You can teach English on a one-to-one basis in your home (perhaps combining this with renting a room – see Renting Rooms and Property) or in one of the many specialist language schools in and around London and the regions. This is an ideal-part time occupation which can easily be fitted in with other (e.g. family) responsibilities. It also opens up the possibility of travelling to other countries across the world, where trained and experienced English language teachers are in high demand.

Most of the students you work with will be young adults of all backgrounds and nationalities (though a number will be older). Some will have a smattering of English, whilst others will be starting from scratch. Modern teaching methods emphasise the importance of placing language teaching in a real-life context. As well as classroom work, therefore, you are likely to find yourself taking students on visits to amenities such as pubs, cinemas and bowling alleys, where they can practise their English and improve their knowledge of English life and culture.

What do I need to get started?

It goes without saying that you will need excellent communication skills and the ability to get on well with people from all nationalities. You will also need all the traditional attributes of teachers, including patience and perseverance. A sense of humour is a great asset as well.

You will also need good spoken and written English yourself, including a knowledge of grammar, spelling and punctuation. Many native English speakers have an intuitive grasp of these matters, but to teach the subject to others you will also need a theoretical understanding of how English works. TEFL training courses will help fill in any gaps in your knowledge, of course.

There is no legal requirement to have a qualification to teach English as a foreign language, but you are unlikely to obtain a position with a reputable language school without one. Apart from this, the knowledge you gain through studying will be of immense benefit to you in your teaching work. Many institutions offer short, introductory courses in teaching English as a foreign language. The standard qualification, however, is the Cambridge/RSA Certificate in English Language Teaching to Adults (CELTA). This highly practical course includes classroom management, lesson planning, and developing skills in reading, listening, speaking and writing. Full-time courses take around four weeks, part-time around twelve. The fees are around £1,000 in each case.

Who will my customers be?

You will be working with people of all nationalities who, for work or domestic reasons, need to improve their spoken and written English. Some will be students, others foreign nationals working in this country, and still others the foreign-born husbands and wives of English nationals. You might also obtain work with one or more language schools, for whom you will provide tuition on a part-time or full-time basis. Language schools can be found all over the UK, though especially in London and the Southeast.

How much can I make?

Earnings in this field are not spectacular. If you work as a tutor for a language school you can expect to be paid in the region of £12 to £20 per hour. If you choose to offer one-to-one tuition in your home the rate will be negotiable but probably somewhat lower, around £6 to £12 an hour being typical. If possible, try to find out the 'going rate' for TEFL teaching in your area by contacting a few other local providers.

How can I sell my services?

In areas with a high proportion of non-native English speakers, try advertising in the local free papers and on newsagents' and supermarket notice boards. If your local college or university has many overseas students, a card in the students union building could well reap dividends.

If you wish to work for a language school, you can obtain a list from ARELS (the Association of Recognised English Language Services). They have over 220 member colleges, all of which are inspected regularly to ensure that they continue to meet the Association's high standards. There is a fairly high turnover of TEFL teachers, so vacancies arise on a regular basis.

Where can I get more help?

A wide range of institutions offer courses in teaching English as a foreign language. One of the best known is International House London (IHL). They train over 1,500 teachers from the UK and overseas every year. IHL offer a week-long introductory TEFL course, and full- and part-time courses for the Cambridge/RSA Certificate in English Language Teaching to Adults (CELTA).

International House London
106 Piccadilly
London
W1V 9FL
Tel: 020 7491 2598
Web: www.ihlondon.com

It is also possible to study for a TEFL qualification by distance learning. One of the leading providers here is the English Language Centre. Their TEFL Certificate course by distance learning costs around £230.

The English Language Centre
Suite 3C, Standbrook House
2–5 Old Bond Street
London
W1X 3TB
Tel: 01925 470903
Web: www.addnet.demon.co.uk/index.htm

Finally, information and advice about training to teach English as a foreign language is available from ARELS (The Association of Recognised English Language Services). They will also provide you with a list of their member colleges on request. This information is also available via their website.

ARELS
56 Buckingham Gate
London
SW1E 6AG
Tel: 020 7802 9200
Web: www.arels.org.uk

TELEWORKING

Teleworking (or telecommuting as it is sometimes called) involves working remotely from an employer using the phone and new technology (including the internet). There are an estimated 250,000 teleworkers in the UK today. Many work from home, and others from specialist centres called telecottages. Some are self-employed, while others are employees whose employers have made special arrangements to allow them to work in this way.

Teleworkers include a wide range of occupations. Among the most common are software developers, data inputters, website designers, researchers, consultants, writers, charity workers, salespeople, accountants and solicitors. Many large employers now allow some of their staff to work from home; the Automobile Association, Lloyds TSB and British Telecom are three examples of organisations employing significant numbers of home-based teleworkers. A particular growth area at present is 'virtual call centres'. This involves people working from home answering telephone calls to company helplines, support desks, sales enquiry numbers, and so on.

Finally, there are many self-employed teleworkers: people with specialist skills such as computer programmers who hire themselves out to a range of clients on short-, medium- and long-term contracts.

What do I need to get started?

If you are used to working in an office or similar environment, you must be able to cope with the changes working from home will bring. One of these (mentioned in Part A of this book) is that you will be working in isolation for much of the time. Many home-based workers find that they particularly miss the gossip and camaraderie of the office. Another potential drawback is that your presence in the organisation will be less visible. You may therefore be the last person in your organisation to hear important news, and are more likely to get passed over for promotion. Whether you are employed or self-employed, you will need to be well organised and self-disciplined to resist the competing temptations working from home can present. For many types of telework, you will need to be confident about using new technology.

The cost of setting up as a teleworker depends largely on whether you have a supportive employer who has agreed to your working in this way. If so, there should be little or no cost to you, as your employer will pay for your phone, computer and any other necessary facilities. If you are to be self-employed you will need to spend a fair amount (probably upwards of £3,000) equipping your home office. Alternatively, you may decide to work for some or all of the time from a local telecottage. In this case equipment such as computers will be provided, but you will have to pay the centre a service charge.

Who will my customers be?

Your options here are three-fold. First, you may be able to persuade your current employer to allow you to work from home. Second, you may be able to find a new job with an employer who operates a teleworking policy. And third, you could set yourself up as a self-employed teleworker. In the latter case, your potential clients will include a wide range of organisations who require the services of skilled individuals willing and able to work in this way.

How much can I make?

Employed teleworkers should receive a similar rate of pay to staff doing a comparable job from their company's offices. In addition, their phone bills (or at least the business-related component) should be paid, as should any other expenditure incurred in the course of their work (e.g. the cost of postage and stationery). Self-employed teleworkers may be paid by the hour, by the day or per contract. Rates vary considerably according to the nature of the work.

How can I sell my services?

People who are currently in jobs but wish to switch to working from home will obviously need to raise the matter with their employer. It helps a lot if other staff in your organisation are doing this already, and/or the organisation has an official teleworking policy. Even if this does not apply, however, employers generally are becoming more aware of the need for flexibility if they wish to retain their experienced staff. If your employers value your services, therefore, they should at least be willing to entertain such a request. If this is not an option, a growing number of jobs in which the person appointed can work from home are being advertised, so applying for these is an alternative option.

Self-employed teleworkers have a range of marketing methods open to them. Members of the Telecentre, Telework and Telecottage Association (see below) are regularly notified of new teleworking opportunities. There are also a growing number of websites (e.g. www.smarterwork.com) where would-be teleworkers can read advertisements from companies seeking home-based staff, and advertise their own availability. Finally, you could try writing directly to potential clients (including perhaps your former employers) offering your services on a home-based, flexible basis.

Where can I get more help?

The Telecentre, Telework and Telecottage Association (TCA) is one of the leading national – and international – organisations for teleworkers. Members receive a bi-monthly magazine called Teleworker which includes information on new teleworking opportunities. Members with internet access also receive regular updates by e-mail.

The TCA also publish 'The Teleworking Handbook' by Imogen Bertin. This book is widely regarded as the teleworkers' bible. It covers such areas as company schemes, union agreements, business ideas, marketing, insurance, health and safety, equipment, e-mail/online services, training and so on. TCA members receive the book as part of their membership package, or it can be ordered separately from the TCA or any bookshop.

The Telecentre, Telework and Telecottage Association
The Other Cottage
Shortwood
Nailsworth
Stroud
Gloucestershire
GL6 0SH
Tel: 01453 834874
Web: www.tca.org.uk

TOURIST GUIDE

As a tourist guide, you will spend your time conducting groups of tourists around various places in your local area, telling them about the history and other aspects of what they are seeing. In general, the area will be defined by geographical boundaries, and your level of knowledge about this area must be high and very detailed. It is one thing to be able to give a standard talk about a town, quite another to give a satisfactory answer to such questions as, 'Say, didn't I read somewhere that Henry V's wet-nurse came from near here?'

In addition to such tours, you might develop a speciality, such as tours of gardens, industrial archaeology, or the music of a certain period of history, and these may take you further afield.

Most guides will accompany groups in whatever transport is provided for them, but some take small groups in their own cars or mini-buses; these are known as 'driver' guides.

What do I need to get started?

There is no legal requirement for tourist guides to hold any form of qualification, but you will find it difficult to get well-paid work without one. The recognised qualification is called the Blue Badge, which you get after attending a course and sitting exams set by your local tourist board. The courses which lead to the exams are held in mid-winter over two years, and cost £2,500. They are difficult to get on to, as there is great demand. For more details of the courses, telephone the British Tourist Authority on 020 8846 9000 and ask for the training and education department. The Blue Badge is linked to a specific area, so if you move to another area you will have to take an 'endorsement' course and sit some supplementary exams. As well as information relating to the specific area, you will need a detailed knowledge of English national history and geography.

As a driver guide, you will need a public service vehicle (PSV) driving licence, and appropriate insurance. Blue Badge guides are advised by their Association to have public liability insurance, which is available through the Association at reduced rates.

Who will my customers be?

Your ultimate clients will be the actual tourists. However, it will be the tour operator who pays you. The latter include organisations such as those who run the open-topped tourist buses in big cities, or London Walks, who take groups around the historical areas of the capital.

How much can I make?

You will negotiate your own fees, which will depend on what you offer – special interest tours are obviously worth more than general tours. The rates recommended for certified Blue Badge guides by the Guild of Registered Tourist Guides are £83 per half day, £124 per full day for London, and £70 per half day, £100 per full day elsewhere. Its affiliated association, the Association of Driver Guides, publishes a list of recommended mileage rates for driver guides who supply their own vehicle, which depend on the size of the vehicle. The customers are expected to pay for your lunch, coffee and tea.

For tours which you conduct in another language, you charge an additional £12 per half day, and where the tour is conducted in more than one language, you charge an additional 50 per cent.

Guides who do not have the Blue Badge earn lower rates. Although you may have some chance to negotiate these fees, if working for organisations such as those which provide the open-topped tourist buses in big cities you will find they have their own set rates.

Although you should not count on this, quite often the tourists you are guiding will also give you a tip at the end of the tour.

How can I sell my services?

As a Blue Badge guide and a member of the Guild, you will be listed in the Guild's annual directory of guides, and will find much of your work comes from that listing. For additional work, or if you do not have the Blue Badge, approach your local tourist board offices, or appropriate tour operators. A good way to find these tour operators is to attend either holiday exhibitions which are open to the general public, or one of the world travel trade fairs which are held in London in November and at the National Exhibition Centre (Birmingham) in February each year. For more details of these trade fairs, contact the organisers, Reed Travel Exhibitions. They also publish a vast catalogue of all the stand holders at these exhibitions, which you can buy if you are unable to attend one of the fairs.

Where can I get more help?

The following organisations (both referred to above) can provide more information about becoming a tourist guide.

The Guild of Registered Tourist Guides (and the Association of Driver Guides)
Guild House
52d Borough High Street
London
SE1 1XN
Tel: 020 7403 1115
Web: www.blue-badge.org.uk

Reed Travel Exhibitions
Oriel House
26 The Quadrant
Richmond
Surrey
TW9 1DL
Tel: 020 8910 7805/10 7929
Web: www.travel.reedexpo.com

TOY MAKING

As with all hand-made products, making toys puts you in

competition with the cheap plastic items coming in from the Third World, and you therefore need to aim your toys at fond parents who are prepared to pay extra for a good quality toy. Such parents are often of the 'green' persuasion, and will look more kindly on toys made from natural materials (such as wood) from sustainable resources. They also like educational toys and those of traditional patterns, such as chickens on a board which peck when you pull a string, rocking horses or Noah's Arks. Here you have to find the right balance between toys which will appeal to children and those which their parents (who pay for them) think appropriate.

Another possibility is making specialised items for the enthusiasts who collect such things as teddy bears, dolls' houses or antique-style dolls.

What do I need to get started?

Before you start making any toys for children, you need to be aware of the regulations which restrict the materials used for toys. These cover hazards like sharp wires inside soft toys, small pieces which could be swallowed and toxic paints. Ask the trading standards officer at your local council for a leaflet on these regulations. Note that the regulations apply only to toys for children; toys made for the adult collectors' market are not covered.

Other than that, you need a good idea of what toys will sell well, which is best gained by going to craft fairs where most hand-made toys are sold, and the ability to produce well-finished toys.

And, of course, you need ideas, patterns and materials to make toys. All of these are freely available in craft shops, which will stock books on toy-making and patterns, as well as fabrics, paints and the essential eyeballs in many shapes and sizes! There are also strict regulations on labelling which require you to include a mark declaring that you take responsibility for safety. This should include your name and address and, where relevant, give warnings and instructions for use.

Who will my customers be?

Your customers will be either the parents (or other relatives) of the children who will use the toys, or the shop owners who will be selling them for you.

For collectors' items such as teddy bears, your customers will be enthusiasts or the specialist shops which cater to them.

How much can I make?

Since this field is so varied potential earnings are difficult to state, but you should aim to earn at least a living wage after paying for your raw materials and marketing expenses. If your product proves popular, you may be able to move on to employing additional workers and thus earn rather more. Another possibility is making and selling toys in kit form for people who want to make them up themselves.

One problem with toy making is that a high proportion of your sales will be seasonal, most coming just before Christmas. If you sell at craft fairs, your income will be erratic, with many weeks passing while you build up your stock for each fair.

How can I sell my services?

One way to sell hand-made toys is to supply gift shops, although these usually want to take items on a sale-or-return basis, and pay only a fraction of what your toys will fetch on the retail market.

Craft fairs are a good place to sell toys so long as they are not too expensive (£10 is about the limit at these events). You could also investigate the possibility of opening a stall in the foyer of your local children's hospital, where visitors will be looking for gifts for young patients.

Collectors' toys can be sold at specialist toy fairs, by mail order or through websites on the internet. There are some special fairs which are better than ordinary craft fairs for these collectors' items. One such as the Miniatura Fair for dolls, dolls' houses and teddy bears, held at the NEC in Birmingham each March and September.

Where can I get more help?

The magazine *Toy Trader* is published monthly and is full of articles and advertisements which will spark your imagination on what to make. Other good sources of ideas are toy museums and antique shops which specialise in toys; and, of course, your local library should have a good selection of books both on antique toys and toy-making techniques.

British Toymakers Guild
124 Walcot Street
Bath
Avon
BA1 5BG
Tel: 01225 442440

British Toy & Hobby Manufacturers' Association
80 Camberwell Road
SE5 0EG
Tel: 020 7701 7271

The Guild of Master Craftsmen
86 High Street
Lewes
East Sussex
BN7 1XN
Tel: 01273 477374

TRANSLATION

If you have a good knowledge of a foreign language, offering a translation service could be the ideal home-based business for you. Much translation work is technical or commercial, so in addition to your language skills it will help if you have some specialist knowledge of a particular topic: computers, medicine or the law, for example. Highly technical translations are generally the best paid (and most difficult). The more obscure languages command the highest rates of pay (see How much can I make? below), though the demand for such translations is likely to be less frequent than for 'mainstream' languages such as French and German.

Unless you are genuinely bilingual, it is normally preferable to translate from the foreign language into your mother tongue rather than vice versa. You may be able to make a passable job of translating into the foreign language but, as numerous leaflets and manuals translated into English in the Far East testify, you are unlikely to have the grasp of current usage and idioms possessed by a native speaker. In general it is best to stick to subjects you feel confident with. Avoid taking on jobs where you know you are out of your depth just to 'oblige' a client. Rather than keeping your customer happy, you are more likely to leave him displeased and disillusioned.

Translation work tends to be irregular, and many freelance translators combine it with other work such as language teaching and interpreting.

What do I need to get started?

Clearly the essential requirement is that you have an excellent knowledge of the language concerned. You will probably have studied the language at an advanced (i.e. degree) level and have spent some time living and working in a country where it is spoken. Many translators have a knowledge of two or more languages other than English, and this can help greatly in broadening the range of work available to you. In some parts of the UK there is a particular demand for translators who have a good knowledge of Asian languages.

You will need some tools and equipment to help you, including foreign language dictionaries and tapes (for pronunciation). You may also find it helpful to obtain foreign language books and magazines to keep up to date with changes in the language and any new terms which have entered it. For some types of translation work (e.g. literary translations for publishers) you are likely to require a computer with word processing software. You should expect to pay in the region of £1,000 for a suitable machine and printer.

Who will my customers be?

Your customers will include companies (especially multi-nationals and those with overseas customers and suppliers), publishers, solicitors, charities and associations, students and private individuals. For example, a manufacturer of microwave ovens might want you to translate its operating instructions into the language of a new market. A childcare charity might need its information leaflet translating into a number of Asian languages. A product design agency receiving a sales enquiry from a German company might need this translating into English. Or a publisher might have acquired a book in Spanish needing to be translated into English before it can be published in this country. These examples reveal the wide range of assignments translators can expect to be offered.

How much can I make?

The 'NUJ Freelance Fees Guide 1999–2000' recommends the following minimum rates per thousand words for translators:

	Books	Magazines	Newspapers
French/Italian/ Spanish/German	£60.75	£66.80	£73.00
Afrikaans/Danish/ Dutch/Latin	£70.35	£77.40	£84.40
Arabic/Greek/ Hebrew/Swedish	£81.95	£90.00	£98.00
Chinese/Japanese/ Korean	£90.00	£99.00	£108.00
All Other Languages	£100.00	£110.00	£120.00

These figures provide a useful guideline, but for many types of work it may be more appropriate to charge by the hour or by the page. This applies especially where the material is particularly complex. In cases where travel is required the translator should also charge for the time involved, though this will be at less than the full rate for actual translation. Overheads in this occupation are minimal, comprising mainly telephone and other office-related expenses and reference books. A successful full-time translator can expect to achieve a net income of £25,000 to £40,000 a year or more depending on the local demand, competition and language/s offered. It is also possible to run this business very successfully on a part-time basis.

How can I sell my services?

An advertisement in Yellow Pages and Thomson's local directory (if there is one serving your area) should provide a steady stream of enquiries. It is also worth preparing a leaflet setting out your services (including details of your experience and qualifications) and sending this to potential clients: local businesses, solicitors, advertising and PR agencies, and so on. If you decide to approach publishing houses, you should also submit a sample of your work (preferably accompanied by the foreign language original). Another option is to apply for work to translation agencies; they often use freelances, especially for the more obscure languages. One drawback here is that you will obviously be paid by the agency at a rate lower than the fee it is charging its client.

Where can I get more help?

The Translators Association is a subsidiary group within the Society of Authors. Members receive free legal and general assistance on all matters relating to translation work, including vetting of contracts and information on current rates of payment.

To become a member you must normally have had your work published in a book or magazine or produced for stage, TV or radio.

The Translators Association
c/o The Society of Authors
84 Drayton Gardens
London
SW10 9SB
Tel: 020 7373 6642
Web: www.writers.org.uk/society/Pages/specfrm.html

The Institute of Translation and Interpreting (ITI) is a professional organisation aiming to promote high standards in translating and interpreting. Membership is open to anyone with a 'genuine and proven' interest in translating and interpreting. Members receive a range of services, including information (and discounts) on courses and conferences, and a bi-monthly bulletin. The ITI also offers a free referral service, whereby enquirers can be given the names of suitable members for any translating or interpreting assignment.

Institute of Translation and Interpreting
377 City Road
London
EC1V 1NA
Tel: 020 7713 7600
Web: www.iti.org.uk

TYPING AND WORD PROCESSING

If you have good typing skills you could put these to use running your own home-based typing and/or word processing business. There is still a need for basic copy- and audio-typing services, but increasingly nowadays clients are likely to expect word processing as well.

To offer a word processing (not just typing) service, you will need a modern computer word processor. This will allow you to perform many additional tasks not possible – or possible only with difficulty – on an ordinary typewriter. A few examples include automatic spell-checking, bold and italics, and the facility to incorporate tables, graphs, photographs and so on into a finished document. With a word processor you can tinker with your document's text and layout as much as you wish till you and your client are happy with it before printing it out. You can also save documents in electronic form (e.g. on floppy disk), to be stored, updated and printed again later as required.

You may find your services easier to sell if you offer a range of additional secretarial and clerical services, e.g. telephone answering, filing, envelope-stuffing, and so on.

What do I need to get started?

Clearly you must be a competent typist. You should be able to type at a rate of at least 60 words per minute; and the faster you type, the more you will be able to earn. Speed is no good without accuracy, however, and you must ensure that this does not suffer in your quest for profit. It will also help if you can spell and have a reasonable grasp of grammar and punctuation.

This is above all a customer-service business, and you will need to take an interest in your clients' work and be constantly on the lookout for ways in which you can do it more efficiently and effectively. Many jobs will have tight deadlines, and you will need to be conscientious and reliable about meeting these (disappoint a client once and he is likely to go elsewhere in future).

You will also need the appropriate equipment: either a modern electric typewriter or a computer word processor. As already indicated, the latter is highly preferable, as it will open many more possibilities for you. A good quality IBM-compatible computer with modern word processing software (preferably Microsoft Word) is ideal. You should also have a high quality printer. For general typing and word processing, a black-and-white laser model (e.g. the Brother HL range) will produce highly professional-looking documents at modest cost. If you want the facility to print in colour as well, an inkjet or bubblejet printer (e.g. the HP DeskJet series) will provide good results without breaking the bank.

Who will my customers be?

Your clients will typically be small businesses who cannot justify employing a full-time typist. You may also obtain work from larger businesses who need extra assistance, perhaps for a special project, to provide holiday cover, or during a particularly busy period (e.g. the run-up to Christmas). You may also find clients among other home-based workers; possible examples include travelling sales executives and the regional officers of many national charities.

Other potential clients include writers and publishers, who may need you to type up manuscripts for them; and students, who may need your services in connection with their theses or dissertations.

How much can I make?

Your earnings in this business will depend on a range of factors. These include the type and level of service you offer, the amount of competition in your area, and (not least) how fast you can type. Setting a price for your work can be difficult at first, but in time you will learn to assess jobs very quickly. As a rule of thumb, begin with your target minimum rate per hour, add around 20% for overheads such as stationery, and try to set all your prices on this basis.

There are various ways of charging for typing and word processing work, each appropriate to a different type of job. With long manuscripts, the usual method is to charge a fixed price per 1,000 words. Fees being requested for this type of service in *Writers News* range from £2.50 to £3.50 per 1,000, with more if additional services such as grammar and spell-checking are included. For smaller jobs such as typing letters and short reports, you could charge a set price per item (e.g. letter or invoice), per page or per hour.

How can I sell my services?

You will need to advertise your business widely. A good place to start would be newsagents' and supermarket notice boards. Have an advertising card prepared describing your service and asking potential clients to call you for further details. You could also have a handbill printed (most high street printers will do this very cheaply) and deliver it to businesses in your local area. Another approach – though costlier – would be to mailshot local companies, perhaps getting the addresses from Yellow Pages.

If you have a college or university nearby, call and ask if you can advertise your services. Most will have a students' notice board where you can put up a card free of charge. To sell your services to authors, you could try taking out a classified advertisement in *Writers News* (01667 454441) or *The Author* (020 7373 6642). Note that in the case of *The Author* you will be required to provide a small sample of your work and two or more letters of reference.

Where can I get more help?

If you need to polish your typing or word processing skills, most colleges and adult education centres offer a range of part-time courses. Your local library should be able to give you more information. Useful books on this subject include 'Complete Typing Business Guide: Everything You Need to Know to Start and Successfully Operate a Home Typing Business' by Frank Chisenhall (Supertext) and 'How to Start a Home-based Secretarial Services Business' by Jan Melnik (Globe). Both books are American but available on special order from bookshops or through internet booksellers such as Amazon (www.amazon.co.uk). For the names and contact details of publishers, buy or borrow 'The Writer's Handbook' (Macmillan) or 'The Writers' and Artists' Yearbook' (A & C Black).

VIDEO PRODUCTION

Modern camcorders are lightweight, inexpensive and – used with a modicum of skill and judgement – can produce highly professional-looking results. This has presented an ideal opportunity for home-based businessmen and women to turn an interest in this form of photography into a paying business.

The range of potential markets for video photographers (or videographers, as they are sometimes called) is vast. Wedding videos are probably the single largest source of work. Nearly every couple today wants a video of their big occasion as a permanent memento – and because there is only one chance to get it right, most are willing to pay a reasonable fee to have the job done by a professional. However, there is a huge range of other potential markets as well (see Who will be my customers? below). Another, related service offered by many video production businesses is converting old cine-films to video.

What do I need to get started?

There is more to producing a video than simply pushing a button on the side of a camera. To produce videos of a professional standard, you will need a good understanding of video photography, including lighting effects, panning and zooming, editing, music and sound recording, and so on. You will need to be fully confident and competent in using your camcorder and accessories. And on a personal level, you will need be able to get on well with all sorts of people: gently (but firmly) encouraging them to co-operate with the filming whilst always remaining the epitome of courtesy and charm. Qualifications are not essential in this field, but there is no substitute for experience. Take an evening class or college course, therefore, and practise by filming family occasions before you start charging anyone for your services.

So far as equipment is concerned, you will need a good quality camcorder, with a tripod for holding it steady, and a good supply of video cassettes. You will require a video cassette recorder (VCR) and television in order to monitor your recordings. You will also need a video-editing machine. The latter is a device such as the Sony XV-AL100 which enables you to mix one scene into another, add titles, and incorporate other professional-looking effects into your videos. Your total expenditure on equipment is likely to be at least £2,000.

Who will my customers be?

As mentioned above, the bread-and-butter work of many videographers is wedding videos. Other events at which their services may be required include christenings, school events, business conferences, VIP visits, speeches, concerts, dance and theatrical productions, parties, sporting events and award presentations. Some estate agents engage videographers to produce videos of houses to show to prospective purchasers; whilst up-and-coming pop groups and bands may require a videographer's services to produce a 'promo' for them.

Commercial work is another huge field: businesses engage videographers to produce training and internal communications materials, induction videos for new staff, promotional materials and video press releases (short video clips sent to TV stations in the hope of getting broadcast news coverage). Finally, it is also quite possible to write and produce your own videos and market them yourself – anything from 'how-to-do-it' guides to low-budget horror films. This is obviously a more speculative approach; but if your video sells well or even achieves cult status (e.g. George Romero's 'Night of the Living Dead'), the rewards can be substantial.

How much can I make?

The going rate for a typical wedding video is around £200 to £300. This allows a half-day for setting up the equipment and filming the event – usually from the guests arriving at the church to the cutting of the cake and the speeches. Some companies also offer a 'whole day' option, in which case the video will continue through the evening at the reception, ending at around 11 pm. The fee for this will obviously be higher, typically £350 to £400. The fee will include a master copy of the video for the bride and groom. In most cases you will also be asked to supply additional copies for the couple's friends and family, and this can help to increase your profit margin (£15 per copy is a typical charge).

Rates for other types of video photography are negotiable, but will be along similar lines to the above. Videographers working for commercial clients may be able to charge higher rates if they have specialist skills and experience. A typical videographer offering a broad range of services should be able to earn £40 to £50,000 a year in fees, though overheads such as equipment hire and purchase, music licences, video tapes and so on can eat up to 30% (or more) of this.

How can I sell my services?

An advertisement in Yellow Pages under 'Video Services' should bring in a steady stream of enquiries. For weddings, try advertising in magazines such as *You and Your Wedding* aimed at couples who are planning to go down the aisle shortly. In the spring especially, many local newspapers run special features aimed at such couples, and advertising in these will normally prove profitable.

Leave your business cards in shops such as florists and bridal wear outlets, and hand them out to guests at other functions you attend. Church and parish notice boards are good places to advertise, and it is also well worth introducing yourself to the minister: if you get on well, he or she will be in a good position to refer enquiries your way (maybe in exchange for a small donation to parish funds?). Finally, consider setting up a website advertising your services. For one example of what can be done, see the site of Spectrum Videofilms on www.nennius.demon.co.uk.

Where can I get more help?

The main organisation serving and representing video photographers is the Guild of Professional Videographers. Anyone is welcome to join the Guild as an Affiliated member. However, to become a Registered member (and entitled to use the Guild logo in your advertising) you are required to prove your skills by submitting a completed video which meets the Guild's minimum standards. All Guild members receive a range of benefits, including meetings, a monthly newsletter and the opportunity to buy equipment at trade prices. The Guild also refers enquiries from potential clients to suitably qualified members. Though UK-based, the Guild has an international membership.

The Guild of Professional Videographers
11 Telfer Road
Radford
Coventry
West Midlands
CV6 3DG
Tel: 024 7659 0949
Web: www.professional-videographers.co.uk

WEBSITE DESIGN

Website designers design, produce and maintain websites (internet pages on the world wide web). Their work involves combining technical, writing and design skills to produce attractive-looking web pages which show their clients to good effect and help them sell more of their products and services.

Website designers advise clients on the best way to promote themselves via the net, and show them examples of what can be done. In consultation with their clients, they decide on the general approach to be taken. Clients provide at least a rough draft of the text they want on their site and any artwork or photographs. Website designers then create the sites on their computer, using programs specially designed for this purpose. Once clients are satisfied with their sites, the designer makes the necessary arrangements to publish them on the world wide web.

As well as creating and publishing sites, website designers also often assist clients in promoting them, e.g. by ensuring that they are listed on all the leading internet 'search engines'. Finally, they may retain responsibility for revising and updating sites (for which they receive an additional fee).

What do I need to get started?

Clearly you will need an interest in working with computers. You will also need some familiarity with the main programming languages used for this purpose, including HTML and Java.

Modern website creation programs are increasingly automating the actual programming, however, meaning that in future design and writing skills are likely to be of relatively greater importance in this field.

There is no need to possess qualifications before setting up as a website designer, and in fact few formal qualifications currently exist. Clients will, however, expect to see examples of your work; so before you start trading you will need to have a portfolio of existing sites you have designed. You could create mock-ups for imaginary companies initially, or offer to design sites free or at low cost for friends and neighbours.

You will, of course, need a computer with internet access for this occupation. To make best use of the latest design and programming tools, this will need to be as up-to-date as possible. Additional equipment required is likely to include a colour printer (for turning out 'hard copies' of web pages) and a scanner (for inputting your clients' logos, artwork, photographs, and so on). So far as software is concerned, you can start by using free programs such as those provided with the web browsers Microsoft Internet Explorer and Netscape Navigator; and DTP programs such as Microsoft Publisher also offer a good range of web design features. Sooner or later, however, you are likely to need professional web page creation software such as Adobe PageMill or Microsoft FrontPage, which can cost anything from £100 to £500 or more.

Your basic computer set-up is likely to cost a minimum of around £3,000, although if you are contemplating entering this field it is very likely that you will already possess at least some of the equipment needed to get started.

Who will my customers be?

Your clients will be mainly small businesses who want (or need) a presence on the net. Even the smallest businesses are now recognising the benefits of going online, so the potential market here alone is huge. You may also be able to obtain work from charities, associations and private individuals. In addition, larger companies sometimes require freelance assistance with a specific project (e.g. a drinks company might engage a freelance to create a web page advertising a new alcoholic soft drink). Advertising agencies and specialist design companies also sometimes sub-contract work to freelance website designers.

How much can I make?

Clients will normally expect you to quote a set fee for creating a website for them. Fees typically start at around £100 to £200 for a basic web page, with much more for elaborate sites with animations, video clips and so on. Once your service is up and running you will have a range of templates you can adapt to meet the needs of your clients, meaning you should be able to create at least one and perhaps two or more websites in a day. This occupation therefore has very high earning potential – £1,000 a week plus – and the overheads are minimal once you have all the necessary hardware and software.

How can I sell my services?

All the usual local advertising media should prove productive (local papers, business directories, Yellow Pages, etc.). You should also – of course – set up your own website to advertise your service (for an example, see www.cc-website-design.co.uk). In this occupation your business website really will be your 'shop window', so you will need to devote some effort to ensuring that it represents an excellent advertisement for your services.

You could try mailshotting local businesses, but a more selective approach might be more effective. Try targeting businesses which are not currently on the web but have competitors who are. Look for a firm which has a website, then search through Yellow Pages for its competitors. Check with a few search engines whether these companies have websites. If they do not, send them a copy of the competitor's site, with a note about the dangers of being left behind and an outline of the service you offer. If you have time, you could even knock up a simple website for the company concerned as an example of what you could do for them. Done well, this simple approach should have a high success rate.

Where can I get more help?

Courses in website design are not yet widely available, but it is nevertheless worth checking with local colleges to see what they have to offer. There are also many good introductory books on website design, e.g. 'HTML Publishing on the World Wide Web' by Mac Bride (Teach Yourself Books). As you might expect, there are also many websites offering advice and information in this field. A few of these – all free of charge – are listed below:

How to Build a Web Page – http://polaris.ncs.nova.edu/buildwebpage.htm

Web Monkey – www.webmonkey.com
HTML Tutorials in Web Design – www.bfree.on.ca/HTML/index.htm
HTML Help – www.htmlhelp.com
The Barebones Guide to HTML – http://wms.luminet.net/training/barebones.html
How Do They Do That With HTML? – www.nashville.net/~carl/htmlguide/index.html.

A range of distance learning courses in website design is offered by the Liverpool company Visual Software Training. Their WebCrawler course is intended for complete newcomers to the internet, while their WebMaster and WebExpert courses incorporate advanced web design and programming. Students on VST courses also receive a range of internet design software at no extra cost.

Visual Software Training
191 St Mary's Road
Garston
Liverpool
L19 0NE
Tel: 0151 475 2898
Web: www.visualsoftware.co.uk

WILL WRITING

Will writing, rather like conveyancing, is one of those legal tasks which do not have to be carried out by a qualified solicitor, and which has developed into a separate profession. Many will writers also offer a service which helps lay executors obtain grants of probate, and some (by no means all) are also prepared to serve as executors themselves.

What do I need to get started?

You can buy a will writing franchise from various companies, but these will cost you between £15,000 and £40,000, and will not necessarily provide adequate training or backup services. Some of these franchises provide you with a piece of computer software which has 'template' wills for you to complete as appropriate; with other companies you obtain the customer's instructions and forward these to the franchisor, who then draws up the will for you. The Institute of Professional Will Writers, the body which has been set up to represent and assist professional will writers, does not recommend buying such a franchise. The Institute's membership fee is £125 a year.

You need to have a certain level of legal knowledge to do this job, and this cannot be acquired on a short course if you have no previous knowledge of the law. This means you need to have a background which includes a minimum of A level Law, which will allow you to absorb the more detailed knowledge you need from short courses and your own studies. Many will writers go on to take a more advanced course such as that of the Institute of Legal Executives.

The Institute of Professional Will Writers recommends that its members have professional indemnity insurance covering them for up to £2 million per claim.

You will also need a computer with word processing software and a good printer; and if you also wish to offer the service of providing safe-keeping for your customers' wills, you will need a fire-proof document safe.

Who will my customers be?

Your clients will be people who do not have their own solicitor, but who realise the wisdom of making a will. Many people today have been through divorces, and especially where they have children from previous marriages they need proper wills to ensure that their property is allocated as they would wish. The laws of intestacy will not necessarily give the children of previous marriages their fair share of an estate, so a proper, professionally drawn-up will is essential.

How much can I make?

This depends on how hard you work and how good your business contacts are. For a simple will for a single person, you will charge between £40 and £80 (between £65 and £100 for a pair of 'mirror' wills leaving all the property between husband and wife). For a more complex will, such as one involving the children of previous marriages, or with large and complex estates, you can charge more. A simple will, by the time you have seen the customer, taken their instructions and prepared the will, will occupy about three hours of your time. Some will writers make £50,000 a year, working full-time. Others work shorter hours and make less.

How can I sell my services?

Although it is worth taking a single line entry in Yellow Pages, to help people who have forgotten your telephone number or don't know it, this is not a business where you will easily pick up casual customers. Most professional will writers are either themselves financial advisers and write wills as part of their financial planning services, or get a lot of customers through recommendations from financial or other professional advisers, or other commercial contacts. The Institute of Professional Will Writers receives a fair number of enquiries from the public and passes these on to members.

Where can I get more help?

The Institute of Professional Will Writers offers advice and assistance to members and prospective members. It offers a one-day introductory course (cost £65) to people who are thinking of taking up will-writing and want to know more about it. This is not a training course, just an introduction to the profession. They then offer a two-day intensive course (cost £195) to teach the basic technical knowledge. They recommend studying two books – 'Parker's Modern Will Precedent' and Barlow, King and King's 'Wills, Administration and Taxation'.

The Institute of Professional Will Writers
14 Foregate Street
Worcester
Worcestershire
WR1 1DB
Tel: 01905 611165
Web: www.ipw.org.uk

WINDOW CLEANING

If you enjoy working in the open air and have a reasonable head for heights, window cleaning could be the business for you. The actual requirements to get started in this field are fairly minimal (see below). And one big advantage of the window cleaning business is that, once you have built up a round, your customers will want you back every three weeks or so to repeat the job.

One possible drawback of window cleaning is that it is somewhat seasonal. It is impossible to work in very bad weather, and clients will generally not expect to see you in the depths of winter. Because of this, many window cleaners have another source of income to help see them through the darker months, e.g. interior decorating or 'odd-jobbing'.

What do I need to get started?

Clearly you must be willing to work outdoors in all weathers. You must also have a good head for heights, as to reach upstairs windows you will need to go up and down ladders. You will need to be physically fit, and strong enough to carry a ladder around. Working at heights is potentially dangerous, so you must be safety aware and have a good sense of balance. Successful window cleaners build good long-term relationships with their customers, so it will help a lot if you have a pleasant manner and are reasonably presentable.

The equipment you will need is minimal. You will require an extension ladder or ladders and a car or van long enough to transport them on. Apart from this, all you really need is a bucket, a chammy leather or squeegee (a rubber blade which scrapes water off a window like a car's windscreen wiper) and some window cleaning fluid, and Bob's your uncle – you're in business!

Who will my customers be?

Your main customers initially are likely to be private householders. Cleaning the windows is one of those tasks few people have the time or the inclination to do themselves, and most are more than happy to pay a 'professional' a few pounds to get the job done. Reasonably well-heeled suburban areas are likely to be the most productive. By contrast, areas with a high proportion of rented or council property are likely to be less remunerative – unless, of course, you are able to contact the landlords and agree a price to clean all the windows of their properties for them.

As your business grows, you may wish to consider offering your services to local companies. Shops, restaurants, offices, factories and so on all need someone to clean their windows for them. If you wish to go down this route, however, you will probably need to consider employing other staff. You may also need to invest in special equipment such as cradles, hoists, scaffolding, safety harnesses and so on, which are required when cleaning the windows of tall buildings.

How much can I make?

Fees vary according to the area and size of properties, but typically range from £4 to £6. With large houses you should charge more, though this may have to be negotiated with the householder. Your earnings will be determined by the amount you charge per house (of course) and the number of houses you can clean in a day. Twenty houses a day would be a reasonable target, which at £5 a time would give you a gross income of £100 a day or £500 a week. Your overheads will be limited, mainly petrol for your van and cleaning consumables. A successful full-time window cleaner can expect to earn in the region of £16–£24,000 a year. If you decide to employ others and are able to obtain industrial work, the potential earnings are considerably greater.

How can I sell my services?

While you might think that most areas are already well served by window cleaners, in reality this is often not the case. Choose an area, therefore, and call door-to-door. Ask the householder if they need a window cleaner and give them a copy of your business card (if there is no-one in, drop this through the letterbox). You could consider giving a discount for the first job or even offer to do it free 'so that you can see just how good my service is'.

It is also worth putting advertising cards in newsagents' windows and on supermarket noticeboards. Other places to advertise include the local newspaper and Yellow Pages (and Thomson's Directory, if there is one covering your area). Note that members of the National Federation of Master Window and General Cleaners (see below) can participate in the Federation's corporate advertising scheme in Yellow Pages.

Where can I get more help?

The National Federation of Master Window and General Cleaners provides information on all aspects of window cleaning. They also stock a wide range of professional window cleaning equipment, available to members at trade prices, and a range of promotional aids (stickers, tee-shirts, 'window cleaner called today' leaflets, and so on). Guidelines on pricing work and dealing with income tax are also available, and the Federation can provide a tailor-made insurance package for window cleaners including public liability, personal accident/sickness and employer's liability insurance.

National Federation of Master Window and General Cleaners
Summerfield House
Harrogate Road
Reddish
Stockport
Cheshire
SK5 6HH
Tel: 0161 432 8754
Web: www.nfmwgc.com

WRITING

Writing is one of the most popular home-based business opportunities. The range of potential outlets for freelance writers is vast, including magazines and newspaper articles, short stories, non-fiction books, novels, TV and radio, filmscripts, plays, advertising copywriting, poetry, greetings card slogans, and more.

Writing is, however, a highly competitive field, and it can take time – perhaps several years – to build enough business to generate a respectable full-time income. Many people start part-time, perhaps writing articles or short stories in the evenings and weekends, and this approach has much to recommend it.

What do I need to get started?

The good news is you don't have to be Shakespeare to make money as a writer. A reasonable grasp of grammar, spelling and punctuation is certainly helpful, and it may be worth taking an evening class on improving your written English if you know you have weaknesses in this area.

Even so, freelance writers don't (usually) need perfect English – editors and proofreaders are always on hand to make any necessary minor corrections. More important attributes are persistence, a good imagination and reliability. You should be thorough and conscientious, e.g. when researching factual information for books or articles. You must also be prepared to write what the market (in the first instance, your editor) requires – even if this is not what you, personally, are most interested in. Finally, you must be professional in all your dealings, and not get too irate when an editor chops the last 300 words from your carefully-wrought article and mangles your opening paragraph!

You can make a reasonable sideline income writing readers' letters and fillers (short items such as household tips) by hand, but for anything more than this you are likely to require at least a typewriter, and preferably a computer word processor. More and more publishers are asking writers to submit their work in electronic form (either on floppy disk or via e-mail), and if you do cannot do this you will miss out on many opportunities. Nowadays it is possible to buy a basic home computer and printer for around £500, and if you are serious about making a career as a freelance writer you should regard this as an essential investment.

Who will my customers be?

The people who will buy your work are usually editors or publishers. With some types of writing (e.g. advertising copywriting) you will be working for business managers and owners. In the case of TV and radio scripts, your customers will be BBC or ITV producers. You can also, of course, sell your work to broadcasters and publishers overseas.

How much can I make?

Someone, presumably a frustrated writer, once remarked that it is possible to make a fortune as a writer, but very hard to make a living. In other words, there is a small core of very highly paid writers, but a lot more who barely scrape by. There is some truth in this, but with persistence, a degree of talent and a little luck, you can certainly find a niche for yourself in this field.

Rates for magazine writing vary considerably, from nothing at all to £400 and upwards per 1,000 words. The National Union of Journalists' Freelance Fees Guide divides magazines into four categories, ranging from Group A (top paying consumer magazines such as *Woman's Own* and *Cosmopolitan*) to Group D (mainly trade and special interest titles such as *Nursing Times*). The NUJ recommended minimum rates per 1,000 words are as follows: Group A - £400; Group B - £275; Group C - £225; and Group D - £160. In practice, new writers may not always be able to get NUJ rates, but they can be used as a starting point for negotiation.

Fees for broadcast material are generally the subject of national agreements negotiated by the relevant union. For example, at the time of writing the BBC pays from £510 for an episode of The

Archers on Radio 4, up to £5,605 for a single episode of a TV serial drama such as Casualty. With books, payment is often in the form of royalties (a proportion, typically 10%, of the amount the publisher makes on every copy of your book sold). Authors usually receive an advance on royalties. For new authors this can be as little as £500, but authors of potential best-sellers may receive advances running into five, six or even seven figures. The advance is normally paid in stages, perhaps half when the book is commissioned, half when the typescript is accepted for publication. Advances are not repayable, but no further royalties will be due until the entire amount of the advance has been 'earned back' from sales.

How can I sell my services?

Many beginners start by writing an article then look around for someone who may be interested in buying it. A better approach – certainly more professional – is to start by sending out a query letter and outline. This sets out an idea for an article and summarises the proposed contents. If the editor likes what she sees, she may give you a definite commission for the article itself, or at least express an interest in seeing it. Either way, your chances of acceptance will be much better than if you simply send in your article 'unsolicited'.

A similar approach can be adopted with non-fiction books. Here it is customary to submit a synopsis of the proposed book and one or two sample chapters (so the publisher can assess your writing style/ability). With other types of writing such as short stories, plays and novels, this approach is unlikely to be successful. In this case you will have to write your piece first, preferably with a definite market in mind, then submit it to a publisher whose needs you believe it will meet.

So far as copywriting is concerned, you will need to find a way of bringing your services to the attention of local businesses. One way of doing this is by means of a mailshot, preferably including samples of your work. It is also well worth contacting local advertising and PR agencies, as these often require freelances to provide extra cover during busy periods.

Where can I get more help?

One popular approach is to take a correspondence course. The UK's leading provider of such courses is the Writers Bureau.

Accredited by the Open and Distance Learning Quality Council, they offer a comprehensive course in creative writing as well as more specialised courses in specific areas such as short story writing and journalism.

The Writers Bureau
Sevendale House
7 Dale Street
Manchester M1 1JB
Tel: 0161 228 2362
Web: www.writersbureau.com

If you wish to become a freelance journalist, it is well worth joining the National Union of Journalists (NUJ), who have an active freelance branch.

National Union of Journalists
Acorn House
314 Gray's Inn Road
London WC1X 8DP
Tel: 020 7278 7916
Web: www.gn.apc.org/media/nuj.html

Two other organisations offering support and other services for writers are The Society of Authors and The Writers' Guild. While there is considerable overlap between these organisations, the Writers' Guild has more members who write for performance (TV, radio, plays, films, etc.), whereas members of the Society of Authors write predominantly for the printed page.

The Society of Authors
84 Drayton Gardens
London SW10 9SB
Tel: 020 7373 6642
Web: www.writers.org.uk/society

The Writers' Guild
430 Edgware Road
London W2 1EH
Tel: 020 7723 8074
Web: www.writers.org.uk/guild

Appendix One

FURTHER READING AND REFERENCES

The following books can assist you with various aspects of running your home-based business. They can be ordered from any bookshop, or via internet bookshops such as Amazon at www.amazon.co.uk.

Advertising for the Small Business by Nick Daws
(2nd Edition, Otter Publications, 2000)

'Daily Telegraph' Guide to Working for Yourself by Godfrey Golzen and Helen Kogan (Kogan Page, 1999)

Going Freelance by Godfrey Golzen
(4th Edition, Kogan Page, 1994)

How to Plan Direct Mail by Iain Maitland (Cassell, 1997)

How to Plan Exhibitions by Iain Maitland (Cassell, 1997)

How to Plan Press Advertising by Iain Maitland (Cassell, 1997)

How to Plan Radio Advertising by Iain Maitland
(Cassell, 1997)

How to Write Business Letters by Ann Dobson
(How To Books Ltd, 1995)

How to Work From Home by Ian Phillipson
(2nd Edition, How To Books Ltd, 1995)

Law for the Small Business by Patricia Clayton
(Kogan Page, 1998)

Make Money at Home by Gordon Wells (2nd Edition, Management Books 2000 Ltd, 1997)

Marketing on a Restricted Budget by Bernard Katz and Mark Katz (Management Books 2000 Ltd, 1997)

Spare Room Tycoon by James Chan
(Nicholas Brealey Publishing Ltd, 2000)

Starting Up by Gary Jones
(Financial Times Management Books, 1998)

Stress-busting by Nick Daws (Need2Know, 1997)

Teach Yourself Book-keeping and Accounting for Your Small
Business by Mike Truman (Teach Yourself Books, 1997)

The Complete Small Business Internet Guide by Tom
Heatherington and Lori Heatherington (Que, 1998)

The 24 Hour Business Plan by Ron Johnson
(Random House Business Books, 1997)

The Teleworking Handbook by Imogen Bertin
(2nd Edition, TCA, 1998)

The Which? Guide to Working from Home by Lynn Brittney
(2nd Edition, Which? Books, 1999)

Working for Yourself: 2000 Edition by Godfrey Golzen
(Kogan Page, 2000)

Appendix Two

USEFUL ORGANISATIONS

The Advertising Standards Authority
Brook House
2 Torrington Place
London
WC1E 7HW
Tel: 020 7580 5555
Web: www.asa.org.uk

Association of British Insurers
51 Gresham Street
London
EC2V 7HQ
Tel: 020 7600 3333
Web: www.abi.org.uk

Banking Ombudsman
70 Gray's Inn Road
London
WC1X 8NB
Tel: 020 7404 9944
Web: www.obo.org.uk

British Agents Register
24 Mount Parade
Harrogate
North Yorkshire
HG1 1BP
Tel: 01423 560608
Web: www.agentsregister.co.uk

British Chambers of Commerce
Manning House
22 Carlisle Place
London
SW1P 1JA
Tel: 020 7565 2000
Web: www.britishchambers.org.uk

British Franchise Association
Thames View
Newtown Road
Henley-on-Thames
Oxon
RG9 1HG
Tel: 01491 578050
Web: www.british-franchise.org.uk

British Standards Institution
389 Chiswick High Road
London
W4 4AL
Tel: 020 8996 9000
Web: www.bsi.org.uk

British Trade International
(formerly British Overseas Trade Board)
Kingsgate House
66–74 Victoria Street
London
SW1E 6SW
Tel: 020 7215 5000
Web: www.brittrade.com

Business in the Community (BITC)
44 Baker Street
London
W1M 1DH
Tel: 020 7224 1600
Web: www.bitc.org.uk

Chartered Institute of Patent Agents
Staple Inn Buildings
High Holborn
London
WC1V 7PZ
Tel: 020 7405 9450
Web: www.cipa.org.uk

Crafts Council
44A Pentonville Road
London
N1 9BY
Tel: 020 7278 7700
Web: www.craftscouncil.org.uk

HM Customs and Excise
Dorset House
Stamford Street
London
SE1 9PY
Tel: 020 7202 4227
Web: www.hmce.gov.uk

Data Protection Registrar
Wycliffe House
Water Lane
Wilmslow
Cheshire
SK9 5AF
Tel: 01625 524510
Web: www.dataprotection.gov.uk

Department for Education and
Employment
Sanctuary Buildings
Great Smith Street
London
SW1P 3BT
Tel: 0870 000 2288
Web: www.dfee.gov.uk

Department of Trade and Industry
1 Victoria Street
London
SW1H 0ET
Tel: 020 7215 5000
Web: www.dti.gov.uk

Direct Mail Information Service
5 Carlisle Street
London
W1V 6JX
Tel: 020 7494 0483
Web: www.dmis.co.uk

Direct Marketing Association
Haymarket House
1 Oxendon Street
London
SW1Y 4EE
Tel: 020 7321 2525
Web: www.dma.org.uk

Direct Selling Association
29 Floral Street
London
WC2 9DP
Tel: 020 7497 1234
Web: www.dsa.org.uk

Factors and Discounters Association Ltd
2nd Floor, Boston House
The Little Green
Richmond
Surrey
TW9 1QE
Tel: 020 8332 9955
Web: www.factors.org.uk

Federation of Small Businesses
Whittle Way
Blackpool Business Park
Blackpool
Lancashire
FY4 2FE
Tel: 01253 336000
Web: www.fsb.org.uk

Finance and Leasing Association
15–19 Kingsway
London
WC2B 6UN
Tel: 020 7836 6511
Web: www.fla.org.uk

Forum of Private Business
Ruskin Chambers
Drury Lane
Knutsford
Cheshire
WA1 6HA
Tel: 01565 634467
Web: www.fpbusiness.co.uk

Highlands and Islands Enterprise
Bridge House
20 Bridge Street
Inverness
IV1 1QR
Tel: 01463 234171
Web: www.hie.co.uk

Home Business Alliance
The Firs
High Street
March
Cambridgeshire
PE15 9LQ
Tel: 01945 463303

Inland Revenue
Somerset House
The Strand
London
WC2R 1LB
Tel: 020 7438 6622
Self Assessment Helpline: 0645 000 444
Web: www.inlandrevenue.gov.uk

Inland Revenue Self Assessment
Orderline
PO Box 37
St Austell
Cornwall
PL25 5YN
Tel: 08459 000 404
Web: www.inlandrevenue.gov.uk
For ordering extra tax return pages,
helpsheets and leaflets

Institute of Directors
116 Pall Mall
London
SW1Y 5ED
Tel: 020 7839 1233
Web: www.iod.co.uk

Institute of Management
Management House
Cottingham Road
Corby
Northants
NN17 1TT
Tel: 01536 204222
Web: www.inst-mgt.org.uk

Market Research Society
15 Northburgh Street
London
EC1V 0AH
Tel: 020 7490 4911
Web: www.mrs.org.uk

Ministry of Agriculture, Fisheries and
Food (MAFF)
Whitehall Place
London
SW1A 2HH
Tel: 020 7238 3000
Helpline: 0645 335577
Web: www.maff.gov.uk

National Federation of Enterprise Agencies
Trinity Gardens
9–11 Bromham Road
Bedford
MK40 2UQ
Tel: 01234 354055
Web: www.nfea.com

Office of Fair Trading
Fleetbank House
2–6 Salisbury Square
London
EC4Y 8JX
Tel: 020 7211 8000
Web: www.oft.gov.uk

OwnBase
Birchwood
Hill Road South
Helsby
Cheshire
WA6 9PT
Tel: 01928 723254
Web: www.ownbase.org.uk
Membership organisation for home-based
workers

Patent Office
Concept House
Cardiff Road
Newport
South Wales
NP10 8QQ
Tel: 01633 813930
Web: www.patent.gov.uk

The Prince's Trust
18 Park Square East
London
NW1 4LH
Tel: 020 7543 1200
Web: www.princes-trust.org

Registrar of Companies
Companies Registration Office
Crown Way
Maindy
Cardiff
CF4 3UZ
Tel: 029 2038 8588
Web: www.companieshouse.co.uk

Scottish Enterprise
120 Bothwell Street
Glasgow
G2 7JP
Tel: 0141 248 2700
Helpline: 0845 607 8787
Web: www.scottish-enterprise.com

Shell Livewire Programme
FREEPOST NT805
Newcastle-upon-Tyne
NE1 1BR
Tel: 0345 573 3252
Web: www.shell-livewire.org

Telecentre, Telework and Telecottage
Association
The Other Cottage
Shortwood
Nailsworth
Stroud
Gloucestershire
GL6 0SH
Tel: 01453 834874
Web: www.tca.org.uk

INDEX